THE SCOTTISH
BOTHY
BIBLE

The complete guide to Scotland's
bothies and how to reach them

GEOFF ALLAN

IN MEMORY OF MY DAD WHO INSPIRED MY LOVE OF THE HILLS,
AND JAMIE, JIM, ART AND WENDY – ADVENTURERS ALL
WHO LEFT US FAR TOO YOUNG

Looking west to An Stac from Glenpean, Western Highlands

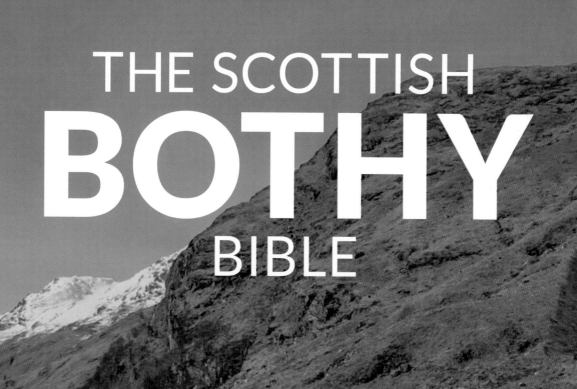

THE SCOTTISH
BOTHY
BIBLE

GEOFF ALLAN

Walking to Oban Bothy from Glen Pean, Western Highlands

CONTENTS

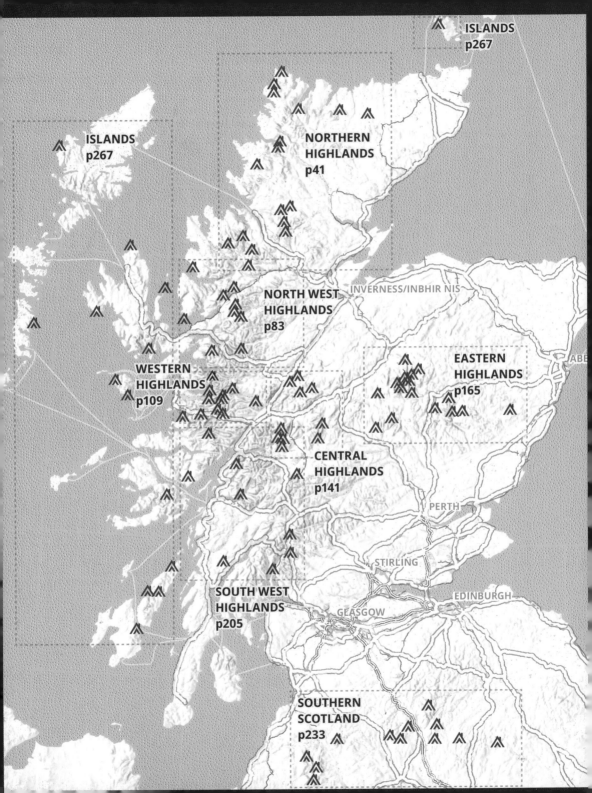

ISLANDS
p267

ISLANDS
p267

NORTHERN
HIGHLANDS
p41

NORTH WEST
HIGHLANDS
p83

INVERNESS/INBHIR NIS

EASTERN
HIGHLANDS
p165

ABE

WESTERN
HIGHLANDS
p109

CENTRAL
HIGHLANDS
p141

PERTH

STIRLING

SOUTH WEST
HIGHLANDS
p205

EDINBURGH

GLASGOW

SOUTHERN
SCOTLAND
p233

BOTHIES

Dawn over Beinn Dearg Mòr from Shenavall, North West Highlands

FOREWORD

A whiff of smoke on the chilly air is often the first sign. Then a faint glimmer of light floats in the darkness ahead. After walking another hundred yards through crisp snow, the beam of my headtorch picks out a chimney, stone walls, and a single glowing window thick with condensation. My journey's end.

Approaching the wooden door, which I know will not be locked, is exciting and slightly scary. Who will I meet in this little cottage, far from anywhere? Will I be welcome? Will I find a warm reception, a spot by the fire, a space to roll out my sleeping mat and bed down for the night?

A couple of hours later, my belly is full and my hands cradle a mug of steaming tea. Leaning back in a rickety old chair I soak up the atmosphere of this cosy little space: the homely scent of coal smoke and food cooked over camping gas mixes with the soft, earthy smell of the building itself. Boots clump on wooden boards and sleeping bags, socks and mitts hang on a line. My new friends pass me a bottle of whisky, while around the room candles burn gently in the necks of already empty bottles, each testament to a past night just like this one.

Strangers who would be unlikely to exchange even the merest greeting on a city street share talk of politics, tales of mountain epics, and wax lyrical about the wild places of this land. Food that has been carried many a country mile is shared around. Later on perhaps a guitar comes out, or maybe a moothie (mouth organ), and the evening passes in a warm fug of song, laughter and chat until the flames fade in the grate and only the red embers glow.

Set in a wonderfully diverse landscape, the bothies of Scotland are something quite unique and a resource to be cherished and shared. Visited by a similarly unique and diverse range of characters, they are sure to offer the traveller an experience that is both stimulating and memorable. And Geoff Allan is just the kind of character one might hope to meet in a bothy. I am fortunate to count Geoff as a close friend, and together we have shared many unforgettable bothy days and nights. This guidebook is a labour of love, and an engaging and extraordinarily detailed reference work. The result of many years of research and travel, it is Geoff's personal ode to our bothy heritage. It is also a fine testament to some of the most beautiful and life-enriching wild lands of Scotland. I hope *The Scottish Bothy Bible* will inform and inspire, and contribute to the preservation and growth of our incredible bothy network.

Jamie Andrew OBE is an international mountaineer, quadruple amputee, and a lover of the Scottish hills

The view from Essan Bothy, Western Highlands

INTRODUCTION

"A simple shelter in remote country for the use and benefit of all those who love being in wild and lonely places."

Definition from the Mountain Bothies Association (MBA) members' handbook.

In the wilderness areas of Scotland, an eclectic collection of basic accommodation has grown into what is now a well-established network of mountain huts, known as bothies. The term comes from the Gaelic *bothan* (via the Old Irish *both*) meaning hut, and originally described rudimentary accommodation provided by landowners for bachelor farm labourers or estate workers who tended crops or livestock. In recent times, a bothy has come to mean a shelter that is freely available for anyone to stay the night or use as a lunch stop. The vast majority of bothies are single-storey crofts, farmsteads or estate houses that were abandoned, then saved from ruin and renovated. They vary in size from Easan Dorcha, affectionately known as 'The Teahouse' which is little bigger than a garden shed, to a bothy like Craig, a former youth hostel which has two reception rooms and three bedrooms upstairs. The network was formalised by the Mountain Bothies Association (MBA), which now maintains 81 properties with the agreement and support of the landowners and estates which own them.

As well as their historical associations, bothies differ from other systems of mountain huts and refuges around the world, in that very few are purpose built and the locations of the majority are not the result of strategic planning, so they may not necessarily lie close to a particular peak or along a recognised long-distance trail. Neither are bothies attached to particular national parks: they are randomly scattered across Scotland, some in very remote places that are rarely visited. And, except in a very few cases, the word bothy is not found on any OS maps – only the names can be recognised. In the landscape there are few physical clues to their whereabouts. On the well-trodden West Highland Way, for example, Rowchoish Bothy, which is just 2 miles from a popular beauty spot, is not signposted at all. This reticence to advertise locations is particularly marked at some visitor centres, where the bothies in the area are not included on the noticeboards displaying walks and bike trails. Another distinctive aspect of the culture which sets bothies apart is the concept of 'bothying', an eccentric ethos that revolves around purely going to a bothy for its own sake, without any other objective in mind, some regulars adopting a particular bothy as a home from home. This means there is a much wider cross section of the population out and about than would ordinarily be expected in a wilderness environment.

Fords of Avon

A desire to protect the shelters from over-use explains the aura of secrecy that has always surrounded them, even though this runs contrary to the ethos of 'open to all'. In 2009 however, the MBA put the locations of all the bothies it maintained online – prior to this, the information was officially only available to members. There are many more non-MBA estate bothies in the Highlands, their whereabouts closely guarded, details only passed on by word of mouth or hinted at in online forums or bothy book entries. Of these, a number of the better-known, non-MBA bothies are listed in this book.

FROM THE CLEARANCES TO MODERN TIMES

Many of the properties now used as open shelters were originally built to house shepherds and ghillies in the decades after the forced evictions known the Highland Clearances – events that occurred in the aftermath of a failed Scottish uprising in 1745 against the ruling Protestant government of George II. The rebellion of clan chiefs was led by Catholic Charles Edward Stuart, better known as 'Bonnie Prince Charlie'. In the years following the defeat, their power and wealth broken, many clans sold their land to new absentee landlords who turned to large-scale sheep farming and later deer stalking. Descendants of clan chiefs, too, became English speaking landlords and put profit before community. As a result, many crofters were driven from the land they had occupied for generations but to which they held no written title. Many families emigrated to the

Ruins of Carnoch township, Western Highlands

new worlds of Canada, America and Australia, embracing an opportunity to start life anew, though others were forcibly shipped out of the country. The remaining crofters were often coerced onto marginal land, and by the time a right of tenancy was enshrined in law in 1886, the extent of depopulation had already left its mark.

Life in the Highlands in the 18th century before the Clearances was, however, uncertain: many communities were little more than one failed harvest away from starvation, and malnutrition left people prone to illness and disease. By the early 19th century, with better infrastructure allowing export of surplus commodities, and agricultural innovations that led to increased crop

yields, particularly of potatoes, the population had recovered. However, the price of dependency on the potato was the decimation of crops by blight between 1846 and 1856, though the impact was not felt as harshly as in Ireland. In the late 19th century, many left for work in the factories of Glasgow, and subsequently, the tragic loss of life following two world wars sounded the death knell for many rural communities. Farms and cottages were abandoned and left as ghosts in the landscape all across the Highlands.

THE WORK OF THE MBA

In 1965, a chance remark in the bothy book at Backhill of Bush (p235) sparked the imagination of Bernhard Heath, a cyclist from Huddersfield. Realising

THE BEGINNINGS OF BOTHYING

Bothying, in the recreational sense, dates from the 1930s when the urban population had more leisure time and the pursuits of hill-walking and climbing were no longer the preserve of the middle classes. Week-end groups of mainly young men, hitch-hiking or scraping together enough cash to travel on buses, headed to the hills, and the partly derelict cottages soon became places to congregate and sleep for free. In some cases their use was clandestine, but, increasingly, various estates gave their tacit consent. Following World War II, this trend continued, enhanced by the growing popularity of 'Munro-bagging' – a quest to climb all the mountains in Scotland over 3,000 feet (914m). (See p298 for more on how hills of different height categories are named). Ex-army kit lowered the cost of being equipped for the mountain environment, and a number of guide books appeared which encouraged people out into the hills. By the 1960s, however, the fabric of many bothies began to suffer through misuse and lack of maintenance. A few were cared for by climbing clubs, but the remainder received only sporadic attention. Alastair Borthwick's *Always a Little Further* details the exploits of the 1930s pioneers and the seminal text *Mountain Days and Bothy Nights* by Dave Brown and Ian Mitchell provides anecdotes from the post-war period.

that some kind of effort was needed to make these refuges habitable, Heath and a few of his hill-walking and cycling friends decided to turn the ruins of Tunskeen Farm, Galloway (p257), into a basic shelter. At the end of that same year, he and a number of like-minded individuals gathered in a nearby village hall and the Mountain Bothies Association was born.

During the late 1960s and early 1970s the MBA extended its network from Galloway to the Cairngorms, Knoydart and then across the country, as well as taking over the upkeep of bothies maintained by various climbing clubs. By 1975, the number of bothies had reached 35 and the list steadily increased as many estates accepted requests to transform redundant properties.

A home for the night at Invermallie

Hutchison Memorial Hut, recently renovated by the MBA

Today there are more than 80 MBA bothies in Scotland and well over 90 in the UK as a whole, and enthusiasts continue to be on the lookout for more restoration projects to add to the roster. In 2015 the MBA celebrated its 50th anniversary and received the Queen's Award for Voluntary Service, the highest accolade for a voluntary group in the UK.

The MBA works collaboratively with landowners and relies extensively on the voluntary work of its members, with regular, well-attended work parties carrying out maintenance in each of its 7 regions. Every individual bothy has a maintenance officer (MO) who is expected to visit at least 2 or 3 times a year to check the building's condition, note jobs that need doing, and take away any rubbish. Many estate owners and their employees also take an active part, often providing transport and materials. As an MO myself, I would certainly encourage anyone to join the MBA, but you can always offer practical help by giving feedback or reporting problems, either using bothy note cards or online (www. mountainbothies.org.uk). Even simply saying that a bothy is in good condition is useful, as it can help a MO decide the best time for a visit.

This is a very positive time for the MBA network, with more bothies boasting new stoves and sleeping platforms, and a number of buildings treated to extensive renovations. Gelder Sheil (p181) and Gleann Dubh-lighe (p117) among others, now offer '5 star' bothy accommodation. Bothies at Cruib (p273) and Dryfehead (p247) are fine recent additions, while a new bothy at Camasunary on Skye (p285) was opened in May 2016 after the estate took back the original building to turn it back into a home. The organisation has had a generous amount of money bequeathed to it in recent years to pay for renovation projects, and was gifted its first property, Over Phawhope (p255) in the Borders region. This has been lavished with attention, and is a shining example of what is possible under the guardianship of this dedicated band of volunteers.

WHAT TO EXPECT

Although bothies come in many shapes and sizes, the most common layout is a simple cottage with 2 rooms, often referred to by its Scots term, *but and ben*, the *but* referring to the kitchen and living room, and the *ben* the bedroom. From the entrance vestibule there is typically a room to the left and one to the right, and occasionally a small additional chamber straight ahead. If a bothy has an attic space, entry is gained from secure internal stairs. Generally speaking, the upper floor rooms are used as sleeping accommodation only, although if a bothy is particularly full, different parties have the option to stay together in their own space and set up for the night.

Bothy accommodation is very rudimentary, and in almost all cases, there are no facilities. This means no gas, or electricity or a tap. You should expect only a wind and waterproof building that offers somewhere dry to sleep. If you are staying overnight, you will need to carry in all the equipment you would normally take camping, plus candles, and if there is a fireplace,

With the owner's permission this bothy is maintained by the
MOUNTAIN BOTHIES ASSOCIATION
A charity registered in Scotland, no. SC008685
Please keep the place tidy

Evidence of a work party at Uisinis Bothy, Islands

Fire

A good fire, affectionately known as "bothy TV", is an essential part of the bothy experience. Although you can collect fallen wood close to a number of bothies, it is best to assume you will carry in your own fuel. Coal is the most effective but briquettes and fire logs can suffice. A few bothy fires have occurred over the years and problems have led to some fireplaces being blocked up. Never leave a fire unattended and make sure that the embers are extinguished before you leave. Carbon monoxide alarms are currently being installed into MBA bothies with stoves, along with fire blankets and extinguishers.

fuel to burn. As a bare minimum, bothies will have a table and a couple of chairs, but many also have sleeping platforms. Water comes from a nearby stream, and although some bothies have latrines or loos, answering calls of nature will involve a walk and the use of a spade. Bothies can look romantic in photos, but in reality can be cold, dusty, damp, and pretty dark. Yet in the evening, with the fire blazing and candles burning, hot food on the table and a glass of wine at your elbow, the place is transformed. Some of the more remote bothies retain their original wood panelling and mantelpieces; others have sofas, bunk beds and even books. A few have the feel of a hostel rather than a shelter. Ultimately, it is how you make yourself at home that will shape your bothy experience.

Water

Water from Highland streams is usually safe to drink if you follow a few simple rules. Only take drinking water from a fast-flowing stream, never from standing water, and avoid water downstream of a bothy or any other habitation. If you have any concerns, boil your water first, or use a filter purification kit or iodine tablets. It is also considerate to wash up downstream of a bothy, and pour waste on the ground where it is less likely to flow back directly into the water. For the same reason, please avoid polluting streams by washing or brushing your teeth in them.

Toilets

Only a handful of bothies have toilet facilities but each bothy should be equipped with a toilet spade. The simple rule of thumb is to select a location at least 200 yards (180m) from the bothy, well away from nearby streams or standing water, dig a hole at least 6 inches (15cm) deep, and bury your deposit. You are also advised to burn your toilet paper, or bag it and carry it out.

WHAT TO TAKE

Many items are similar to those you would take camping. The most important are listed here.

Clothing

Even in summer you need to keep warm so don't forget thermal mid-layers (including a set for sleeping in) and a waterproof jacket and overtrousers. Bring hats and gloves, outdoor trousers, not denim jeans which are too difficult to dry. For tops avoid cotton and choose synthetic, wicking or merino t-shirts. Sturdy boots with ankle support are essential. Partner these with good socks (bring spares) and a pair of gaiters. Bring a pair of sandals for indoors.

Food

Dried foods such as pasta, couscous, noodles, and cup-a-soup sachets, are quick to cook and light to carry. Porridge or breakfast bars are efficient in the mornings, and take plenty of chocolate, biscuits and sweets to keep up sugar levels and morale. Tea, coffee and dried milk are standard, and don't forget lunch items: pitta bread, and tortillas stay fresh longer than rolls. Condiment and sugar sachets (from cafés or ferries) are very useful additions. Many seasoned bothy goers, myself included, like cooking and take fresh vegetables, meat or fish, even eggs and milk. A bottle of wine is a welcome tonic and a hip flask is good to share. Carrying in an extra meal and rations, in case you are delayed by injury or trapped by bad weather, is also a wise move. And do hang up food supplies in a plastic bag. Mice can be a problem in bothies particularly in the summer.

Fuel

A fire is essential outside the summer months. Bringing in coal is well worth

The loo at Bob Scott's

BOTHIES WITH LOOS

Strabeg	p67
Lochivraon	p79
Ben Dronaig Lodge	p87
Craig	p95
Bob Scott's	p169
Corrour	p175
Glas-Allt-Shiel	p183
Ruigh Aiteachain	p189

the effort; briquettes are a lighter but bulkier alternative. Some kindling and firelighters are also useful.

Carrying in tents

At some popular bothies it is wise to add a lightweight tent or bivvy bag: bothies in this category are clearly indicated in the description. It is also quite acceptable to camp outside a bothy, using the communal space for cooking and socialising before retreating to your own personal space. In the majority of bothies, there are multiple rooms so you can set yourself up independently from another group. However, from a purist's point of view, not carrying in a tent when you are going to a bothy out of season, or you are pretty certain it is not going to be full, adds an extra frisson to your trip.

Descent to Shenavall

ESSENTIAL ITEMS

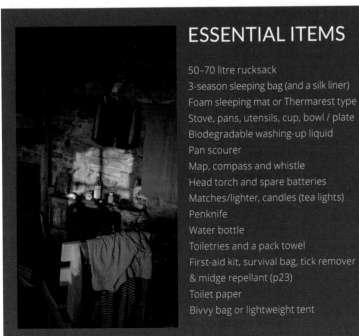

50–70 litre rucksack
3-season sleeping bag (and a silk liner)
Foam sleeping mat or Thermarest type
Stove, pans, utensils, cup, bowl / plate
Biodegradable washing-up liquid
Pan scourer
Map, compass and whistle
Head torch and spare batteries
Matches/lighter, candles (tea lights)
Penknife
Water bottle
Toiletries and a pack towel
First-aid kit, survival bag, tick remover & midge repellant (p23)
Toilet paper
Bivvy bag or lightweight tent

It may seem obvious, but without a tent, you simply have to locate the bothy, which can be quite a challenge if you are arriving in the dark. During daylight you may think that there was no way you would have difficulty finding even a familiar bothy, but the number of times I have walked in after dark and my heart has started to race because I should be there by now, or perhaps I have walked by the bothy without noticing. The complete relief when the tell-tale gable end looms up out of the darkness is one of the best rushes of the whole bothy experience.

BOTHY ETIQUETTE

Although there are no formal rules, there is a bothy code formulated by the MBA and posted at every property the association maintains. Put simply,

it is the common-sense philosophy of treating others with respect, and leaving a bothy in the condition you would wish to find it in. Most importantly, no one has an exclusive right to a bothy and the concept of "first come, first served" does not exist. Bothies are open shelters, available to all, and the overriding ethos is that, however full, there is always room for one more. This is rarely a problem, as long as you take heed of the cautionary note about the popularity of certain bothies at Easter and in the summer months. The practicalities of carrying enough food and fuel for any more than 3 or 4 days, means few people stay for extended periods, and doing so is discouraged though nothing is formally set in stone. Also, while it is advisable

THE BOTHY CODE

The bothies maintained by the MBA are available by courtesy of the owners. Please respect this privilege and note that bothies are used entirely at your own risk. And finally, please record your visit in the Bothy Log-Book.

Respect Other Users

Please leave the bothy clean and tidy with dry kindling for the next visitors. Make other visitors welcome. If they are not MBA members set a good example.

Respect the Bothy

Tell us about any accidental damage. Don't leave graffiti or vandalise the bothy. Please take out all rubbish which you can't burn. Avoid burying rubbish; this pollutes the environment. Please don't leave perishable food as this attracts vermin. Guard against fire risk and ensure the fire is out before you leave. Make sure the doors and windows are properly closed when you leave.

Respect the Surroundings

If there is no toilet at the bothy please bury human waste out of sight. Use the spade provided, keep well away from the water supply and never use the vicinity of the bothy as a toilet. Never cut live wood or damage estate property. Use fuel sparingly.

Respect Agreement with the Estate

Please observe any restrictions on use of the bothy, for example during stag stalking or at lambing time. Please remember bothies are available for short stays only. The owner's permission must be obtained if you intend an extended stay.

Respect the Restriction on Numbers

Because of over crowding and lack of facilities, large groups (6 or more) should not use a bothy nor camp near a bothy without first seeking permission from the owner. Bothies are not available for commercial groups.

An evening's entertainment

not to leave valuables lying around when you go out for the day, there is a fundamental element of trust between bothy goers not to interfere with the possessions of others while they are left unattended.

Consideration for others

Good social skills are definitely an asset and bothy goers tend to have a strong community spirit. People help each other out by sharing food, hot drinks as well as advice and experiences. Occasionally you may encounter an antisocial group and the two bothies on Loch Lomond side, Rowchoish (p227) and Doune Byre (p215) do have a reputation for rowdiness along with Tunskeen (p257) and Backhill of Bush in Galloway (p235). Some go to bothies for solitude, others for reunions and gatherings, taking guitars and a repertoire of songs. It is important to go with the flow, and maybe contribute your own party piece.

If there is a particular issue with a bothy, this is prominently indicated on the MBA website, and also in forums on internet sites (check out Ukhillwalking.com, Walkhighlands.com and Grough.co.uk). Recently, when a gable end collapsed (now repaired) word got round the bothy community pretty fast so no one got stranded at that particularly remote location. It is also a bothy tradition to leave some essentials behind for the next person to use. Arriving cold and tired to find a kind, considerate person has left coal or chopped wood and kindling is a godsend. Occasionally, people leave beer and, more regularly, the odd packet of biscuits, tea bags or

A model of good practice. Wood left at Ruigh Aiteachean

pasta, although this is not encouraged because it attracts mice. Nevertheless, many bothies have a tin box or plastic container for storing food items. Before you leave, spend a little time tidying up, collecting and chopping wood for the next person, and maybe leaving something – candles and spare matches are always welcome. It is heartening how much this happens, especially out of the summer season. Also, do leave reading material, especially books. Many of the more remote bothies have a small library but even well out of date newspapers are worth a read on a slow bothy evening and make perfect kindling.

Rubbish

One of the biggest bothy bugbears, for the MBA and regular bothy users, is

people leaving rubbish behind. Always carry out all your rubbish, including bottles. If you arrive at a bothy, and find rubbish there, burn what is combustible and take away what you can. If you are already overloaded, send a bothy report card to the MBA or post details on the website.

Wood collection

Collect as much fuel as possible before setting up properly and unpacking to ensure you will have a fire for the whole evening. On approaching a bothy, I am already on the search for timber (good locations are indicated in the entry) and will scout for wood up to a mile around the property. The best time to collect wood is after a storm or flood, when dead wood accumulates under the

tree canopy or along a river bank. For that reason, autumn and early winter are favourite times for stalwarts to go bothying. However, there is always something to be found if you have keen radar, with the exception of a few bothies in the Cairngorms, (Faindouran and Hutchison spring to mind, see p179 and p187) as well as places like Kinbreack (p125) and Suileag (p75), stuck out in barren moorland. The absolutely sacrosanct rule is never to cut live branches; this damages trees and green wood will not burn. Avoid bog wood – the drowned roots of ancient forest – it is almost always completely sodden. Around a couple of bothies where habitat requires preservation you are asked not to pick up fallen wood, such as at Ruigh Aiteachain (p189)

THE BOTHY BOOK

In the majority of MBA bothies there is a bothy book and you are encouraged to record your visit. It is also good practice to write details of your itinerary, in the very rare event that a rescue party has to work out where you were heading if you get into difficulties. The bothy book is always worth a read and you can pick up useful information about navigation, the best places to find wood or unusual walk in routes people have taken. Some people are even inspired to poetry or prose, and you also occasionally find drawings and endearing entries from enthusiastic kids out on their first bothy adventure. Many bothies have fewer than 100 entries a year, and none for weeks on end during winter. Old books are generally taken away by the maintenance officer for safe-keeping, but at Clennoch (p243) there are laminated old bothy books going back over 20 years.

Two contrasting entries in the bothy book at Glencoul (p49) stick in the memory because of the starkly differing experiences. The first, written in tight, measured handwriting is the idyllic account of a couple who paddled into the bothy from Kylesku, picking scallops from the shallows, mussels from the shore and toasting their good fortune with a bottle of chilled Sauvignon blanc. The very next entry was scrawled with manic urgency and was a veritable tale of woe. A guy had stumbled across the moor from Inchnadamph, a good 6 miles through some tough terrain, in awful weather. The sense of relief in reaching the bothy was replaced by anguish when he realised he had used an envelope to light the fire containing a £50 note – all the money he had for the week!

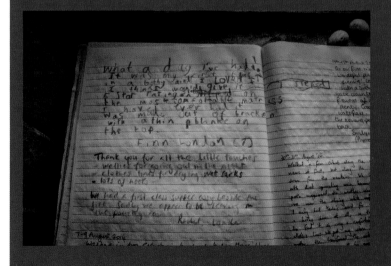

Bothying in winter

I find winter is the best time to go bothying, as long as you have additional kit and you can guarantee a fire. Carrying in fuel, a good sleeping bag and mat, spare warm clothes and enough hot drinks and food at this time of year is absolutely essential. Get it right and you'll enjoy a winter-wonderland vista of Scotland; get it wrong and you'll spend the night in a freezer, resolved to go bothying only in the warmer months. When visiting in the winter, the objective is to minimise risk. For cooking and boiling water on gas, a 70/30 butane/propane mix works much better in cold temperatures than straight butane. I generally take in a 500ml canister and cook a two-portion meal on the first night to guarantee eating the next evening. Fuel for the fire is essential (many regulars take a 10kg sack of coal), plus firelighters, maybe some packaged kindling, and candles. In winter, bothies can be grim places without a fire.

where the estate supplies logs. Other estates also supply wood from time to time, but you can't rely on it. Some of the more remote bothies, and a few coastal ones, have a peat cutting close by, which can be utilised well into October if the estate, or bothy goers, have been diligent over the summer. At a coastal bothy there is no guarantee of finding driftwood, but there is normally a storm beach in the vicinity (usually described in the entry). Most bothies have a saw, and occasionally an axe to cut timber down to size, though it can often be an onerous task when the teeth are rusted or the axe blunt.

HILLCRAFT AND STAYING SAFE

Although the walk into a bothy is not as challenging as heading up to the high peaks, don't put yourself in undue danger and don't assume help will come. Common sense, resilience and experience should get you out of all but the most extreme situations.

Maps and navigation

Always take a map and compass; they are essential items for any trip. The OS Landranger 1:50,000 scale sheets applicable for each bothy are given in the information boxes and if precise navigation or detail is required the 1:25,000 scale Explorer maps have been added. Never go out on your own if you are not confident about your map-reading and navigational skills. Better to consult Eric Landmuir's *Mountaincraft and Leadership* or go on a course (Scotland's Outdoor Training Centre at Glenmore Lodge, and the Mountaineering Council of Scotland

offer excellent tuition). Although GPS has now become a very accurate tool and is used by a lot of hill-walkers, it should be regarded only as a backup to map and compass. If batteries fail or there is a software glitch, you are stuck. In addition, while pinpointing your location on a map using GPS is useful, and especially reassuring in zero visibility, it cannot tell you where to go next, unless you have entered way markers before you set off. Phones have similar issues of limited power supply, malfunction, and in more remote areas coverage may be non-existent. When you buy a new OS map you get the additional option of downloading a scanned version of the map for your phone or tablet, which can be a useful back up. And most importantly, follow best practice by leaving a route description with a friend or relative or a note on a car dashboard, especially if you are travelling alone, including the estimated time that you plan to return.

Medical conditions

Remember to take any personal medication you require, and if part of a group, make everyone aware of medical conditions, such as diabetes, and how to deal with them. Get into the habit of carrying a first-aid kit and a survival bag.

Weather

Before setting off on trips to the hills, study the weather forecast and always take note of tightening isobars, indicating that strong winds are imminent. In addition to the BBC and Met Office, an excellent resource is the Mountain Weather Information

Service (www.mwis.org.uk), which produces forecasts for 8 different mountain areas across the UK, 5 in Scotland. A new forecast for the following 3 days is posted by 4.30pm every day. However, even when you are armed with the forecast, be aware that the weather in Scotland can change suddenly, reducing visibility on summits, or bringing heavy rain after a sunny morning as a front moves in from the Atlantic.

Midges, ticks and snakes

Midges appear with unerring regularity from the beginning of June, get worse in July and August, before disappearing in mid-September. I have found the best repellant is 'Avon's Skin so Soft' in combination with mosquito coils, though there are various other products available containing DEET. A head net is an extreme measure but may be useful in the height of summer.

Ticks can be problematic in areas where there are high numbers of deer or sheep. They are hard to spot and have a painless bite, but once embedded in the skin are difficult to dislodge. When walking through bracken or tall grass, wear long trousers. Once attached, ticks burrow their heads into your flesh: armpits, neck, head and groin are particularly susceptible. Tick removers (from outdoor shops or vets' surgeries) do the best job. Some ticks carry Lyme disease, a debilitating condition which can become quite serious if left untreated. Removing infected ticks within 36 hours seriously reduces the risks of catching the disease.

The adder is Britain's only venomous snake and you may see them sunning themselves in open moorland, woodland edges and heaths. They are unlikely to bother you unless you bother them, and most people who are bitten were handling them at the time. A bite can cause dizziness, vomiting and a painful swelling.

In an emergency

If one of your party or someone in a bothy gets injured, try to stay calm and assess the situation rationally. The basic first-aid procedure follows a simple acronym ABC: checking airways, breathing and circulation. Make the casualty as comfortable as possible, and if unconscious put them in the recovery position. Try and work out your exact position and consider whether to seek help, which may involve one of the party walking out if you cannot get a mobile signal. Telephone 999 and ask for the Police and Mountain Rescue, and be ready to explain the situation in detail, including supplying a grid reference. Mountain Rescue provides an excellent service, but don't plan a trip on the assumption you can call them out if you happen to get into difficulties. Only contact them in a real emergency. If you are in any doubt about your own competence or, more crucially, that of the weakest or least experienced member of a group, make plans conservatively.

RIVER CROSSINGS

Rivers in spate are one of the most serious hazards when visiting a bothy, so treat fast-flowing water higher than knee-deep with extreme caution. In

Paddling into Essan, Western Highlands

periods of thaw or heavy rainfall, run-off from large areas of high ground channels into a single water course lower down in a glen, and the level of rivers and even small burns can rise alarmingly quickly, especially if the ground is already saturated. It is often necessary to wade through shallow streams on your way to a bothy and these fording points are indicated in the description information boxes. When encountering a crossing where the water level has risen, always walk upstream to where you can cross more safely but if this is not possible, take a detour to the nearest bridge, even if it means going miles out of your way. It is preferable to putting yourself in danger. A worst-case scenario would be to cross one swollen stream, come up against

another that is even more fast flowing, and on your return discover that the first is running higher than before!

RIGHT TO ROAM

Scotland's access rights are amongst the most liberal in the world, and the right to roam was enshrined in statute by the Land Reform Act (Scotland) in 2003. Always act responsibly and with due consideration of others, whether landowners or outdoor enthusiasts. Although the interests of these two parties do not often coincide, bothies represent one area where a successful relationship has been forged. By law, landowners must not put up fences, walls or signs that prevent people from crossing their land, but you are advised to keep to paths and tracks

where possible, especially during the stag-stalking season. This runs from 1st July to 20th October and during these times bothies may be closed, or access restricted. The Heading for the Hills web service (www.outdooraccess-scotland.com), enables walkers and climbers to find out where deer stalking is taking place on higher ground and plan their trips accordingly. Information is also often posted at popular parking spots. Your co-operation is appreciated and if you are planning a trip in the stalking season or to a remote bothy, make a call to the estate as a common courtesy. The appropriate phone numbers are given for each bothy.

CROSSING A RIVER

When crossing a swollen stream, assess the situation calmly and look for a stretch of water that is wide and shallow, with perhaps only the final step into a fast-flowing channel. Avoid points immediately above waterfalls or large rocks – you could be swept into them. Plot your route carefully and don't rush. Ensure your spare clothing is safely stowed in plastic bags, undoing hip and chest straps so your rucksack does not drag you under. Do not go barefoot: the shock of cold water and sharp stones can make you lose your balance and your boots will have a much better grip. Walking poles, too, are a great help. If able, walk diagonally upstream across the channel, focusing on the point where you aim to climb out onto the far bank. If you are in a group and contemplating a mutually supportive team shuffle, pay closest attention to the weakest member of the party, and put the strongest body upstream.

Over the years I have taken a number of dubious decisions to wade through deep water. On one November trip, I intended to head to Meanach (p157), which, coming from Luibeilt, is over on the far bank of the Abhainn Rath, a sizeable river. It had been raining off and on all afternoon and I saw the crossing wouldn't be straighforward. Walking upstream to find a safe place, I trudged over half a mile before teetering across from boulder to boulder. I had no walking poles, just an ice axe. Having made it to the far bank, I marched quickly towards the bothy, taking little heed of the terrain, and fell straight into a chest-deep bog. Stuck miles from help with a full pack and shockingly cold, I managed to hook onto solid ground using the axe and pulled myself out. The evening was spent wringing out my sodden clothes. Lesson learned.

River Avon, walking into Faindouran, Eastern Highlands

En route to Glendhu, Northern Highlands

There is no right of access for motor vehicles on private estates, and access to some bothies is restricted during the lambing season when the shelters are used by shepherds. Burleywhag (p241) and Achnanclach (p43) are in active use every year. Keep dogs on a lead at all times where animals are grazing. A farmer has the lawful right to shoot any dog worrying livestock on sight. Other activities that may affect bothy access are heather-burning, grouse-shooting and, increasingly, forestry felling. Large swathes of conifers that were planted in the decades after World War II are now being harvested, with new forestry tracks bulldozed in to take out the valuable timber. Many areas of the Highlands and Borders have been denuded, and although unattractive, this is still an important part of the rural economy. New forestry tracks have improved access to a number of bothies, as have roads to wind farms and hydro-electric power schemes, although this can make them feel less remote.

GETTING AROUND ON PUBLIC TRANSPORT

I am a big fan of public transport and have relied heavily on it over the years, especially in the writing of this book. The combination of train, ferry and bike has taken me to the furthest corners of the country and proves that a car is not essential. Transport options for each bothy are listed along with contact details for service providers.

Trains

Train services run regularly from Glasgow and Edinburgh to the hubs of Fort William and Inverness, and the West Highland Line train from Glasgow Queen Street to Mallaig is considered one of the finest railway journeys in Europe. The view down to Loch Shiel when you cross the Glenfinnan viaduct (the Harry Potter Bridge) is breathtaking. Beyond Inverness there are two services, one heading west to Kyle of Lochlash, and the other north to Bonar Bridge and on to Wick and Thurso. Remember that you must book your bike on every Scotrail service north and south of the Central Belt. There is an allocation of 6 spaces on the West Highland Line, but a more limited one on services to Inverness and Wick.

The classic stopping points for bothying by train are the stations at Corrour and Glenfinnan. Corrour, as featured in the film *Trainspotting*, sits on the edge of Rannoch Moor, and provides access to one of my favourite bothies, Staoineag, and also nearby Meanach (p161 and p157). Stepping onto the platform here effectively saves you a 10 mile walk in from either Rannoch or Spean Bridge, and is quite a surreal experience if you arrive at 8am after catching the sleeper from London Euston. The walk in north from Glenfinnan heads up to Knoydart and the Rough Bounds via Corryhully p113). This is the start of a classic multi-day trip through to Glenpean (p119), A'Chùil (p111) and Sourlies (p135), ending at Inverie where you can catch a boat back to Mallaig and the train back south.

Buses and coaches

The national coach routes in Scotland are also very reliable, especially for Glen Coe and Glen Shiel on the A87 heading to Skye, with interconnecting buses from the main towns (such as Oban to Inverness). Unfortunately the post bus system was drastically cut back in 2009 but Royal Mail still offers a limited service. In many areas local bus operators have filled in the provision, although this is often restricted to a single daily service (check www.bustimes.org.uk). Most local buses have no space for bikes, except for two very useful services from Inverness to Durness.

Ferries

One of the sources of particular national pride are the services sailing to the islands off the west and north coasts of Scotland, run predominantly by Caledonian Macbrayne, known as Calmac (www.calmac.co.uk), on which bikes get free passage. Bothies on Islay, Rùm and Mull are all accessed from a Calmac service. Train and ferry services are integrated at both Oban and Mallaig, and there are useful local ferries from Islay to Jura, Mallaig to Inverie and Knoydart, and across the Kyle of Durness and on to Kearvaig (p55) and Cape Wrath.

Bikes and paddling

Many bothies have tracks up to the door suitable for access by bike and quite a few are situated on the coast or beside lochs and reachable by kayak. With the advent of 'bike packing' and 'fat bikes' pretty much all bothies are now within reach, but there will be compromises on what you can carry in. The listings indicate all the bothies that you can mountain bike to: graded easy (locations that you can cycle to with panniers without any issues) and straightforward (stress free mountain biking, plus cycling with panniers but involving dismounting and pushing where necessary). Some bothies that can be reached by kayak require a high level of experience to negotiate tides and landing. Those noted have a relatively easy approach.

HOW TO USE THIS GUIDE

There are 8 sections representing different areas of the country, from the far Northern Highlands, to a whole section devoted to Island bothies. The selection in each region combines all the MBA bothies, plus the most well-known private shelters maintained by estates or groups of enthusiasts, plus notes on bothies that are either closed or in disrepair, and a summary of other non-MBA properties that are worth exploring. The selection is as complete as I can make it without betraying any confidences. Part of the appeal and quirkiness of bothying is the voyage of discovery that you set out upon, to find out about the secret haunts only known about by those who have spent years exploring the country.

Bothy listings

The start of each entry gives: the year the MBA took over maintenance or began renovating the bothy, a description of size and sleeping arrangements, GPS latitude/longitude coordinates, grid reference, elevation, and the appropriate 1:50,000 OS Landranger map number.

Information boxes indicate the need to bring in supplies of fuel or where to find it, plus a helpful summary of distance, time and terrain of the

Burnmouth Cottage, Islands

easiest walk in routes starting from the nearest car park. The 1:25,000 Explorer map number has been added if extra navigational details are required, including the Gaelic names of geographical features such as streams and rock outcrops that are not printed at 1:50,000 scale. Key attractions include the best hills to climb, waterfalls, woodland walks and archaeological sites within easy reach, as well as recommended cafés and pubs. All the public transport options are given and special notes indicate bothies that are locked or occupied during the stalking or lambing seasons.

Layout and sleeping arrangements are described, with LHR and RHR denoting left-hand or right-hand room as you walk in through the bothy door. The

room that is most commonly used is referred to as the communal area. Sleeping platforms and alpine-style bunk beds have been built in more and more bothies over the last few years – definitely preferable to the floor. The specified number of people refers to how many this provision can accommodate, without reference to additional space on the floor. Attics increase the number that can be catered for, as they are almost exclusively used as dormitories.

Walk in times err on the generous side, taking into account a full rucksack and an average level of fitness. This equates to approximately to 2 miles an hour, but a speedy party may cover up to 3 miles an hour without stops or navigation

TERRAIN

Terrain is divided into 3 categories that cover the majority of walk ins. Additionally, there are three walk ins designated 'very tough', two on Jura plus the walk in to Oban (p129) from Lochailort.

Easy Along a track or clearly identifiable path with minimal navigation required.

Straightforward Along tracks and paths with some navigation involved; also covers those over 4 miles in length, and those with short uphill sections or stretches of boggy ground. In this category are routes that may be easy in good weather, but include a stream or river crossing that could be challenging after heavy rain or snow melt. This is denoted by 'river crossing' in the information box. When rivers are 'in spate' the water level is high.

Challenging Involves sections following faint trails or pathless terrain that may be particularly rough or boggy and which require good navigation skills. This category also describes straightforward routes that are over 6 miles long or have long uphill sections, typically over a bealach or pass, or have multiple river crossings to negotiate.

The vast majority of the bothies listed are reachable with a bit of determination, and many are accessed very simply with a fair wind. A few of the more remote bothies do require a high level of competency in navigation and hillcraft, and even a trip to the bothies west of Corrour, or into Knoydart and the Rough Bounds, can put you in a compromising situation if the weather seriously deteriorates. When you pass a sign on the walk in advising caution, do pause for thought.

issues. Allow extra time in inclement weather, and especially when there is a potentially hazardous river crossing.

The descriptions and the Top 5 lists should enable you to choose the right bothy for your particular needs. There is no grading system, which would be arbitrary and subjective, but the few bothies that have a particular reputation for rowdy and antisocial behaviour are noted, as are those shelters commonly used only as a lunch stop. Whether you are travelling solo or with a few friends or family, the doors of Scotland's bothies, each with its own unique atmosphere and set in a range of superb locations, are open. Welcome to the wonderful, eccentric, unpredictable and thoroughly rewarding world of bothying.

TAKE CARE

You are entering remote, sparsely-populated, potentially dangerous mountain country.

Please ensure that you are adequately experienced and equipped to complete your journey without assistance.

Kearvaig Bothy, Nothern Highlands

TOP 5 FOR
COAST & BEACHES

TOP 5 FOR
FAMILIES & BEGINNERS

TOP 5 FOR
WILDLIFE

Eagle's Nest, Islands

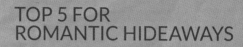

TOP 5 FOR
ROMANTIC HIDEAWAYS

TOP 5 FOR
SOLITUDE

TOP 5 FOR
HISTORY & LEGENDS

Suileag, Northern Highlands

TOP 5 FOR
SPECTACULAR SCENERY

TOP 5 FOR
MUNROS

TOP 5 FOR
WILD & REMOTE

Staoineag, Central Highlands

NORTHERN
HIGHLANDS

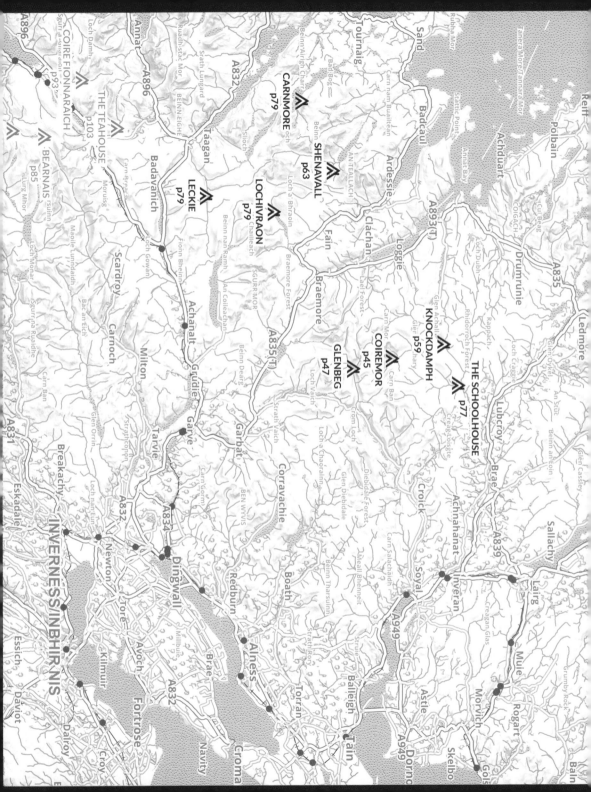

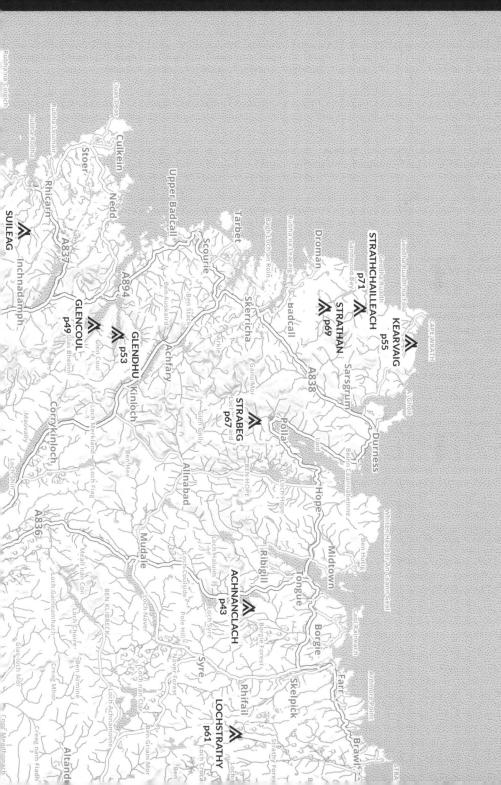

FUEL SUPPLY Some fallen branches and kindling in woodland on slopes of Sron Ruadh.

KEY ATTRACTIONS The ridge of Ben Loyal (765m) is a classic day out. More mellow options: Beinn Stumanadh (527m) S of the bothy or a stroll to the ruined Caisteal Bharraich with views over the Kyle of Tongue. Torrisdale Bay is one of a number of fine beaches dotted along the N coast.

PUBLIC TRANSPORT Scotrail Northern Highland Line Inverness to Wick, stops at Lairg and Thurso. Durness Bus service 803 Durness to Thurso (01971 5112230); Postbus service 134 Lairg to Tongue.

SPECIAL NOTES Not officially available during stag stalking, 1 September to 20 October, but in practice it is left unlocked. Local estate workers have priority. Bothy is best avoided during the lambing season.

⩜
ACHNANCLACH

Working estate cottage close to the road, in a wonderfully remote location (1982)

SIZE Large; plenty of sleeping space
LOCATION LAT/LONG 58.4269, -4.3463, NC 631 512, 148m, LR Map 10

Achnanclach, 'the field of the stones', is one of the most far-flung bothies in the country. Caught between the heather-clad slopes of Beinn Stumanadh and the waterlogged blanket bog that stretches up to the rugged North Atlantic coast between Tongue and Bettyhill, it is a perfect destination for soaking up the intoxicating emptiness of this precious, windswept and lochan-studded landscape. The steading, known locally as Poole Cottage, was commissioned in the early 1900s to serve as the schoolhouse for the small township that had flourished on this fertile strip of pasture for well over 200 years. The sheep here are still prized for their hardiness and ability to lamb without close supervision, and you can still see the distinctive lines of ridge and furrow that stretch back towards Loch Craggie. Also visible are numerous stone foundations and tumbledown enclosures scattered through the tall grass and bracken.

The building is a long, elongated structure made up of 4 rooms, 3 of which are connected, and a storage outbuilding accessed by a separate door. Generally found in good condition, it is one of the few MBA bothies kept in service for estate management and here is a maze of stock control fences outside the building that are in regular use. The RHR contains a large working fireplace, a sleeping platform in the far corner, and 2 tables. The 2 iron bed frames in the second room are, alas, without mattresses. At the back with its own little skylight, there is also a small, snug box-room with a raised sleeping platform that extends across the whole floor area. The LHR is referred to by the local estate workers as the 'Green Room' because of the perpetual build-up of mould caused by damp seeping through the concrete floor. Although this is periodically cleaned, the room is rarely used.

ROUTE 1
Situated near the top of Loch Loyal, this is one of very few bothies that can be seen from the road. From 50 yds S of the layby, take the grass track down to the bridge between two lochs. Path continues around the shore and up to the bothy. Some choose to walk on to Lochstrathy Bothy (p61), skirting the forestry plantations and negotiating the wetlands of the Flow Country, on the way to the RSPB reserve and train station at Forsinard.

DISTANCE 1½ miles
TIME 30–45 minutes
TERRAIN Easy. Path all the way
PARKING for 2 cars at small layby (NC 614 506)

FUEL SUPPLY Sometimes wood accumulates at the head of the loch. Bring supplies.

KEY ATTRACTIONS Perfect base for an ascent of Seana Bhràigh (927m), one of the most remote and spectacular Munros in the country.

PUBLIC TRANSPORT Scotrail service from Inverness to Thurso and Wick, stops at Culrain and Lairg. Macleod's Dial-a-Bus runs Tuesday to Thursday (01408 641354) from Lairg to Oykel Bridge. Postbus service 123 Drumbeg–Ledmore Junction–Lairg stops at Oykel Bridge; no return service.

SPECIAL NOTES Please check with the Corriemulzie Estate (01403 891765) before visiting during the stag-stalking season 1 September to 20 October. Crossing the Corriemulzie River and tributary Allt a' Choire Bhuidhe when in spate is dangerous. Accessible by bike if you are prepared to negotiate the fords.

COIREMOR, MAGOO'S BOTHY

Luxury converted stables hidden in remote wilderness (1967 and 2002)

SIZE Large; 3 separate bothies, plenty of sleeping space
LOCATION LAT/LONG 57.8565, -4.8582, NH305 888, 318m, LR Map 20

Only when you make the final approach to the upper reaches of Strath Mulzie does the scale of the spectacular ridge of Creag an Duine, and the procession of steeply gouged coires protecting the high plateau of Seana Bhràigh, reveal itself. Sheltering beneath these imposing cliffs, Coiremor Bothy seems to cling to the sanctuary of Loch a' Choire Mhòir's eastern shore. The conversion of the stables was one of the MBA's first projects and no mean feat given the site's remote location. Later, in 2002, the ruins of the main farmstead were also restored as a lasting memorial to a dead airman, Mark 'Magoo' Maguire. The RAF helped transport materials and equipment to the site, and the renovation took just over two months. The bothy now consists of a terrace in 3 separate sections: the main body of the building – the memorial bothy; a self-contained compartment; and the original MBA bothy at the end of the terrace.

Coiremor is the closest a bothy comes to being some kind of boutique hotel, although it lacks a sign, unlike its distant cousin Fèith Uaine, the 'Tarf Hotel'. Magoo's has an open fireplace, a large dining table and a makeshift kitchen area. In its adjoining bedroom, the large bunk-bed sleeping platform sleeps 4 people. The second section has its own external door, a king-sized sleeping platform with two single mattresses, a table-bench and a small stove. Lit only by a small window in the back wall, this intimate space could, with some imagination, make for a romantic destination. The E end of the building is the original bothy, which consists of 2 wood-panelled rooms: one with a chintzy set of armchairs and a sofa; the other acting as a sleeping area. There is also another welcoming stove. You almost expect a hotel bar to complete the illusion! One of the best Scottish MBA bothies, Coiremor combines a remote location and spectacular scenery with luxurious accommodation. It is very special yet criminally under-visited.

ROUTE 1

Most approach from N via Glen Einig and Strath Mulzie. Unusually for the Highlands, you can drive along the track from Oykel Bridge to Corriemulzie Lodge. Park just before the lodge at NH 327953 and then it's a straightforward walk up the glen. Care is needed crossing the river at NH 293912 and NH 293906. There are stepping stones but the water level can rise quickly. Walking or cycling from Oykel Bridge adds a further 6 miles. Follow directions to the Schoolhouse (p77) at Duag Bridge, cross bridge over Abhainn Dubhag, then turn L along the track to Corriemulzie Lodge.

DISTANCE 5 miles
TIME 2–2½ hours
TERRAIN Straightforward. Track all the way to the bothy. River crossings
PARKING Before lodge (NH 327953)

FUEL SUPPLY Bring supplies.

KEY ATTRACTIONS Strategic base for climbing the surrounding Munros, including Beinn Dearg (1084m), Cona Mheall (980m), Am Faochagach (951m) Meall nan Ceapraichean (926m) and Seana Bhràigh (927m). A gentler stalkers' path up from the weir leads to atmospheric Loch Srùban Mòra. Fine bar and bunkhouse at the Old Drovers Inn, Aultguish.

PUBLIC TRANSPORT Citylink service 961 from Inverness to Ullapool 3 times a day; request stops at Black Bridge and Inverlael. Nearest train station: Ardgay on North Highland Line from Inverness to Wick. No public transport to Croick.

SPECIAL NOTES Not officially available during stag stalking, 1 September to 20 October but in practice it is left unlocked. Bothy's future remains uncertain.

GLENBEG

One of the most secluded bothies in the Highlands

SIZE Small; 2 rooms, limited sleeping space
LOCATION LAT/LONG 57.8088, -4.8402, NH 313 834, 349m, LR Map 20

Set in the wilderness of the Freevater Forest between Ullapool and Bonar Bridge, Glenbeg is one of the most secluded bothies in the Highlands. It sits high up in Gleann Beag, E of the imposing plateau of Beinn Dearg, and S of Seana Bhràigh, one of Scotland's most remote Munros. On arrival, you really feel you have entered a lost world, as very few people now venture out here. There were originally 2 bothies on the site: a stone-built cottage maintained by the MBA, and a white corrugated-iron hut belonging to the Inverlael Estate. The hut burned down in April 2012, and after an acrimonious dispute, the MBA pulled out. Although the bothy is no longer maintained, it is cosy with 2 small rooms and an external storage area at the W end of the building. The LHR has a big fireplace, windows front and back, and a token table and chairs. The back room is an empty dormitory with one window. Unfortunately the present uncertainty about the bothy's future means you set out with more trepidation than in the past.

ROUTE 1

Continue on the metalled estate road leading to Alladale Lodge, and just after the tarmac ends and the track climbs steeply to the house, turn L down to a bridge over the Alladale River. The track kinks R then L up the far bank, through pines and birch, and after skirting Sròn Ugaidh, enters the wide strath of Gleann Mòr. Continue along the valley to the bridge that crosses the Abhainn a' Ghlinne Mhòir and on to Deanich Lodge. Soon after pick up the track from Black Bridge, and continue to a 2nd bridge over to the N bank of the river. After a mile, re-cross the river just before a small weir. The boggy path to the bothy is not marked on the 1:50000 map beyond the weir but is clearly visible. It can be difficult to cross after sustained rainfall.

DISTANCE 9½ miles

TIME 4 hours

TERRAIN Challenging. Well-defined track. River crossing

PARKING Glencalvie Lodge (NH 464 891)

ROUTE 2

Follow the metalled road past the farm at Lubriach, and head up the track on the E side of the glen, rather than crossing the bridge to Strathvaich Lodge. Contour up onto the moor; ignore the track branching R, and continue past the dam on Loch Vaich to the ruined settlement of Lubachlaggan. From here continue up the glen, ignore a track leading R and, soon after, pick up the track from Gleann Mòr to the bothy.

Straightforward cycle from both Glencalvie Lodge and Black Bridge but crossing the bog for the final stretch is laborious.

DISTANCE 10½ miles

TIME 4 to 5 hours

TERRAIN Challenging. Well-defined track. River crossing

PARKING Black Bridge on the A835 (NM 373 708)

⩓
GLENCOUL

Pocket-sized bothy with spectacular lochside views (1998)

SIZE Small; 2 rooms, both with raised platforms, sleeping 4
LOCATION LAT/LONG 58.2281, -4.9468, NC 271 305, 11m, LR Map 15, Explorer Map 442

Looking down to Glencoul Bothy from the Stack of Glencoul's precarious summit cairn, the long, deep fjord stretches back gracefully towards Unapool and Kylesku. To the W, the peaks of Sàil Gorm and Sàil Gharb on Quinag's N shoulder catch the eye, and, for a fleeting moment at least, you can happily feel the master (or mistress) of all you survey. This heavily glaciated scene, carved from rocks subjected to a massive shift of tectonic plates over 400 million years ago, really draws you in, yet until recently, surprisingly few people ventured out to this intoxicating spot. Located at the head of Loch Glencoul, which means narrow glen in Gaelic, the bothy is a small *but and ben* that abuts the gable end of a larger house in a slightly peculiar fashion – the 2 buildings seem pinned together like blocks of pre-constructed Lego. The bothy was originally used as a school, and its close proximity to the main house allowed direct access between the two buildings. The main house is locked and the windows boarded up.

Much of the history of the first tenants who lived here in the early 1890s was collected by poet Alistair Elliot, whose grandfather John Elliot was the gamekeeper up until World War I. He and his wife Margaret brought up a family of five boys – William, Alistair, Matthew, John and James – all born in the house over a ten-year period up to 1901. A copy of a journal written by John has been left in the bothy. One passage describes the family's self-sufficiency in mutton, ham, chicken and eggs, which were supplemented by an allowance of venison from the estate. Another explains the practicalities of getting to the nearest shop in Scourie: a journey of 5 miles by boat and a further 9 in a borrowed horse and cart. Sadly, both William and Alistair (the poet's great uncle) died separately on the Western Front, and a white marble memorial to them stands on the hillside above the house. It was financed by the Duke of Westminster, whose family still owns the estate. James, the poet's father and youngest of the boys, won

a bursary to Edinburgh University and became a respected physician. Some of Alistair's poetry, such as 'Some Scottish Music', was inspired by his years growing up in Glencoul. The poem describes the family listening to classical music on a wax cylinder, including some whimsical speculation on its proximity to the peat fire. The family finally left in the 1950s, moving to Glendhu Bothy, though farm buildings on the site are still in use today.

This traditional bothy comprises 2 rooms accessed by a small hallway. The LHR is the living area – a snug space containing the original fireplace, a single bed frame, 2 wooden

armchairs, and a table under the NW-facing window. The RHR had a hastily built breeze-block chimney and a cramped cold feel, but has recently been refurbished. Unless you are planning to arrive by kayak, or take a boat trip from the Kylesku Hotel, there is no direct route to Glencoul, and approaches from W and N both require concentration and good navigation skills, particularly in poor weather conditions.

ROUTE 1

750 yards before the car park on the zig zag bend at the head of Loch Gainmhich, south of Unapool, a stalker's path leads off to the west signposted to Glen Oykel via Eas a Chual Aluinn. There is space for two cars on the verge, or alternatively use the official parking area. Follow the path, initially quite boggy, round the S side of the loch, crossing the outline of a track known as the 'Marble Road' after 200 yards. Climb steeply round to the N side of Loch Bealach a' Bhùirich, and continue to a small cairn marking a path to the top of the falls on the W side of Poll Amhluaidh. Ignore this and continue SE, crossing the channel by some stepping stones, and round to a nameless lochan about a mile further, where the Cape Wrath Trail from Inchnadamph joins from the W. (This is an alternative walk in but a couple of miles longer, and climbs the bealach (620m) between Glas Bheinn and Beinn Uidhe). Shortly after this junction strike steeply downhill ignoring the path which continues to contour above the glen, zig-zagging R then L before it peters out. Pick your way down to the valley floor, and cross

to the N bank of the Abhainn an Loch Bhig, wherever you feel it is safest. There are numerous streams to ford from Loch na Gainmhich but this is by far the most serious. Once across, follow a rough path downstream to Loch Beag, passing the waterfall on the way, and continue round the loch side to a jetty. Here, cut inland to the bothy.

DISTANCE 8 miles

TIME 3 to 4 hours

TERRAIN Challenging. Track and faint path

PARKING Layby S of Loch na Gainmhich (NC 238 285)

ROUTE 2

The walk in from the N follows a route that is easier to navigate but considerably longer. From Kylestrome,

follow the lochside track to Glendhu Bothy (p53), cross the bridge over the Abhainn a' Ghlinne Dhuibh and pick your way along the southern shore, before climbing steeply to the headland of Beinn Aird da Loch. Here the path peters out across the boggy flat but resumes a little uphill from the point. Descend the increasingly more obvious path towards the bothy, ignoring deer tracks down the slope which are false trails, down to Loch Glencoul. Cross the Glencoul River by a new footbridge, and proceed to the sanctuary of the bothy.

DISTANCE 5 miles

TIME 3 hours

TERRAIN Challenging. Stalkers' path, faint trails. Serious river crossings

PARKING Kylestrome (NC 218 345)

FUEL SUPPLY Bring supplies.

KEY ATTRACTIONS A visit to the spectacular 200m waterfall Eas a' Chual Aluinn (waterfall of the beautiful tresses), the highest in the UK is a must. The Corbetts Glas Bheinn (776m) and Beinn Leòid (792m) are both readily accessible from the bothy. Kylesku Hotel serves excellent fresh sea food, and organises boat trips to the bothy and waterfall. Recognised stopping off point on the Cape Wrath Trail.

PUBLIC TRANSPORT D and E Coaches (01463 222444) service 61 Inverness to Ullapool. Durness Bikebus service 804 from Inverness operates mid-May to mid-September; must be booked 24 hours in advance. The Durness Bus (01971 511223) offers a similar service.

SPECIAL NOTES Phone the Reay Forest Estate (01971 502220) in advance if intending to visit during the stalking season, 12 August to 20 October.

FUEL SUPPLY Bring supplies.

KEY ATTRACTIONS UNESCO Geopark visitors' centre in Unapool has a cafe and free wifi. Kylesku Hotel serves excellent fresh sea food. The sweeping Kylesku bridge over the Caolas Cumhann is an impressive site, with a viewpoint at either end. Recognised stopping off point on the Cape Wrath Trail.

PUBLIC TRANSPORT D and E Coaches service 61 Inverness to Ullapool (01463 222444). Durness Bike Bus service 804 from Inverness runs mid-May to mid-September: book 24 hours in advance. Durness Bus (01971 511223) offers a similar service.

SPECIAL NOTES Phone Reay Forest Estate (01971 502220) beforehand if intending to visit during stalking season, 12 August to 20 October. A red plastic warning tag attached to a sign is raised when shooting is in operation. Permission required to launch a boat from the road end pier. Easy to mountain bike.

GLENDHU

Superior estate house by a remote loch (1999)

SIZE Medium; 2 ground floor rooms, plus 2 rooms in the attic
LOCATION LAT/LONG 58.2586, -4.9279, NC 283338, 25m, LR Map 15

Walking up the rutted stalkers' path that hugs Loch Glendhu, the steep crags of Cathair Dhubh rear up and the interlocking spurs in the narrow valley beyond seem to tighten with every step. Glendhu, meaning 'Black Glen' in Gaelic, is well-named. There are 3 buildings at the head of the loch: an old stalkers' cottage, the byre where ponies were kept, and the well-appointed bothy. It was once used for storing the deer carcasses shot by paying guests, who travelled in by boat from Kylesku. The Elliots, who had moved from Glencoul bothy (p49) in the late 1950s, finally left for Scourie a few years later.

The renovation of the bothy was undertaken by the Duke of Westminster's family, who own Reay Forest Estate. The layout follows the typical *but and ben* configuration of 2 ground-floor rooms and a set of stairs leading up to 2 attic dormitories. Originally ghillies lived upstairs, using the RHR as their living room, and the LHR for hanging the carcasses. Downstairs, the RHR remains the communal area with its original hearth, mantelpiece and white-washed wood-panelled walls. A large table sits under twin sash windows, and there are a couple of comfortable chairs to draw up to the fire. The LHR is cold and stark with a concrete floor. The attic rooms are wood-panelled, each with a skylight. The tiny RHR has a working grate and is particularly snug. One of the MBA's most well-maintained bothies.

ROUTE 1

From the small carpark at Kylestrome, just after the turning from the main road down to the old pier, walk down the metalled road signposted to Loch Glendhu, past the estate house and down to the shore. Just before an old stone bridge that leads onto Eilean na Rainich, turn L up another signposted track and proceed along the loch side before joining the access road to the Maldie Burn. Once across the new bridge above the dam, ignore a track to the R, and continue down to the lochside and on to the bothy.

DISTANCE 4 miles
TIME 1½ to 2 hours
TERRAIN Easy. Track all the way
PARKING Kylestrome (NC 218 345)

ROUTE 2

From the parking spot on the track down to a small jetty, cross the A838, and head past the estate houses, then L up through Achfary Forest. After about a mile, leave the trees and ascend steeply to the Bealach nam Fiann. Ignore a path leading R and a second on L, and continue to a footbridge over the Allt Bealach a' Phollaidh. Here, take the track to the L descending to Loch an Leathiad Bhuain and on down to Loch Glendhu, where it meets the new access road from Kylesku. Turn sharp L here and follow the track across the bridge and on to the bothy.

DISTANCE 7 miles
TIME 2½ to 3 hours
TERRAIN Straightforward. Stalkers' path and track all the way
PARKING On verge (NC 301 387)

KEARVAIG

Nestled in its own secluded bay in the far northwest (1987)

SIZE Large; raised platform sleeps 2, plus attic
LOCATION LAT/LONG 58.6085, -4.9410, NC 292 727, 9m, LR Map 9

Wandering in the soft light of an early summer morning along the pristine beach at Kearvaig Bay, gentle rollers lapping at your feet and the first of a spectacular series of sea stacks coming into view, is a truly unforgettable experience. Galvanising yourself for the steep ascent of the towering cliffs, you reach the dizzying heights and witness guillemots, razorbills, and kittiwakes busy in the rocky crannies, while puffins dart out to retrieve sprats from the foaming waves for their ever-demanding chicks. Back at the bothy, which is set above the beach, you put water on the boil and hunt for that last breakfast muesli bar. All the while, you marvel that this spick-and-span accommodation is provided free – the finest expression of the voluntary, non-commercial ethos of the MBA.

Cape Wrath was once home to a clutch of crofting communities, but by 1845 the remaining tenants were shepherds who grazed sheep on the peat-rich moorland of the Parph. At Kearvaig, the site of a traditional 'black house' was found during an archaeological survey, and the farmstead built above its foundations was occupied for nearly 200 years. A note scribbled on the plasterboard in the shelter's end room is dated 1966 and was photographed and framed during the bothy's renovation. Together with a linked entry in the logbook 20 years later, it reveals something of the migration of the original tenants. RW Nicoll states that her father, Edward John McCallum, was born at the farm in 1862, and her grandfather worked the land before the Stevenson lighthouse was built at Cape Wrath in 1828. She was born at Sheigra, further down the coast towards Kinlochbervie in 1912. The bothy book entry is by Elizabeth Redmond, John McCallum's great, great granddaughter, on her fourth visit from Victoria, Australia. She revealed that the family had 14 children: 3 emigrated to Australia, while the rest married locally, one daughter, Kitty, staying on in the cottage.

The bothy itself is a hunting lodge built on the site in 1877, 20 yards from the farm cottage, which now lies in ruin, the date carved into one of the extended beams beneath the roof. The building was abandoned 40 years ago and had become a little the worse for wear when an MBA renovation team extensively refurbished both the interior and exterior in 2009. The building comprises a cottage with an additional one-room apartment attached to its E gable end, both with a single entrance on the S side. The RHR was originally the parlour, and is still the main communal room. A granite fireplace, which has a brick insert added later, sits in the E-facing wall, and there is a press at the S end. The room is wood-panelled throughout. A table sits under the S-facing sash window, and there are chairs to pull up around the fire. The LHR, once the kitchen, has whitewashed walls, another table and more chairs, plus a single-person sleeping platform. The fireplace has, unfortunately, been blocked up. A steep staircase in the centre of the internal wall leads up to a 2-room attic lit by skylights. There is also access to a small cloakroom behind the stair. Entered through a small internal lobby, the one-room apartment is effectively an independent, well-finished, and very snug little bothy in itself, with its own hearth and a sleeping platform running the length of one wall. A small stone-walled outbuilding with a window in its W end has been constructed on the N side of the apartment.

ROUTE 1

Kearvaig is most easily accessible via a single-track road which runs from a jetty on the W shore of the Kyle of Durness to the Cape Wrath lighthouse (see box for details of crossings). From here it is a 7-mile hike along a metalled road, ascending steeply from Daill and then out onto the moor, before turning R down a curving track for the final stretch to the bay. This is a very wild spot once the summer season is over and there are stories of people getting stranded on the bothy side, which effectively becomes an island in bad weather and when the ferry does not run. Take a couple of days' extra food if you think there is a possibility of being caught out. Alternatively, if you are feeling up to an epic scramble, you could head down the Durness estuary and across a rickety bridge over the Grudie River (NC 349 628).

DISTANCE 7½ miles

TIME 2½ to 3 hours

TERRAIN Straightforward. Metalled road and track

PARKING W side of the Kyle of Durness (NC 369 661)

ROUTE 2

The alternative, more gruelling route to Kearvaig involves trekking up the coast from Blairmore and Sandwood Bay – part of the final stretch of the Cape Wrath Trail. From Strathchailleach Bothy (p71) it is a serious undertaking, as the terrain is unforgiving and mostly trackless. From the bothy, cross the Strath Chailleach and head directly over Cnoc a' Gheodha Ruaidh, aiming to reach the Keisgaig River, a short distance inland from the cliffs. Just before this you need to climb the barbed wire fence that marks the boundary to the Cape Wrath MoD firing range (red flags indicate when firing is taking place but you are advised to check in advance). Descend steeply to the river and climb the slope ahead: the most straightforward route, where the ground is easier, is between Sithean na h-Iolaireich and Cnoc a' Ghiubhais. Here, leave the Cape Wrath Trail route to the lighthouse, and take a bearing NE across the moor to the single-track road, close to the Kearvaig River. Walk along the road then turn L along the track that leads down to the bay and the bothy.

DISTANCE 12 miles (6 miles from Strathcailleach Bothy)

TIME 5 to 6 hours

TERRAIN Challenging. Tracks, faint trails and open moorland

PARKING John Muir car park Blaimore (NC 195 601)

FUEL SUPPLY Bring supplies.

KEY ATTRACTIONS Cape Wrath Lighthouse and Ozone Cafe and Clò Mòr cliffs, the highest in mainland Britain. Also visit Sango Bay beach, Smoo Cave and Balnakiel Craft Village.

PUBLIC TRANSPORT D and E Coaches (01463 222444) service 61 Inverness to Ullapool. Durness Bike Bus service 804 from Inverness runs mid-May to mid-September: book 24 hours in advance. The Durness Bus (01971 511223) offers a similar service. Cape Wrath Ferry (capewrathferry.wordpress.com) operates daily June to September from Keoldale, 3 miles south of Durness across the Kyle to the single-track road towards Cape Wrath. Sailing time and frequency depends on tides, weather and amount of traffic. In May the ferry runs at 11am and 1.30 pm. From October to May the ferry must be booked (John Morrison 01971 511246). Between Easter and mid-October there is a regular minibus service to the lighthouse at Cape Wrath that coordinates with the ferry. Ask to be dropped at the turnoff to Kearvaig, just over 3 miles away.

SPECIAL NOTES No-smoking bothy located just outside an MoD firing range. Twice-yearly exercises can last up to two weeks but once-daily access is generally permitted. The Post Office in Durness displays firing times, go to visitcapewrath.com/mod. Route 1 easy to cycle.

FUEL SUPPLY Bring supplies.

KEY ATTRACTIONS On the two alternative routes of the Cape Wrath Trail (Inverlael by Loch Broom/Ullapool to Inchnadamph section). Excellent coast-to-coast cycle route from Ullapool to Croick, all off-road. The Ceilidh Place in Ullapool is an excellent place to relax.

PUBLIC TRANSPORT Scotrail service from Inverness to Thurso and Wick, stops at Culrain and Lairg. Macleod's Dial-a-Bus, from Lairg to Oykel Bridge, Tuesday to Thursday (01408 641354). Postbus service 123 Drumbeg–Ledmore Junction-Lairg stops at Oykel Bridge; no return service. D and E Coaches (01463 222444) service 61 Inverness to Ullapool.

Durness Bike Bus service 804 from Inverness runs mid-May to mid-September: book 24 hours in advance. Durness bus (01971 511223) offers a similar service.

SPECIAL NOTES Please check with the Corriemulzie Estate (01403 891765) before visiting during the stag-stalking season, 1 September to 20 October.

⋀
KNOCKDAMPH

Meditative spot in a remote sweep of moorland (1976)

SIZE Medium; 3 ground-floor rooms, plus small attic
LOCATION LAT/LONG 57.9149, -4.8948, NH 286 954, 233m, LR Map 20

Staring into the fire at the old stalkers' cottage on an autumn night during the yearly rut, you cannot escape the mournful chorus of young testosterone-fuelled stags. It is a hypnotic sound heard over countless lonely Highland moors, but perhaps has particular significance here as the Gaelic *Cnoc Daimh*, meaning stag hill, is marked on even the earliest Scottish survey maps dating back to the beginning of the 19th century. The empty expanse of heather and bog was once a bustling thoroughfare for drovers and their cattle and a number of farmsteads and townships sprang up along the route then disappeared during the Clearances. Further E at Croick in Strathcarron, there are messages etched in the stained glass windows of the church by families forcibly evicted from their properties in 1845. Today the careworn tracks are only traversed by hardy backpackers on the Cape Wrath Trail, and the odd party intent on soaking up the solitude.

A typical *but and ben*, the bothy has retained much of its original character. From the small hall, there are 2 large communal rooms on the ground floor, each with a working fireplace, long tables and benches. A lovely old staircase leads up to a tiny room in the attic that has 2 beds with mattresses and a wee window in the gable end. There is also a sleeping platform in the LHR downstairs, and a small back room. The outbuilding extending to the back is locked and used for storage.

ROUTE 1

The closest access to the bothy is from Oykel Bridge, passing the Schoolhouse at Duag Bridge (p77) on the way. From here, cross the bridge and take the track leading R 200 yards further on, passing a small sheepfold before heading W across the moor. Note that the fording point of the Abhainn Poiblidh at NH 319 977, just after the confluence of the burn with Rappach Water, may be impassable in times of spate. Once across it's a gentle 3 miles to the bothy.

DISTANCE 8 miles
TIME 2½ to 3½ hours
TERRAIN Straightforward. Track all the way. River crossings
PARKING Gob na Fòide (Okyel Bridge) (NC 389 004)

ROUTE 2

Head up to and cross the A835, and follow the private road up Glen Achall, past 2 quarries. Just after the 2nd, take the L fork on the track, crossing a bridge over the Ullapool River, and continue on along the N shore of Loch Achall, to East Rhidorroch Lodge. From here the track climbs onto the open moor. Just as Loch an Daimh comes into view, take a track L that contours 50 yards above the shore, rather than going down to the boathouse at the head of the loch. After 2 miles, you see the bothy.

DISTANCE 10½ miles
TIME 3½ to 4½ hours
TERRAIN Straightforward. Unmetalled road and track
PARKING Tesco, Ullapool (NH126 941)

FUEL SUPPLY Wood usually available in the outbuilding, or gather from surrounding plantation.

KEY ATTRACTIONS RSPB Forsinard Flows nature reserve with lookout tower, trails and new visitor centre. Excellent Strathnaver Museum in Bettyhill for historical context. Ancient Pictish Farr stone nearby and many archaeological sites in Strathnaver including brochs, neolithic tombs and Achnanlochy Clearance Village. Free camping above the dunes near the beach at Strathy East (NC 838 657). Welcoming bar at the Strathy Hotel.

PUBLIC TRANSPORT Scotrail Northern Highland Line Inverness to Wick, stops at Forsinard and Thurso. Durness Bus (01971 511223) service 803 Durness to Thurso.

SPECIAL NOTES Open all year round.

CROFT HOUSE, LOCHSTRATHY

Remote spot on the edge of Sutherland Flow country (1997)

SIZE Large; plenty of sleeping space
LOCATION LAT/LONG 58.4124, -4.0668, NC 793 490, 160m, LR Map 10

It is hard to believe that the Croft House at Lochstrathy actually exists until you poke your nose through the fading yellow bothy door. A portal between the conifers stretching back to the coast and the cinemascopic skies of the Sutherland Flow Country that lie beyond, it feels miles from anywhere, and once ensconced, the sense of complete isolation never seems to leave you. From the bothy, there is direct access to the empty expanse of peat bog, cotton grass and sphagnum that is recognised as one of Europe's most unique and precious landscapes. Wandering out to nearby Loch na Saobhaidhe, as the light fades, feels like an immense privilege, and while human impact cannot be ignored, this remains one of the most out-of-the-way places in northern Scotland.

The bothy is a typical *but and ben*, with an annexe built onto the N gable, used for storage. From the small lobby there are rooms R and L. The latter has panelled walls and a large fireplace. The RHR retains the original stone hearth and flagstones. Both rooms have 2 single wooden bed frames. A steep staircase leads up to a 2-room attic with wood panelling and skylights. Although rarely visited, the bothy has a surprisingly homely feel.

ROUTE 1

Parking just beyond the end of the lane from Strathy, follow the wide gravel track heading S, which joins the vehicle access road from the E. Ignore the R turn to Strathy South wind farm and continue on the rougher track that follows the course of the river Strathy. 2 miles before the bothy, ignore another track on R and persevere until the bothy comes until view. Here there is a ford to cross which could be an obstacle in times of spate.

DISTANCE 12 miles
TIME 4 to 5 hours
TERRAIN Straightforward. Track all the way, best by bike. River crossing
PARKING Strathy (NC 839 643)

ROUTE 2

From the layby, head along the private road, crossing the river by an old Victorian bridge. Once through the farm, turn R, and after 200 yards pick up an ATV track that ascends to the S side of Beinn Rifa-gil before petering out. From here cross the blanket bog, following a faint trail to Loch Rifa-gil, and then either make straight for the plantation and follow the boundary fence to the bothy, or keep to higher ground, skirting round the slopes of Meall Bad na Cuaiche to the N bank of Loch Strathy. Here cross the river and head on to Loch na Saobhaidhe, before turning N to the forest clearing. The terrain is very boggy, so expect to double back on yourself. Very challenging in wet weather.

DISTANCE 5 miles
TIME 2½ to 3½ hours
TERRAIN Very tough. ATV track, faint trails, pathless open moorland and blanket bog
PARKING Rhifail, layby near farm road (NC 724 494)

SHENAVALL

Classic bothy in truly spectacular location (1966)

SIZE Large; plenty of sleeping space
LOCATION LAT/LONG 57.7768, -5.2541, NH 066 810, 128m, LR Map 19

A flagship MBA bothy, Shenavall is one of the best-known and busiest in Scotland and a visit is the perfect introduction to the delights of bothying. Spectacularly located on the edge of the Fisherfield Forest and close to an area of remote peaks described by Alfred Wainwright as 'the Great Wilderness', it has been a magnet for Munro baggers and walkers for over a century. You can read a wealth of background material from accounts by the people who lived there, to entries in journals and bothy books, including vivid passages in Ken Wilson and Richard Gilbert's classics, *The Big Walks* and *Wild Walks*. Renowned author and mountaineer WH Murray visited in the 1950s, and HRH Prince Charles also hiked out here while still a pupil at Gordonstoun. Unless you are visiting out of season you are unlikely to have the place to yourself, but this region is one of the jewels of the Scottish Highlands and an opportunity not to be missed.

Shenavall derives from the Gaelic *seann bhaile* meaning old town, and possibly refers to an earlier township in the glen Strath na Sealga before the Clearances. Constructed in 1891, the cottage's first occupant was Colin Macdonald, a stalker and shepherd on the Dundonnell estate. According to a 1990 account, the family were virtually self-sufficient: they grew their own vegetables, fished the loch, took venison from the hill, and kept 4 cows. Twice-yearly they bought supplies of meal, paraffin, sugar and tea. They also tended a flock of sheep for the estate, in partnership with 4 other families who lived in the glen. A teacher appointed by the school board stayed with each family for a month to educate the children, in exchange for board and lodging.

David Maclean Urquhart's family were the last permanent residents in Strath na Sealga, living first in Shenavall, and later on in Achneigie, a house located a mile east of the bothy. In his memoir, *Miss Mackenzie couldn't see the wind*, he describes family life, including the necessity of cutting and drying peat and hay before the onset of winter so they wouldn't freeze and the livestock wouldn't starve. In 1950 WH Murray visited the family while on an expedition to climb An Teallach, and was surprised people were still living in such a solitary location. In *Undiscovered Scotland*, published the following year, Murray comments that 'at first glance Shenavall looked a very small cottage, but proved to be surprising commodious within. There were tables and chairs, bed springs and mattresses, and even firewood. The house had been unoccupied for ten years, yet was dry inside'.

The original layout of the bothy, one of the first to be taken on by the MBA in 1966, comprised 3 equal-sized rooms on the ground floor and stairs up to a large attic. Additional outbuildings were demolished after a storm in the early 1990s, though the partly ruined byre to the S remains. Over the years the bothy's popularity had taken its

toll on the fabric of the interior, but during 2013 and 2014 MBA work parties completed major renovations. They extended the ground-floor LHR towards the stairs to make a larger communal area, and demolished the rotting annexe, adding a window in the reconstructed stone work. From an exterior porch, with a large partitioned section for storing wood, you enter a small lobby, where stairs up to the R lead to the attic used as a dormitory. The RHR can now only be accessed through a passageway running along the back of the building, from the LHR. This opens out into a large, bright welcoming space, complete with new inset fireplace and surround and 2 new benches either side. The extended area is to the R, opposite the hearth, and has a long kitchen worktop and a window looking back out into the lobby. The RHR, by contrast, is relatively gloomy with bare wood panelling, a blocked-up fireplace, and a low platform bed sleeping 4. In the attic, 3 Velux windows introduce much-needed light and air.

ROUTE 1

Most head in from the Dundonnell side, following a vehicle track from Corrie Hallie where rights of way are

signposted to Kinlochewe, Poolewe and Gruinard. After a steady climb up through Gleann Chaorachain, cross the river by a footbridge and after another steep climb you reach a prominent cairn. Here take the path branching R that leads directly to the bothy. This stretch is boggy in places as it traverses round the shoulder of Sail Liath, S of Lochan na Bràthan. If arriving after dark, watch out for the steep drop on the final approach to the bothy.

DISTANCE 4½ miles

TIME 1½ to 2½ hours

TERRAIN Straightforward. Vehicle track and heavily eroded path, boggy in places

PARKING Car park Corrie Hallie (NH 114 850)

ROUTE 2

From the cairn, keep to the main track that continues S to Strath na Sealga, before doubling back along the river side and finishing at Achneigie (NH 082 796). From here there is a well-used path to the bothy. Straightforward to mountain bike.

DISTANCE 6 miles

TIME 2½ to 3½ hours

TERRAIN Straightforward. Track and well-used path

PARKING Car park Corrie Hallie (NH 114 850)

There are a number of other approaches across the vast wilderness to the S and W of the bothy. The Cape Wrath Trail heads over the hills from Kinlochewe and another classic

FUEL SUPPLY Bring supplies.

KEY ATTRACTIONS Perfect base to tackle the 'Fisherfield Six', comprising 5 remote Munros – Ruadh Stac Mòr (919m), A' Maighdean (967m) Beinn Tarsuinn (937m), Mullach Coire Mhic Fhearchair (1018m) and Sgurr Ban (989m) – plus Beinn a' Chlaidheimh (914m), now downgraded to a Corbett. Other superlative days out include climbing Corbett Beinn Dearg Mòr (910m) viewed from the bothy door, and the iconic ridge of An Teallach to the N.

PUBLIC TRANSPORT Scotrail Service from Glasgow/Edinburgh–Perth–Inverness or Citylink coach service M90/M91 Glasgow/Edinburgh–Perth–Inverness. Westerbus service 700 from Inverness to Gairloch or Laide stops at Dundonnell.

SPECIAL NOTES Not officially available during stag stalking, 15 September to 20 October, but in practice it is left unlocked. The MBA's use of this bothy is courtesy of the Gruinard Estate. Please assist both these bodies by reporting any illegal fishing activity. Very popular spot so be prepared to camp at Easter and in the summer months.

2-day route weaves its way through mountains from Poolewe, past another basic shelter at Carnmore (p79). This is very challenging country so if you choose these routes you must be fully equipped and ready for any eventuality: help is very far away.

FUEL SUPPLY Permission from Scottish Natural Heritage to collect dead wood and kindling from fenced-off woodland to S.

KEY ATTRACTIONS Conamheall (482m), and the Corbetts Cranstackie (800m) and Beinn Spionnaidh (772m) make a fantastic round trip from the bothy. Wonderful walk up the Srath Coille na Fearna and the adventurous can push on to Foinaven (908m) although it is quite a trek.

PUBLIC TRANSPORT D and E Coaches (01463 222444) service 61 Inverness to Ullapool. Durness Bike Bus service 804 from Inverness runs mid-May to mid-September; must be booked 24 hours in advance. The Durness Bus (01971 511223) offers a similar service. Also service 803 Durness to Thurso.

SPECIAL NOTES Not officially available during stag stalking, 12 August to 20 October but in practice the bothy is left unlocked. Please do not park in front of the gate. Access is required at all times and any vehicle blocking the entrance will be moved.

STRABEG

Perfect farmhouse retreat just a stroll from the road (1989)

SIZE Large; 3 ground-floor rooms plus long, sectioned attic space
LOCATION LAT/LONG 58.4249, -4.7562, NC 391 518, 35m, LR Map 9

In this crowded isle, only on the far north coast of Scotland could you stay the night in a well-maintained, freely available farmhouse that feels like a retreat yet is barely a mile from the main road. Welcome to Strabeg! Bedding down for the night, you might contemplate a morning wander up through the protected native woodland of oak, alder, birch and rowan that hugs the steep quartzite crags above your accommodation, or, if you are feeling suitably inspired, plan an ascent of the rugged peaks that lie to the W. En route, you are unlikely to meet a soul, and you may catch a glimpse of a golden eagle patrolling the skies. Crofting and sheep farming have been the mainstay of this corner of the country for hundreds of years, supplemented by fish from the loch. Census details held in the bothy show a continuous record of occupation since 1674, although the first evidence of settlement at Loch Eriboll goes back much further. A Bronze Age souterrain was discovered just by the roadside in 1960, excavations uncovered a pair of bronze shears on a ledge inside, and later, rotary querns and a triangular glass bead with spiral inlays dating back to the Roman Iron Age were unearthed.

The present steading at Strabeg was built in 1894, and retains much of its original character. From an external porch, you enter a hallway with rooms R and L, the second leading through to an annexe at the back of the building with a kitchen and bathroom. There is a Belfast sink and draining board set below a large window with a lovely view north to the loch, plus a rusting old bath tub and toilet. Although there is no running water, the toilet can be flushed using a bucket. The RHR is the communal space with a fine hearth, table and chairs, and, like many far-flung bothies, a small library. The LHR is mainly used as a dormitory. Stairs from the lobby lead up to a partitioned attic, also used as sleeping accommodation.

ROUTE 1

Park next to the gate at the head of Loch Eriboll and follow the farm track into the bothy which quickly comes into view. After a mile or so the track deteriorates to a boggy path. The only obstacle is a stream just before the bothy, which could be hazard after heavy rainfall.

DISTANCE 1½ miles
TIME 30 to 40 minutes
TERRAIN Easy. Well-maintained track and clearly visible path to the bothy; very boggy for the last 500 yards. River crossing
PARKING By gate (NC 393 538)

FUEL SUPPLY Peat store outside the bothy but best to bring supplies.

KEY ATTRACTIONS Sandwood Bay, maintained by the John Muir Trust since 1993, is one of Scotland's best beaches and you can head for Am Buachaille, the 65m Torridonian sandstone sea-stack just S of the bay. The local summits Creag Riabhach (485m) and Fashven (457m) offer wonderful views back to Sandwood and W to Ben Hope. Oldshoremore beach is another gem.

PUBLIC TRANSPORT D and E Coaches (01463 222444) service 61 Inverness to Ullapool. Durness Bike Bus service 804 from Inverness runs mid-May to mid-September; must be booked 24 hours in advance. The Durness Bus (01971 511223) offers a similar service. North West Community Bus Association's bus 890 runs daily from Ullapool to Kinlochbervie.

SPECIAL NOTES Open throughout the year. Grazing land for sheep.

⌂ STRATHAN

A real connoisseur's hang-out, close to beautiful Sandwood Bay (1976)

SIZE Small; 2 rooms, limited sleeping space
LOCATION LAT/LONG 58.5033, -5.0098, NC 247 612, 62m, LR Map 9

Strathan is a fantastic wee place, on the edge of the remote Parph, a rare, uninhabited 100-square-mile sweep of alluvial moorland, topped with peat and heather, stretching between Kinlochbervie, Cape Wrath and Durness. Once a shepherd's cottage, it is now a much-loved retreat from the world. On arrival at the bothy's cheery bright-red front door, there is little to accomplish other than getting a fire going, wandering down to the beach at Sandwood Bay, and perhaps exploring Strathchailleach further up the coast.

The bothy's attractions led to a bizarre case of squatting in the autumn of 2000. A homeless couple, Robbie and Anne Northway, decided to move in, along with their 40 geese, 12 dogs and a pony. The land is owned by the Scottish Executive and the couple reasoned that because the bothy had originally been bought for the benefit of crofters, they had every right to occupy it. The local Keoldale Sheep Stock Club, who rented the pasture around the property, were not amused, and the MBA quietly seethed and asked walkers to avoid the place. After 4 months, the couple were evicted, although Robbie continued to occupy an old steading nearby, until the following summer. The full story is told in Mike Cawthorne's book *Wilderness Dreams*.

The building is a very simple *but and ben*, with 2 cosy rooms entered from a small lobby. The RHR has a fireplace and is the communal living space. It was enhanced in 2016 by the installation of pine panelling and there is the usual mix of furniture – table under the small sash window and a few chairs to draw up to the fire. The LHR is an uncluttered dormitory, partitioned to make 2 separate sleeping areas.

ROUTE 1
From the small parking near the farmhouse (before the more popular parking for those hiking to Sandwood Bay), follow the track heading straight onto the moor. After just under a mile, look out for a path heading due E, marked by a cairn. There are a couple of false junctions before the turning so be careful, especially after dark. From this point, follow a boggy, intermittent path that skirts round the N beach of Loch Mòr a' Chraisg, which can be a quagmire after heavy rain. Once past the smaller Loch Beag a' Chraisg, the path becomes more obvious, descending into Strath Shinary with a footbridge at NC 244 611 and the bothy within sight. Previously, a rickety wire bridge spanned the river here and there are fraught tales in the bothy book of those risking life and limb to cross the burn rather than trudging back to their cars. The bridge was replaced in the spring of 2012 and the words *'Obair nan Sithichean'* –'Work of the Fairies' – have been inscribed below the bridge's safety notice.

DISTANCE 3½ miles
TIME 1½ to 2 hours
TERRAIN Straightforward. Track and path, often waterlogged
PARKING Small off-road area just beyond Oldshoremore, N of the B801 (NC 205 596)

STRATHCHAILLEACH

Former hermit's home. Unique and unforgettable (1999)

SIZE Medium; 3 rooms, 1 with 2-person sleeping platform
LOCATION LAT/LONG 58.5447, -5.0099, NC 248 657, 95m, LR Map 9

Strathchailleach is a battered old estate cottage set between the wild Atlantic and the Parph, the vast, empty moorland S of Cape Wrath. Once over the threshold, you feel you have entered a living museum. As recently as 1996 the cottage was occupied by James MacRory-Smith, a hermit better known to the locals as Sandy. This loner lived in the bothy for 32 years, collecting his benefits every 2 weeks from the post office at Balchrick, and keeping warm during the winter using dried peat from the surrounding peat bog. With no piped water, sewerage system, electricity or gas, the house lays claim to being the last inhabited place in mainland Scotland without any services. Inside, a series of distinctive murals Sandy painted on the walls during his long stay add a personal touch, and you could easily imagine this remarkable character bursting through the door, and asking you what you were doing there. Sitting in this extraordinary and remote spot, you can begin to appreciate just what it took for Sandy to live out here for all those years, with just a battered old radio and the odd bottle of whisky for company.

One of 16 children, James MacRory was born in 1926 in Dumbarton on Clydeside. His mother died when he was just 17, and soon afterwards he enlisted as a squaddie in the last throes of World War II. After marriage and 2 children, tragedy struck when his wife was killed in a car crash – an event he never came to terms with. After his son and daughter were taken in by their mother's parents, he embarked on a rover's life, eventually gravitating to Sutherland. After a series of temporary homes, he fetched up at the shepherd's house at Strathchailleach. Over the years, locals would often see him combing the beach at Sandwood, lost in his own world. After a violent winter storm destroyed the exposed W gable of the cottage in 1981, the MBA offered to undertake repairs on the understanding that one room would be made available to passing walkers. However Sandy, who could be erratic and moody, did not always uphold his side of the bargain. He wavered between begrudgingly hospitable or spiky and threatening, and occasionally he just left the door locked. In the end the MBA took the bothy off their list, and only when ill health finally took its toll and Sandy moved to a caravan in Kinlochbervie, were there moves to re-establish Strathchailleach as an open shelter. Sandy died in 1999 after a short illness and is buried in the cemetery at Sheigra. A photo hangs on the living-room wall, along with a short

summary of the time he spent at the bothy. For more details, see James Carron's biography of MacRory-Smith *A Ceiling of Stars, The Remarkable Life of a Highland Hermit* and there is also a short chapter in *Wilderness Dreams* by Mike Cawthorne.

According to census records, Strathchailleach – in Gaelic 'the valley of the old woman' – has been occupied since the beginning of the 19th century. It is one of several farmsteads that now lie in ruin on the walk in from Sandwood Bay. A very squat *but and ben* that is similar in style to Strathan, it has 2 tiny inset windows, and a shiny red front door. From a small hallway there are rooms R and L, plus a rather psychedelic kitchen area at the back, decorated in a naïve Pointillist style, with a couple of Sandy's frescoes on display between the shelves. The RHR is the living room, a new hearth and surround recently replacing the old fireplace, and Sandy's home made bellows. On the walls are 3 more of his paintings and the surrounding stonework has been whitewashed to reflect more light. A table sits under the small S-facing window, and there is a low table, chairs and more shelving. The LHR is used as a dormitory and has a 2-person sleeping platform.

ROUTE 1
This route follows the final section of the Cape Wrath Trail. From the John Muir Trust car park, follow the well-trodden track to Sandwood Bay, passing 3 small lochans on the way. Walk down to the beach and traverse the sand to the outflow of Sandwood Loch, a serious obstacle in times of spate. Cross the flow as close to the sea as you can, and then pick up a faint sandy path that ascends the steep slope ahead and then runs along the cliff top. At the N end of the bay, you are confronted by the spectacular sight of the final waterfall of Srath Chailleach, the river draining the catchment around the bothy. Pick up a faint trail along the S bank of the river, which leads all the way to the bothy. Waterlogged and boggy in places.

DISTANCE 6 miles

TIME 2½ to 3½ hours

TERRAIN Straightforward. Track, traverse of sandy beach. River crossing, faint boggy trail to bothy

PARKING John Muir car park Blairmore (NC 195 601)

ROUTE 2
The alternative approach is from Strathan Bothy. From here, pick a line over the steep flank of An Grianan and down to Strathchailleach Bothy when it comes in view. Head for a gate in the sheep fence that stretches across the Parph, a few hundred yards from the bothy at NC 244 656. Please ensure you shut the gate.

DISTANCE 7 miles from Strathan Bothy (see p69)

TIME 3 to 4 hours

TERRAIN Challenging. Track, faint trails and open moorland

PARKING Small off-road area just beyond Oldshoremore (NC 205 596)

FUEL SUPPLY Bags of peat in a lean-to at E gable end.

KEY ATTRACTIONS Sandwood Bay, one of Scotland's finest, is a mile-long stretch of sand with a dramatic waterfall at one end and an impressive sea-stack Am Buachaille at the other. A wander up Beinn Dearg (460m), leads you into the wild interior of the Parph.

PUBLIC TRANSPORT D and E Coaches (01463 222444) service 61 Inverness to Ullapool. Durness Bike Bus service 804 from Inverness runs mid-May to mid-September; must be booked 24 hours in advance. The Durness Bus (01971 511223) offers a similar service. North West Community Bus Association's service 890 runs daily from Ullapool to Kinlochbervie.

SPECIAL NOTES Open throughout the year. Sandwood Bay is a nature reserve owned and managed since 1993 by the John Muir Trust, which aims to preserve the area's wild beauty and biodiversity, as well as maintaining a viable crofting community. Keep dogs under control to avoid disturbing free-roaming sheep and ground-nesting birds.

FUEL SUPPLY Bring supplies.

KEY ATTRACTIONS Ideally situated for ascents of majestic Suilven (731m) and its rather neglected neighbour Canisp (846m). The small fishing port of Lochinver is a popular tourist destination with many fine eateries, all serving local produce, including the Caberfeidh, and the Lochinver Larder.

PUBLIC TRANSPORT Highland Scotbus from Ullapool to Lochinver runs twice a day in the summer season (01463 224410).

SPECIAL NOTES Open all year round. Loch fishing by permit only. No dogs. For all enquires contact the Assynt Foundation (01571 844122). Honesty shop by estate buildings: tea/coffee/snacks. Straightforward to mountain bike from the Lochinver side.

⩓
SUILEAG

A basic bothy beneath iconic Suilven (1984)

SIZE Medium; 2 rooms each with a raised platform bed; sleeps 8
LOCATION LAT/LONG 58.1398, -5.1449, NC 149 212, 137m, LR Map 15

Suileag Bothy is the only maintained open accommodation in Assynt, a region of isolated island peaks, blanket bog and ribbon lochs that was awarded UNESCO Geopark status in 2006. It is owned by the sustainability-focused Assynt foundation, a community organisation that, in a landmark case, instigated one of the first land buy-outs under the provisions of the 2003 Scottish Land Reform Act. Almost £3 million was raised, enough to purchase 44,000 acres of pristine wilderness including not only the peaks of Canisp and Suilven but also Cul Mòr and Cul Beag. This purchase effectively safeguards the natural landscape and its culture for future generations. The shelter is set deep within the unforgiving, ice-scoured landscape of Lewisian Gneiss, which stretches beneath the sandstone pillar of Suilven. It is a long, single-storey stone structure with a locked outhouse at one end. In Gaelic, its name means 'little eye' or 'loop' and probably refers to the acute meander

of the river close to the bothy. The interior, basically an open shell with exposed stone walls and no ceiling panels, can be draughty and is quite cold outside of the summer months. The space is split into 2 rooms by a wooden partition, creating a large communal room complete with dartboard (sadly there are no darts) and a second, more intimate space with a wooden floor laid over the concrete foundations. Both rooms have sleeping platforms (LHR sleeps 6) and working hearths, so 2 groups can co-exist independently.

ROUTE 1

The easiest route in is from the Lochinver side. It is possible to drive along the back road from the village past Glencanisp Lodge and park, saving an additional 1½-mile journey from Lochinver. From here, follow the rutted stalkers' path to the bothy. There are a couple of short, steep sections along the way, which could prove challenging if you are cycling in.

DISTANCE 2½ miles
TIME 1 to 1½ hours
TERRAIN Easy. Track all the way
PARKING Glencanisp Lodge walkers' car park (NC119 219)

ROUTE 2

Climb the stile and follow a boggy path signposted to Suilven down to the bridge over the stretch of water between Lochan an Iasgaich and Loch na Garbhe Uidhe. Continue on a new path which heads off L to the Allt an Tiaghaich, replacing one marked on the OS map bearing R. Once across the burn, head out onto the moor and reach another series of lochans with a ribbon of water between, crossing by a set of stepping stones at NC 148 218. Continue for half a mile before the bothy, tucked behind a small rocky outcrop, comes into view.

DISTANCE 3 miles
TIME 1½ to 2 hours
TERRAIN Straightforward. Boggy, well-worn path. River crossings
PARKING Small layby (NC 158 249)

FUEL SUPPLY No stove or fireplace.

KEY ATTRACTIONS A recognised stopover point on the Cape Wrath Trail (Inverlael by Loch Broom to Inchnadamph section). The Oykel Bridge Hotel offers excellent salmon and trout fishing. One of the few MBA bothies you can actually drive to without unlocking a gate.

PUBLIC TRANSPORT Scotrail service from Inverness to Thurso and Wick, stops at Culrain and Lairg. Macleod's Dial-a-Bus (01408 641354) has a limited service to Rosehall. Postbus service 123 Drumbeg–Ledmore Junction–Lairg stops at Oykel Bridge; no return service.

SPECIAL NOTES Please check with the Corriemulzie Estate (01403 891765) before visiting during the stag-stalking season, 1 September to 20 October. Easy cycle.

THE SCHOOLHOUSE, DUAG BRIDGE

Pint-sized village hall with a restored classroom (2008)

SIZE Medium; 3 rooms, 2 with raised platforms, sleeping 5
LOCATION LAT/LONG 57.935, -4.8053, NH 340 975, 99m, LR Map 20

This small, unassuming shelter was the schoolhouse for the scattering of families who lived in these remote glens until the late 1930s. The ghillies, gamekeepers and shepherds took advantage of the 1870 Education Act, extended to Scotland in 1872, which offered free, compulsory and non-religious education for all children between 5 and 13. The building at Duag Bridge is one of the very few remaining of its type; one other is on the walk in to Knoydart from Strathan, at the end of Loch Arkaig. By the 1920s, up to 20 pupils were supervised by a teacher who probably lived on site. In winter, the children brought peat to add to the classroom stove, and one enterprising family used stilts to cross the swollen river in times of spate. By the start of World War II, the school had closed and the building became a hay store and unofficial doss. Destined for demolition by the Corriemulzie Estate, the derelict eyesore was taken on by the MBA and a succession of work parties replaced all the windows and rebuilt the roof.

The bothy is clad in functional grey corrugated sheets, and consists of 3 self-contained rooms leading off from a small hallway, each carefully restored. The LHR was completely reconstructed from floor to ceiling, with a sleeping platform for up to 4 people added along two walls, and a worktop along a third. The whole space was insulated and a double glazed window inserted, making it very cosy. The slightly larger RHR has been returned to its former state as a classroom, with school desks, a blackboard, and even a bookshelf containing the complete works of Shakespeare! There is no stove but the extensive wind- and waterproofing provides sufficient warmth once any group is ensconced. Tucked between the 2 rooms is a small dormitory with a single raised platform.

ROUTE 1

Follow the well-graded, unmetalled access road that leads from the road end to Corriemulzie Lodge, over a bridge that crosses the River Einig to the S side of the glen, and then climbs gently up through the conifer plantation to the steep bank side of Allt nan Càisean. Here, as the track arcs round and down towards the river, ignore 2 turns L and continue on, contouring above the channel before a gentle climb to the bothy.

DISTANCE 4 miles

TIME 1½ to 2 hours

TERRAIN Easy. Unmetalled road all the way to the bothy

PARKING At bothy or opposite cottages at Gob na Foide (NC 389 004)

Leckie Bothy

ADDITIONAL NORTH HIGHLAND BOTHIES

All on the periphery of the 'Great Wilderness', each within a day's walk of Shenavall

CARNMORE

LAT/LONG 57.7366, -5.3982,
NJ 041 032, 203m, LR Map 19

Very rough and ready open barn, found at the southern end of Fionn Loch, E of Poolewe, a mile above a causeway which separates the main body of water from the much smaller Dubh Loch. Inside the long single room there are a couple of old camp beds above a mud floor. 6 transparent panels in the roof help provide much needed light. There is no fireplace or stove. The bothy is mainly used by climbers attempting routes on the steep Càrn Mòr crag above the shelter, but it is also a strategic stopping-off point on a multi-day trip E to Shenavall (p63) and Dundonnell, or S to Letterewe and Kinlochewe.

DISTANCE 9 miles

TIME 4 to 5 hours

TERRAIN Challenging. Track and well-defined path, boggy in places

PARKING Carpark at Poolewe (NG 979 768)

LECKIE

LAT/LONG 57.6306, -5.1894,
NH097 645, 150m, LR Map 19

Leckie is an old farmstead, formerly used as an estate bothy, which lies above Kinlochewe, E of Loch Maree, 2 miles beyond the route of the Cape Wrath Trail heading to Shenavall (p63). The cottage remains intact with 3 rough-and-ready living rooms, 1 with the original range, and a bathroom with bath and toilet still in place. Unfortunately there is a major hydroelectric scheme under construction in the glen. Work is due to be completed by the end of 2017. Easy cycle.

DISTANCE 3½ miles

TIME 1½ to 2 hours

TERRAIN Easy. Vehicle track all the way to the bothy

PARKING Carpark above Kinlochewe (NH 037 623)

LOCHIVRAON

LAT/LONG 57.7107, -5.1617,
NH 117 734, 260m, LR Map 19

Lochivraon lies next to a large locked estate house, at the western end of Loch a' Bhraoin, in the wide sweep of moorland between the Munros of Fisherfield and the Western Fannichs. The bothy is very well maintained, with a kitchen area, toilet and living room on the ground floor, with an attic above. There is a small stove, and 5 single single sleeping platforms shoehorned into the available space. Issues about restrictions at the bothy appear from time to time on the MBA website, but it is not maintained by the organisation. Booked for 2 weeks every May by a local school. The track along the loch side has a number of shingle sections that are difficult to cycle on.

DISTANCE 4 miles

TIME 2 to 2½ hours

TERRAIN Easy. Track all the way

PARKING Layby on A832 (NH 161 762)

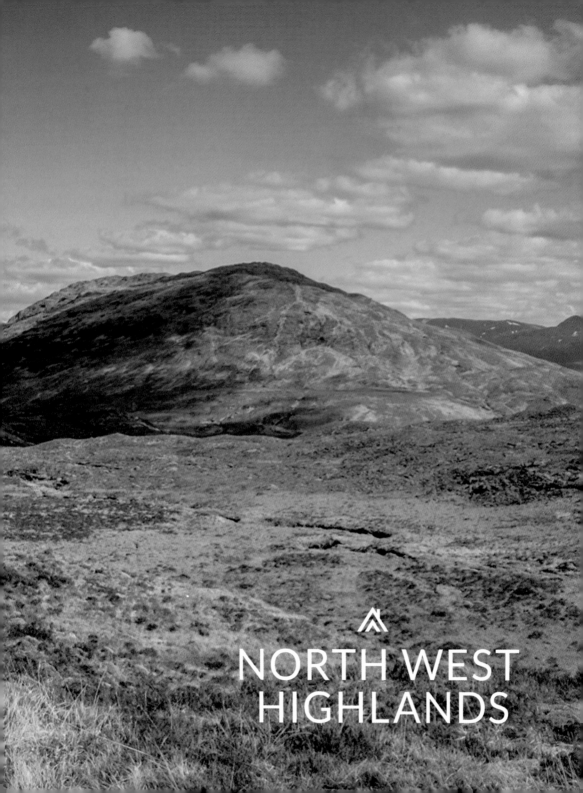

NORTH WEST HIGHLANDS

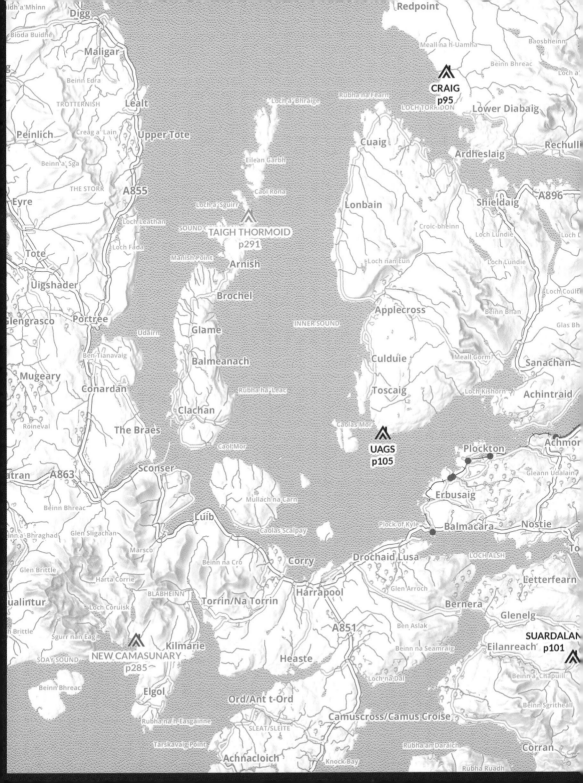

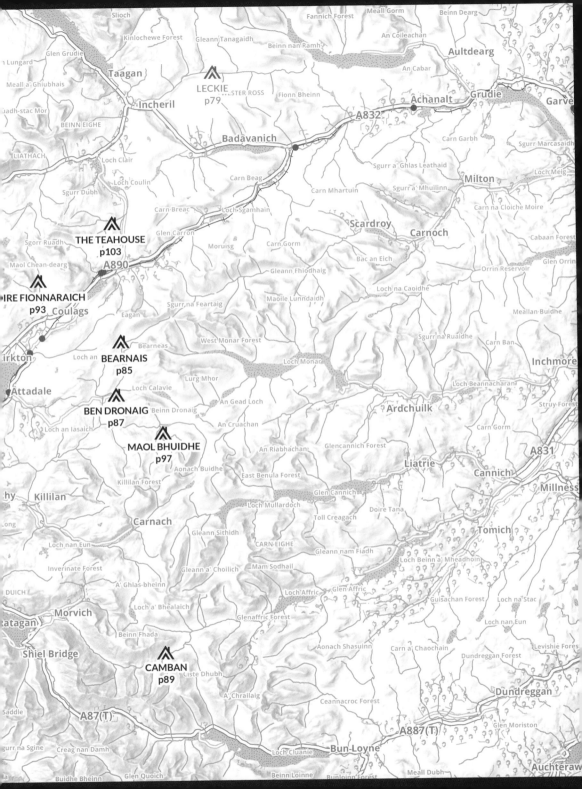

FUEL SUPPLY Bring supplies.

KEY ATTRACTIONS An excellent base for tackling the remote Munros Bidein a' Choire Sheasgaich (945m) affectionately known as the 'Cheese Grater' and Lurg Mhor (985m), as well as the Corbetts Beinn Tharsuinn (863m) and Sgùrr na Feartaig (862m). The 'Kirk Falls', Eas an Teampuill, above Strathcarron are worth a detour en route to the bothy.

PUBLIC TRANSPORT Scotrail West Highland Line from Inverness to Kyle of Lochalsh, stops at Achnashellach and Strathcarron. Lochcarron Garage bus service 704 Inverness to Applecross (01520 722205) stops on request.

SPECIAL NOTES Open throughout the year. During the stalking season from August to October please contact the Attadale Estate prior to using the bothy (01520 722308) or if walking in from Achnashellach (01520 766266).

⌂ BEARNAIS

Snug, unassuming bothy – a real gem (1974)

SIZE Small; 1 room, sleeping platform for 2 people
LOCATION LAT/LONG 57.4344, -5.2984, NH 021 431, 279m, LR Map 25, Explorer 429

Bearnais lies on the periphery of the vast, empty territory of Wester Ross, giving you a taste of adventure without being too committed. The name is a combination of the Gaelic, *bàrr* (top), and *ais* or *eas* (waterfall). Rescued by the MBA from the ruins of an old estate property, only half of the original cottage was reconstructed to make this 1-roomed bothy, along with a large storm porch. There is a well-drawing fire and a narrow platform bed for 2 people sleeping head to toe. Of the two distinctive inglehooks on either side of the fireplace, one has a stone plaque commemorating the life of Eric Beard, a well-known character in the outdoor community back in the 1970s. The room has 2 windows, facing N and S, a small table, plus a low bench and a couple of chairs. The Munros are the main draw here, but if the weather closes in you could take a trip to Maol Bhuidhe Bothy (p97), or walk over to Ben Dronaig Lodge (p87).

ROUTE 1

From the station head S for a short way along the A890 before turning L through the farm at Achintee. At a crossroads take a L (signposted Hill Paths) round to an electricity substation where a track continues up the hill. Shortly after, a signpost indicates Bearnais L and Ben Dronaig straight on. This is not marked on either 1:50000 or 1:25000 map. Take the L fork leading over to the S side of the River Taodail. Climb steeply past the beautiful Eas na Creige Duibhe Mòire waterfall, through a small bealach marked with a tiny lochan at 485m, and down into the Bearneas. There are numerous streams to be forded on both sides of the hill; take care in times of spate.

DISTANCE 6 miles
TIME 2½ to 3 ½ hours
TERRAIN Challenging. Stalkers' path all the way. River crossings
PARKING Strathcarron Station (NG 941 421)

ROUTE 2

The route from Craig is more direct but involves more ascent. From the Forestry car park (NH 039 493), take the path signposted to Strathconon across the railway and down to the River Carron. Cross the bridge, and continue round to a second bridge ignoring 2 turnings L. Follow the track for 2 miles along the valley floor, before finally turning L up a signposted path which heads up the E side of the Allt Coire à Bhàinidh to the cliffs of Creag a' Chaorainn. This is a steady climb, with one steep section along the ridge of Aon Cheum, to the E of the coire wall, and tops out at 630m. The path descends steeply to the bothy, which quickly comes into view.

DISTANCE 5½ miles
TIME 3 to 4 hours
TERRAIN Challenging. Wide vehicle track then steep mountain path up to 630m. River crossings
PARKING Forestry car park, Craig (NH 039 493)

FUEL SUPPLY Wood often supplied by the estate.

KEY ATTRACTIONS A good base for an ascent of the remote Munros Bidein a' Choire Sheasgaich (945m) and Lurg Mhor (985m), as well as the Corbett Beinn Dronaig (797m). Attadale Gardens is a lovely spot for an afternoon stroll. Bearnais bothy (p85) is close by and Maol Bhuidhe (p97) further into the interior.

PUBLIC TRANSPORT Scotrail service from Inverness to Kyle of Lochalsh, stops at Attadale.

SPECIAL NOTES Open all year round. During the stalking season from August to October please contact the Attadale Estate prior to using the bothy. Tom Watson, Head Stalker 01520 722308. For mountain biking follow route 2.

BEN DRONAIG LODGE

A special find with top-drawer accommodation

SIZE Large; 4 rooms, with 3 used as dormitories
LOCATION LAT/LONG 57.3967, -5.3073, NH 014 388, 218m, LR Map 25, Explorer 429

You could be forgiven for walking straight past Ben Dronaig Lodge without realising it was an open bothy. Set close to a locked estate lodge in the wide floodplain of the *Uisge Dubh* (Black Water) SE of Loch Carron, it looks like an unremarkable white corrugated-iron outbuilding. However, don't be fooled. Inside, the bothy boasts not only a toilet but a kitchen area with a sink, offers sanctuary in a tough, challenging environment and is a strategic staging-post to the vast wilderness to the E.

The bothy is maintained by the Attadale Estate, which courted controversy when it extended and upgraded paths into the interior of the remote area N and E of the bothy in 2001-02. This seems ironic now, as there is a major hydroelectric scheme being built in the glen. The work is due to finish by the end of 2017. The bothy itself has 3 windows on the S side, with a small extension on the N for the kitchen and toilet. There is a large communal area, a blocked-up fireplace, table and chairs. The toilet and the dormitories are to the L, and the RHR has another with a working hearth that does not draw very well. Both the 2 small dormitories have excellent little fireplaces but no doors. There is a note requesting that visitors stay no longer than 48 hours, emphasising that the shelter is a refuge and not a holiday cottage!

ROUTE 1

From the station head S for a short way along the A890 before turning L through the farm at Achintee. At a crossroads take a L (signposted Hill Paths) round to an electricity substation where a track continues up the hill. Shortly after, a signpost indicates Bearnais L and Ben Dronaig straight on. Continue up across the moor past a number of small lochans. From the Bealach the path heads down into Uisge Dubh, following a rusting fence from NG 956 394, joining the track from Attadale a mile or so before the bothy.

DISTANCE 6 miles
TIME 2½ to 3 ½ hours
TERRAIN Straightforward. Stalkers' path. River crossings
PARKING Strathcarron station (NG 941 421)

ROUTE 2

Follow the metalled road as it turns L and then R, away from the entrance to the gardens, and along the glen to the holiday cottages at Strathan. Then take the vehicle track up the steep slope to Loch an Droighinn, skirting the edge of a forestry plantation. Continue up a series of zig-zags to a broad bealach just beyond the outflow of Loch na Caillich. From here it is straight down into the Strath Fèith á Mhadaich, before the track loops round the valley floor and after another half a mile the lodge and bothy come into view.

DISTANCE 8 miles
TIME 3 to 4 hours
TERRAIN Straightforward. Vehicle track, steep sections up to 338m
PARKING Attadale (NG 923 386)

CAMBAN

Welcome staging-post en route to remote territory (1969)

SIZE Medium; 2 rooms both with large sleeping platforms
LOCATION LAT/LONG 57.2143, -5.2250, NH 053 184, 279m, LR Map 33

Camban sits high up on the long, lonely pass that links Glen Affric and Glen Lichd, close to the watershed west to Loch Duich, and east through to the Beauly Firth. The name is composed of two elements in Scots Gaelic: *camas* (a bend in a river) and *bàn* (probably 'fair', a reference to the area's light-coloured vegetation). It was once a staging post on an old droving road through from Skye and the NW to the livestock markets in Dingwall and Inverness, but fell out of use in the early 1800s when the new estate owners introduced sheep to graze the land. The cottage was built around this time to house a shepherd and his family, and there are census records going back to the 1830s listing the various occupants. The last tenant, named Paterson, finally moved down the glen between 1917 and 1920 and settled at Alltbeithe, now a youth hostel. Camban was then closed up, but over the years functioned as a rough-and-ready shelter, providing useful refuge in this remote mountain terrain. However, by the 1960s, like so many of these remote outposts, the structure was in a quite ruinous state, and it was only through the initiative of two families who wanted to create a memorial to their lost sons, Philip Tranter and Alistair Park, that new life was breathed into the place.

In 1966 these two experienced mountaineering friends died in separate climbing accidents and the families wanted to set up a mountain refuge as a fitting tribute. After a long search, Camban was made available and the poignant story of its restoration is told in an MBA newsletter article by Nigel Tranter, Philip's father. In the bothy, you can read a summary and look at photographs on a display board. In 2008, when a second, more extensive renovation took place, a new roof was installed and sleeping platforms built to replace the original loft space. The new work, which made a big difference, was partially financed by the Innes family, and was dedicated to Liz Innes, former secretary of the Corriemulzie Club, who was a member of the original working party.

The entrance to the bothy opens into a long hallway with doors R and L leading into 2 spacious, equal-sized rooms. Each has a working fireplace, and bunks along the back wall. The RHR has a table and a couple of benches and the flagstones have been sealed with plyboard sheets. There is no further insulation in the building and the interior stonework is exposed. Transparent roofing panels allow extra light to penetrate into the room, but the LHR has none and is a little gloomy.

ROUTE 1
Follows the start of the new Affric Kintail Way. Walk along the road, and take the track R signposted to Glen Affric and Loch Cluaine along the valley floor to Glenlicht House, a private bothy maintained by the Edinburgh University Mountaineering Club, which has an emergency

shelter at one end. From here a path continues over 2 bridges and up round the waterfalls on the Allt Grannda and on to the bothy.

DISTANCE 7 miles

TIME 3 to 4 hours

TERRAIN Straighforward. Track to Glenlicht House, then well-made path up to bothy

PARKING by the Mountain Rescue Post at Morvich (NG 960210)

ROUTE 2

Take the track signposted to Glen Affric and Morvich up An Caorann Mòr and onto Alltbeithe Youth Hostel (NH 081 200). The path peters out before you reach the low bealach and Fionngleann but reforms heading down the Allt a' Chòmhlain. Although from here you catch sight of the bothy, it is advisable to make for the bridge by the Youth Hostel rather than tackle the river before this. As you return towards Camban, there is another tributary to ford – the Allt Gleann Gniomhaidh. The path diverges here, and there is a choice of a ford or a rather suspect bridge, before the final push along Fionngleann to the bothy.

DISTANCE 7½ miles

TIME 3 to 4 hours

TERRAIN Challenging. Vehicle track part-way, faint trail over a bealach at 400m, then recognisable path into Glen Affric

PARKING Layby on the A87, 1 mile E of Cluanie Inn (NH 091 121)

FUEL SUPPLY Bring supplies.

KEY ATTRACTIONS Fantastic location to tackle the surrounding Munros: to the W is Ben Fhada, also known as Ben Attow (1032m) and to the S Ciste Dhubh (979m), Aonach Meadhoin (1001m) and Sgùrr á Bhealaich Dheirg (1036m), along with the prominent Sgùrr an Fhuarail (987m).

PUBLIC TRANSPORT Scottish Citylink bus from Glasgow and Fort William to Skye, stops at Cluanie Inn; Shiel Bridge services 915, 916.

SPECIAL NOTES Open throughout the year. Alltbeithe Youth hostel close by. Bothy used as a water station on the Highland Cross duathlon held in June.

The land surrounding the bothy is owned and managed by the National Trust for Scotland (NTS). On the hillside above it, the Trust has constructed several enclosures to restore natural habitat decimated by grazing deer. Since the project started in 2000 there has already been a noticeable increase in species diversity, including the first sightings of badgers and black grouse. Unfortunately, following damage to young trees and the scavenging of fence posts for use as firewood the NTS is alerting visitors to the bothy that continued abuses may jeopardise future access to the building. The Trust also recognises that the deer fences are unsightly and restrictive, and the long-term aim is their removal followed by strict control of livestock and deer numbers.

FUEL SUPPLY Bring supplies.

KEY ATTRACTIONS Plan your ascent of Munros Maol Chean-dearg (933m) and Sgorr Ruadh (962m) from the bothy; the Corbetts Fuar Tholl (907m) and An Ruadh-Stac (892m) are also close by. The Lochcarron Hotel in the village is a popular spot.

PUBLIC TRANSPORT Scotrail service from Inverness to Kyle of Lochalsh, stops at Strathcarron. Lochcarron Garage bus service 704 Inverness to Applecross (01520 722205) stops on request.

SPECIAL NOTES Bothy closed during the stalking season from 1 September to 20 October.

A hydroelectric scheme is currently being built on the Fionn-abhainn, a mile below the bothy. The track has been upgraded to the new dam, but remains open at all times. Straightforward to mountain bike.

COIRE FIONNARAICH

Well-appointed, scenic bothy with a short walk in (1986)

SIZE Large; 2 attic rooms, plenty of sleeping space
LOCATION LAT/LONG 57.4755, -5.4209, NG 950 480, 180m, LR Map 25

Coire Fionnaraich is one of those places that is very satisfying to know about and recommend on. Surrounded by dramatic, steep-sided red sandstone peaks, the bothy is an old stalker's cottage run by the Ben Damph Estate, also known as Coulags, after the farm at the roadside before you enter the glen. The name *Fionn, Fiann* or *na Fèinn* means 'bright', 'white' or 'fair' in Gaelic and celebrates the mythical warrior-giant of mainly Irish tradition, transcribed in English as Finn MacCool (*Fionn mac Cumhaill*), who has many geographical features attributed to him, including Fingal's Cave on Staffa. A large pointed boulder, a little wander past the bothy, called the Clach nan Con-fionn is said to have been used by the giant to tether his hunting dogs. Another well-known tale relates how he built the Giant's Causeway as a stepping stone across the water from the Emerald Isle to Scotland.

The bothy stands a little taller than many of its contemporaries, and has a distinctive tiny window above the doorway that lights a wee nook on the landing. Sadly, a mature rowan tree which grew just in front of the bothy no longer stands, but many of the interior features are intact, including the stairs and most of the wood panelling. On the ground floor there are two communal rooms, the RHR with a Dowling stove and the LHR where the hearth has, unfortunately, been blocked up. There are tables in each room, an assortment of plastic chairs and a bench. Upstairs, the 2 attic rooms, each with a small window, make excellent dormitories.

ROUTE 1

From the parking bay, take the new access road on the L after the bridge, signposted to Glen Torridon, to the new dam. Here the original stalkers' path continues, crossing a bridge and on to the bothy. On the way you pass a stone slab which is a memorial to a Breton father and son, Alan and Michael Canon, whose ashes are scattered nearby.

DISTANCE 2 miles

TIME 1 hour

TERRAIN Easy. Initially follows a vehicle track, then clearly defined stalkers' path to the bothy

PARKING Small area on N side of A890, just W of bridge at Coulags (NG 957 451)

Note: If you are planning to catch the train to Strathcarron and then on to the bothy, take the path running along the N bank of the River Carron and cross the bridge on the main road. Although this adds a further 2½ miles, it shortens what would otherwise be a route march along the A890 all the way to Coulags.

FUEL SUPPLY Fallen branches in woodland towards the shore.

KEY ATTRACTIONS Little-known Redpoint beach is a real gem and the Torridon Stores and Cafe is a useful refuelling stop. Free camping by the road junction outside the village. Badachro Inn, a sailing destination on the road to Redpoint, is one of the best hostelries in the Highlands.

PUBLIC TRANSPORT Scotrail service from Inverness to Kyle of Lochalsh, stops at Strathcarron. DMK Motors minibus service 701-2 from Strathcarron to Shieldaig and Torridon village on request (01520 722682); must be booked in advance. No public transport provision on to Lower Diabaig.

SPECIAL NOTES No restrictions, open all year round.

CRAIG

Very comfortable and spacious former youth hostel (2006)

SIZE Large; 3 attic rooms and plenty of sleeping space
LOCATION LAT/LONG 57.6097, -5.7270, NG 774 638, 83m, LR Map 24

Standing serenely above the shores of Loch Torridon, looking across to the Applecross peninsula, Rona, and the Trotternish Ridge on Skye, Craig is as luxurious as MBA bothies get. This large, well-appointed sandstone shepherd's cottage, constructed in the late 19th century, was adopted by the Scottish Youth Hostel Association, and had the distinction of being the most remote hostel in the UK before it closed in 2003, because there was no choice but to walk in from the road end at Diabaig. Three years later the MBA gained responsibility for property's upkeep, and it remains a hostel in all but name.

There are 3 rooms on the ground floor, and 3 bedrooms above. The hostel's gas lighting and piped water supply were removed, but there is an outside toilet that you flush using a bucket. To the L of the entrance hallway is the common room and kitchen area, featuring a large, striking Celtic mural. There is a small Dowling stove, a large dining table, benches,

and a couple of comfortable chairs. The kitchen retains the original work surfaces and cupboards, but there is no sink. The room to the R of the hallway provides further accommodation space. Immediately upstairs is a small cubby-hole with 2 single beds. To the R is the old warden's bedroom with some furniture, books, and 2 further single beds with mattresses. The LHR is empty, and can sleep 6 comfortably.

ROUTE 1

Turn sharp R on the single-track road to Lower Diabaig after negotiating the Bealach na Gaoithe (the Pass of the Winds), and park by the road end. A signpost which reads Gairloch via Craig directs you along a well-engineered path restored by the Footpath Trust. Walk gently uphill, crossing a number of streams by sets of stepping stones before turning N to Lochan Dubh. Just beyond the lochan the path curves to the L and cuts down through crags before levelling out towards the bothy.

DISTANCE 2½ miles
TIME Up to 1 hour
TERRAIN Easy. Well-maintained path
PARKING Lower Diabaig, by the pier (NG 790 606)

ROUTE 2

Take the track signposted to Craig and Diabaig past Redpoint Farm and on to a grassy path over the machair to the beach. Head to the old salmon fishing station at the far end of the bay, and ford the stream beyond it. Continue on across the moor 100yds above the coast, crossing a number of streams. At the last, make a short diversion upstream to a remarkable Mesolithic cave and a shell midden (NG 767 649) below some obvious crags. Return down and L along the Craig River. Cross by a footbridge 500yds upstream and see the bothy.

DISTANCE 4½ miles
TIME 2½ to 3 hours
TERRAIN Straightforward
PARKING Redpoint, at very end of B8056 (NG 732 687)

MAOL BHUIDHE

Very remote mountain bothy with a unique atmosphere (1970)

SIZE Medium; 1 downstairs room but plenty of attic space
LOCATION LAT/LONG 57.3722, -5.2405, NH 052 360, 261m, LR Map 25, Explorer 429

There is a certain mystical quality associated with Maol Bhuidhe, a lonesome homestead which lies in the heart of the remote, roadless territory between Glen Carron and Glen Shiel. The cheery sight of its bright, whitewashed exterior has brought relief to many a weary traveller, and there are numerous tales in the log book of dangerous river crossings and arduous tramping over the unforgiving terrain. A place of pilgrimage for many bothy enthusiasts, the combination of apprehension, satisfaction and invigoration provided by the challenge of heading out here is only complemented by the almost palpable solitude and isolation experienced on your arrival.

The cottage was built during the mid-19th century and its name derives from the Gaelic, *bhuidhe* meaning 'yellow' and *maol*, 'bald-headed' or 'rounded place'. The first recorded occupants were the Renwicks, who raised a brood of 10 children there,

one of them attaining the post of Moderator of the Free Church of Scotland. A second family named Burnet moved up from the Borders to take over the shepherding and game-keeping duties, but found integrating into the local community difficult because they couldn't speak Gaelic. An account by Ian Mackay illustrates the tough experiences the inhabitants faced, especially in winter. There are also many references to the bothy in Iain Thompson's celebrated book *Isolation Shepherd*, inspired by his experiences of living with his wife and two young children in a cottage by Pait Lodge on the S shore of Loch Monar in the 1950s. Abandoned in 1914, Maol Bhuidhe fell into disrepair and its only visitors were the tramps and vagabonds who regularly wandered the glens in the 1920s and 1930s. By the time the MBA intervened in the late 1960s, the windows were gone, as was part of the back wall; fortunately the roof remained relatively weatherproof. A second more extensive refit was initiated in 1979 in

memory of Daniel Gerrard who had been killed in a climbing accident on Beinn Alligin the previous year. The bothy is a typical *but* and *ben* with 2 main downstairs rooms, and a partitioned attic accessed by a set of stairs. These were manhandled over the bealach from Iron Lodge on a small car trailer during the second renovation. The roof space provides ample sleeping room and is lit by two Velux windows. Tucked into the back on the ground floor, the box room's tiny window stops this space from becoming too claustrophobic. Downstairs to the R is a rough-and-ready working area. The exposed interior stonework has been whitewashed and the floor retains much of its original cobbling. To the L, an interior door leads into a communal, wood-panelled room, a little cramped owing to a low ceiling but homely nonetheless. A long bench fills the back wall and a single sleeping platform has been pushed into one corner. A table sits under the small N-facing window, and there are a couple of additional chairs. The hearth has been carefully reconstructed and sports a rare 'swee' – a pot stand on a swinging arm – an interesting piece of ironmongery commissioned by a former MBA maintenance officer from an Inverness blacksmith.

Note: The two most practical approaches to Maol Bhuidhe are from the W but be aware that the bothy is protected on 3 sides by water. Delays or detours in times of spate must be factored in: crossing fast-flowing currents is risky and there is no prospect of rescue should you get into difficulties. After heavy rain, even the final stream crossing on Route 2, just before the bothy, can be challenging. Ben Dronaig Lodge (p87) is a useful staging-post if the weather unexpectedly deteriorates.

ROUTE 1

Follow the metalled road as it turns first L and then R, away from the entrance to the gardens, and along the glen to the holiday cottages at Strathan. Then take the vehicle track,

widened for heavy vehicle use, up the steep slope to Loch an Droighinn, skirting the edge of a forestry plantation. Continue up a series of zig-zags to a broad bealach just beyond the outflow of Loch na Caillich. From here it is straight down into the Strath Feith á Mhadaich, before the track loops round the valley floor and, after another half a mile, continuing on to Ben Dronaig Lodge. Pass it and walk over a rickety bridge or ford the Allt Coire na Sorna before turning E up round to Loch Calavie. Take a faint path R a little beyond the main body of water, crossing the Allt Loch Calavie by a new wooden footbridge, which has replaced two precarious wires, before contouring down across some tough pathless moorland to Loch Cruoshie, and the wide River Ling. Extreme care

should be taken when crossing the river before the final stretch up to the bothy. The best fording point is just before the confluence of the main channel and the Allt a' Chreachail Mhòir, which runs down past Maol Bhuidhe from Aonach Buidhe to the S.

DISTANCE 12½ miles

TIME 4 hours

TERRAIN Challenging. Tracks, established paths and faint trails. Up to 350m

PARKING Attadale (NG 923 386)

ROUTE 2

From Camas-luinie, continue on past the end of the tarmac, through a locked gate and along the S bank of the River Elchaig to an estate cottage. Cross the bridge to the

FUEL SUPPLY Bring supplies.

KEY ATTRACTIONS Perfect for an expedition up the N-facing coires of the Corbetts Aonach Buidhe (899m) to the S, and Ben Dronaig (797m) to the NW. Munros Lurg Mhor (986m) and Bidein à Choire Sheasgaich, the 'Cheese Grater' (945m), lie to the N. Route 2 follows part of the Cape Wrath Trail.

PUBLIC TRANSPORT Scotrail service from Inverness to Kyle of Lochalsh, stops at Attadale. Scottish Citylink bus service 915/916 from Glasgow and Fort Wiliam to Skye; closest stop Dornie.

SPECIAL NOTES Not officially available during stag stalking from August to October but in practice it is left unlocked. Check with Killian Estate (01599 530055 or 07771 777789) for access during this time. Extremely remote territory requires good all-round hillcraft skills, especially in poor weather conditions.

N side of the glen, and follow the winding track as it ascends past Carnoch and Iron Lodge, before heading steeply up to the bealach following the An Crom-allt, which has to be forded at NH 043 311. The track becomes less defined as it heads through the pass and down to Maol Bhuidhe and there are a number of fording points where you must take care. If the water level is high, avoid crossing the Allt na Sean-luibe and stick to the W side of the channel until you see the bothy.

DISTANCE 10 miles

TIME 4 hours

TERRAIN Challenging. Steep in places. River crossings. Up to 465m

PARKING Car park at Camas-luinie (NG 948 283)

FUEL SUPPLY Some wood in the nearby forestry plantation.

KEY ATTRACTIONS The summit of Sgurr Mhic Bharraich (779m), a pathless Corbett on the S side of Glen Shiel, is close as is Beinn Sgritheall (974m) – its W side is rarely visited. The Glenelg Inn is a great place to stop for a drink.

PUBLIC TRANSPORT Scottish Citylink bus service 915 or 916 from Glasgow and Fort Wiliam to Skye, stops at Shiel Bridge. Local bus service 611 run by MacRae, Kintail from Kyle of Lochalsh to Glenelg.

SPECIAL NOTES Open all year round. Bothy occasionally used by local shepherds who have priority.

SUARDALAN

Easy walk in to a tucked-away retreat (1976)

SIZE Medium; 3 rooms, 2 with raised platforms, sleeping 9
LOCATION LAT/LONG 57.1966, -5.5062, NG 883 173, 113m, LR Map 33

Suardalan, derived from the Old Norse *Swarddale*, combining *sward* an expanse of short grass, with *dalr* or *dal* (dale), is an old 19th-century shepherd's cottage, tucked away in a quiet peninsula guarded by the Mam Ratagan Pass. Despite an easy walk in, the bothy receives few visitors – most head for Kintail and Skye. The surrounding glens have been inhabited since 3000BC, and in neighbouring Gleann Beag the most startling remnants are three *brochs*, Iron Age forts, over 10 metres high, that are unique to Scotland.

Access to Glenelg was improved in the 18th century when the military upgraded the route over Mam Ratagan to link Bernara Barracks and Fort Augustus. Later new landlords brought in sheep and cattle. Elaborate sheep *fanks* (pens) are dotted across the hillside in Glen More but the industrial-scale sheep farming failed to produce the expected fortune, and over-grazing soon ruined the old pasture.

The bothy follows a typical *but and ben* layout with a large room at either end of the building, and a neat sleeping chamber with a 2-person platform in between. The LHR has stone walls and a large bunk-bed sleeping platform that comfortably sleeps 8. There is a good-sized stove, a table under the window, and various chairs. The RHR has a large fireplace, a table, more chairs, and original wood panelling remains on both walls and ceiling.

ROUTE 1

From the end of the road, 500 yards past the house at Moyle (NG 885 187), walk down a forestry track and cross the bridge over the Glenmore River. Then turn sharp R onto the moor and follow a faint path up to the bothy.

DISTANCE ¾ mile
TIME ½ hour
TERRAIN Easy. Track, faint path
PARKING Moyle (NG 890 182)

ROUTE 2

From the bridge at Braeside (NG 870 196) the route is longer but more scenic. Follow the boggy path along the course of the river, then turn uphill to go round the shoulder of Sròn Mhòr when the bothy will come into view.

DISTANCE 2 mile
TIME 1 hour
TERRAIN Easy. Path, boggy in places
PARKING Braeside (NG 870 196)

ROUTE 3

Head over from Gleann Beag road, passing Dun Telve and Dun Troddan *brochs*. Park at the farm at Balvraid (NG 847 165). Follow a track uphill beyond the ruins of the third *broch*, Dun Grugaig, under an electricity pylon and round to the plantation at Srath à Chomair. Continue on up onto the moor, ignoring path on the R to Kinloch Hourn, skirt the small Loch Iain Mhic Aonghais, and descend to the bothy. The final stretch is notoriously boggy.

DISTANCE 3½ miles
TIME 1 to 1½ hours
TERRAIN Easy, track, boggy
PARKING Gleann Beag (NG 847 165)

FUEL SUPPLY No fireplace.

KEY ATTRACTIONS The round of Beinn Liath Mhòr (887m), Sgorr Ruadh (962m) and Fuar Tholl (907m) is well within reach.

PUBLIC TRANSPORT Scotrail service from Inverness to Kyle of Lochalsh, stops at Achnashellach. Lochcarron Garage bus service 704 Inverness to Applecross (01520 722205) stops on request.

SPECIAL NOTES Open all year. No fires outside the hut.

THE TEAHOUSE EASAN DORCHA

Quirky, glorified garden shed (1990)

SIZE Very small
LOCATION LAT/LONG 57.5191, -5.3228, NH 012 526, 215m, LR Map 25

Easan Dorcha, affectionately known as the 'Teahouse', certainly boasts a beguiling setting but is little more than an extremely robust garden shed. As its name suggests, it is an ideal spot for lunch or a brew, rather than an overnight stay. Long used by hunting parties, estate workers and walkers as a refuge, the bothy was given a new lease of life in 2010 when the MBA undertook its complete refurbishment, using long-lasting, well-seasoned cedar. The hut nestles in beautiful mixed woodland of Scots pine, rowan and birch just below 2 streams that combine to form the River Coulin. This part of Wester Ross, S of the area's honey-pot attractions – the Torridon Hills and the round of Maol Chean-dearg to the W – is often overlooked. Its Gaelic name means 'dark waterfalls', and the river creates picturesque drops as it crashes down the mountainside from the coires of Beinn Liath Mhòr and Beinn Liath Beag. Inside there is a small table and chair, and the long wooden bench that is not really wide enough to lie on. Windows facing W and E provide ample light, and, if you are so inclined, there is just enough space on the floor for 3 people to sleep with some intimacy.

Many combine the 2 routes to the bothy, one heading W and the other E in a fine circular walk, This is the ideal option if you plan to arrive by train.

ROUTE 1

After parking, follow the private road to Achnashellach Station and go over the gated level crossing. A short walk up to R leads to a signpost. Head W, signed L to Loch Torridon, up the wide forestry track parallel to the River Lair. Once out of the woodland, walk up the hill to a white cairn (NG 991 501). Here a stalkers' path leads off W to the bealach between Fuar Tholl and Sgurr Ruadh. Ignore this and continue on to a second cairn marking the route into Drochaid Coire Làir (NG 990503). Instead of taking this path, head R skirting Drochaid Coire Làir on a gentle gradient, through the wide bealach and down into Easan Dorcha

glen. After half a mile of woodland, cross the bridge at the confluence of two streams just before the bothy.

> **DISTANCE** 3 miles
> **TIME** 1½ hours
> **TERRAIN** Straightforward. Well-made path over bealach (385m)
> **PARKING** Achnashellach (NH 005 484)

ROUTE 2

At the footpath sign, turn R and follow the vehicle track that climbs up the hillside, before kinking R and L and up to the top of Coulin Pass. Follow the track straight down to the valley floor and cross the bridge over the River Coulin. Immediately after take a track L parallel to the river and then head up through the Scots pines of Easan Dorcha glen. The bothy comes into view about half a mile from here. This is by far the easiest route for mountain bikes.

> **TIME** 2½ hours
> **TERRAIN** Straightforward. Track all the way to the bothy
> **PARKING** Achnashellach (NH 005 484)

FUEL SUPPLY Protected woodland. Bring supplies.

KEY ATTRACTIONS Applecross Inn is renowned, with fresh seafood a speciality. Kayak hire and organised trips from Applecross village in the summer months. Bealach na Bà, the high, tightly twisting mountain pass into Applecross is a cyclists' test piece.

PUBLIC TRANSPORT Scotrail service from Inverness to Kyle of Lochalsh, stops at Strathcarron. Lochcarron Garage bus service 704 Inverness to Applecross and Toscaig (01520 722205).

SPECIAL NOTES Open all year. Owned by the Applecross Estate 01478 613489 or email admin@ applecross.org.uk. If the small stream outside the bothy runs dry, go back along the path to find an alternative source. For kayaking launch from Toscaig Pier.

UAGS

Charming coastal bothy with views over to Skye (1998)

SIZE Medium; 2 rooms plus attic
LOCATION LAT/LONG 57.3487, -5.7874 , NG 724 349, 23m, LR Map 24

Set above a little rocky raised beach at the S end of the Applecross peninsula, Uags Bothy is a magical place where you can escape the bustle of modern life. Walking in along a wild, unspoilt stretch of coastline, on a clear day there are views across the Inner Sound to Scalpay, Raasay and Skye, with the Cuillin Ridge just visible on the skyline. Although a rather isolated spot, *Uags* (Old Norse for 'bay') was once part of a small crofting township and the walls and gable ends of other homesteads are clearly visible nearby. The community survived until the early 1930s, before the last inhabitants finally retreated to Toscaig. The Applecross Trust took over the estate in 1975.

The bothy opens into a hallway lit by a window, with rooms partitioned L and R and stairs leading up into the attic. The RHR has whitewashed stone walls, the fireplace has been bricked up, and it is sparsely furnished. With just 2 large tables and benches, it functions more as a lunch stop. The smaller LHR is cosier, with a small inset stone hearth, plus table, bench and comfortable chairs, including a throne (enough said) and a large S-facing window. Upstairs there are two neatly wood panelled rooms with large skylights in the roof, one with a single bed and a rather suspect mattress. This stretch of coastline is surprisingly isolated, and out of the summer months has few visitors. Locally, this is a well-known spot for a day walk, and there is a picnic table outside.

ROUTE 1

Taking care not to block the turning area at Toscaig, take the signposted path to Uags and Airigh-drishaig. Cross a footbridge, walk round towards a barn and after about 200yds come to a second signpost where you turn R right to Uags. Initially, the route is quite sketchy – a faint boggy trail heading up across the moorland – but keep well above and L of a small nameless lochan and you will soon see an area of pasture with some old shielings (NG 717 367). Just before these ruins, ford the Allt Loch Meall nam Feadan, a potential obstacle after heavy rain, and make for a small cairn on the far side of the clearing. Continuing above the sheilings, the path becomes much clearer. Walk up a small rise and contour through the rocky landscape. Just before the bothy, the final stretch is wonderfully atmospheric, passing through rare Atlantic Oak woodland. A protected habitat of temperate rainforest, it is found only in damp regions on the W coasts of Scotland, Ireland, France and Spain. This is one of the UK's last uncultivated and undisturbed vestiges of land. The path marked on some OS maps round the coast to Airigh-drishaig has long since fallen into disuse. Retrace your steps back to Toscaig, rather than attempt a round trip.

DISTANCE 2½ miles
TIME 1 to 1½ hours
TERRAIN Straightforward. Faint path over moor. River crossing
PARKING Opposite end cottages, Toscaig (NG714 386)

WESTERN
HIGHLANDS

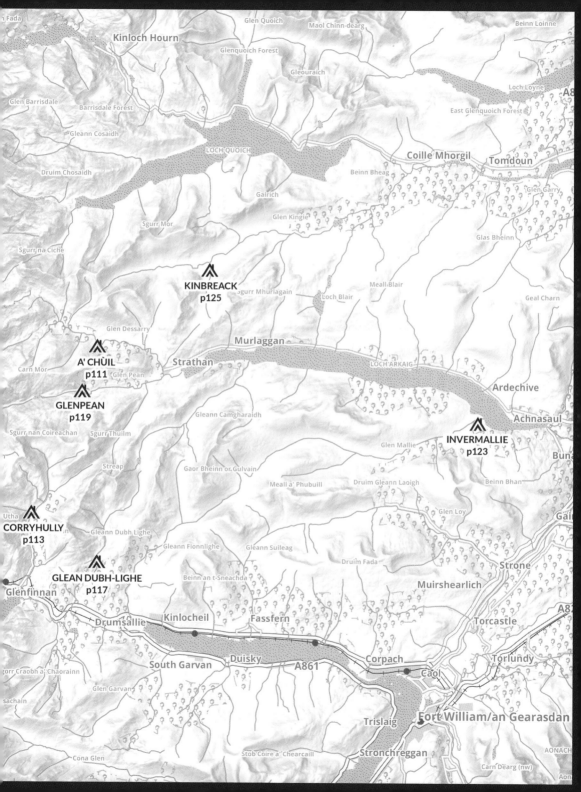

FUEL SUPPLY Fallen timber in surrounding plantation.

KEY ATTRACTIONS An impressive ridge runs to the NW from Sgùrr nan Coireachan (953m), Garbh Choire Mhòr (1013m) and onto Sgùrr na Cìche (1040m). Climbing Corbett Sgùrr Còs na Breachd-laoigh (835m) and Druim a' Chuirn (822m) is less formidable.

PUBLIC TRANSPORT None to Strathan.

SPECIAL NOTES Open throughout the year. Deer control from 1 July to 16 February, with a critical period from 20 August to 20 October. Sign appearing at road end at Strathan indicates stalking. Please stick to the low-lying routes and ridges marked on noticeboard (Glendessary Estate 01397 712406). Major timber felling with removal of the entire plantation into Glen Pean by 2021. Expect some disturbance and heed warning notices. Easy mountain bike.

A' CHÙIL

On the edge of wilderness but easily accessible by car (1968)

SIZE Medium; 3 rooms, 1 with a 2-person sleeping platform
LOCATION LAT/LONG 56.9769, -5.3844, NM 944 924, 137m, LR Map 33/40

When you leave the forestry track and head down through the undergrowth to A' Chùil Bothy, excitement builds as the view of upper Glen Dessarry and the hills leading into Knoydart finally opens up. A' Chùil (from the Gaelic *an cùl* meaning 'back' or 'rear') overlooks the meandering River Dessarry and lies on the boundary of an extensive conifer plantation that spreads all the way round to neighbouring Glen Pean, where wild boar roam. Before the plantations, this area was once part of a huge sheep farm, and the bothy is one of a group of late-19th century shepherd's dwellings. The outposts included properties that have become the sister bothies to A' Chùil in Glen Pean and at Kinbreack, forming a small community centred around Strathan, where there was a school that also doubled up as a church. Taigh nan Saighdearan, a small government barracks dating back to the Jacobite rebellions of the 1700s, was also located at Strathan and its troops controlled an important route

across the Western Highlands. A' Chùil was abandoned after World War II and lay empty until resurrected by the MBA in the late 1960s.

The building is a typical *but and ben* with just 2 rooms. The RHR, which retains its original iron hearth and mantlepiece is smaller and more communal. There is also a 3-person sleeping platform tucked into an alcove, with a small skylight above. The LHR still has a working fire and a long sleeping platform stretching the length of the far wall, accommodating 4. Many people combine a visit to A' Chùil with multi-day itineraries that include walking to Glen Pean or heading on to Sourlies, Inverie and Barrisdale Bay. This is amazing walking country and the lack of access restrictions to the through routes during the stalking season is a real plus. The bothy always seemed a little downbeat but its aspect has been improved as a result of tree felling. It is rarely full but you should always expect company. If you are continuing on up Glen Dessarry, head down to

the bridge (NM 943 929) and take an obvious path back up to the main track, rather than pushing on through the plantation on the S bank of the river.

ROUTE 1
From the large car park at the road end at Strathan (NM 987 916), follow the main track and once beyond the ruins of the barracks, take a L at the junction where there is an impressive signpost, in the direction of Oban, Kinlocheil and Glenfinnan. Head down to a bridge before ascending a little into the plantation. At the next junction, head R along the track which contours round the N slopes of Monadh Gorm. L takes you on to Glenpean Bothy (p119). Continue on this track for just over 2 miles, before taking a small path marked by a cairn through the trees and down to the bothy at the plantation edge.

DISTANCE 3 miles
TIME 1 to 1½ hours
TERRAIN Easy. Forest access road for majority; path for last 500yds
PARKING Car park Strathan NM 987 916

FUEL SUPPLY Some fallen wood in the plantations. Best to bring supplies.

KEY ATTRACTIONS An ideal base for the round of Sgùrr nan Coireachan (956m) and Sgùrr Thuilm (963m) – the 'Corryhully Horsehoe'; also Streap (909m) a very worthy Corbett. Fine views of the Jacobite monument and Loch Shiel SW of Glennfinnan, plus the sweeping viaduct featured in Harry Potter and the Philospher's Stone.

PUBLIC TRANSPORT Scotrail West Highland Line from Glasgow Queen St. to Mallaig, stops at Glenfinnan. Citylink coach service 915/916 Glasgow to Fort William. Daily bus from Fort William to Glenfinnan (Shiel Buses 01397 700 700).

SPECIAL NOTES Open throughout the year. During the stalking season, check access with the Glen Finnan Estate (01397 722203). Easy cycle.

CORRYHULLY

The 'Electric' bothy. Barn with a handy kettle and sofa, en route to Knoydart

SIZE Small; 1 room with platform beds sleeping 5
LOCATION LAT/LONG 56.9038, -5.4290, NM 912 844, 65m, LR Map 40

Corryhully is one of the very few open shelters in the Highlands with its own electricity supply, hence its nickname. There is a kettle, 2 lights and a couple of double sockets all fed by a meter. A nearby hydroelectric dam, with a wide access road cutting across the E side of the River Finnan, is about a mile above the bothy. The building is a long, open shell with an earth floor, and an inset hearth (one is currently blocked up) at each of the gable ends. A permanent 3-person sleeping platform runs down the length of the far wall, split by a table. Additional bed space consists of wooden boards balanced on a bench. The focal point is the fireplace at the W gable end, where a few chairs and a prized sofa have been corralled. The bothy lacks both intimacy and insulation but makes an ideal stopover after a long train or car journey. Expeditions into the Rough Bounds and Knoydart often begin here and it is also the funnelling point for 2 alternative starts to the Cape Wrath Trail.

ROUTE 1

After parking, or walking ½ mile from Glenfinnan station along the main road to the junction just before the bridge, proceed along the metalled road on the W side of the River Finnan, signed Strathan. Walk underneath the celebrated viaduct, then continue up the valley until just before the road starts to turn uphill to the lodge, with the bothy in view. After turning R on a track signed Loch Arkaig, cross a small bridge to the side of a ford and arrive at the bothy.

DISTANCE 2 miles
TIME 45 minutes to 1 hour
TERRAIN Easy. Metalled road to within 200yds and then a track
PARKING Glenfinnan (NM 906 808) and Glenfinnan visitors' centre (NM 902 803)

A FOOTNOTE ON BARISDALE
LAT/LONG 57.0798, -5.5135, NG 872 043, 10m, LR Map 33

On the N coast of the Knoydart peninsula lies Barisdale Bothy, beautifully sited looking out across Loch Hourn to Beinn Sgritheall. In the same manner as Corryhully, the shelter acts as a staging post onto the Round Bounds, and is also on the Cape Wrath Trail. Once an open bothy it is now managed by the Barisdale Estate (£3 per night, no bookings). There is also a campsite adjacent to the bothy (£1 per night including use of the bothy facilities). Access is either via paths along the lochside from Kinloch Hourn, 5 miles to the E, or a track from Inverie, 7 miles to the SW. Or head in over the Mam Unndalain bealach from Sourlies (p135) and the River Carnach on a section of the Cape Wrath Trail. Barisdale is also accessible by boat from Arnisdale.

FUEL SUPPLY Bring supplies.

KEY ATTRACTIONS During the summer months the Jacobite Steam Train from Fort William to Mallaig passes by. Corbetts An Stac (814m), Rois-bheinn (882m) and Sgùrr na Bà Glaise (874m) lie SW of the bothy, and have fine views out to Eigg and Rùm.

PUBLIC TRANSPORT Scotrail West Highland Line from Glasgow Queen St. to Fort William and Mallaig, stops at Lochailort. Walk just over 2 miles along A830 to start of path. Citylink coach service 915/916 Glasgow to Fort William. Daily bus from Fort William to Lochailort Service 500 (Shiel buses 01397 700 700).

SPECIAL NOTES During the stalking season, 1 September to 20 October please contact the Inverailort Estate to check access (01687 470206). Only cross the railway tracks at the approved crossing.

ESSAN

Homely lochside bothy – easily seen, but harder to reach (1989)

SIZE Medium; 3 rooms, 1 with bunk-bed, sleeping 12
LOCATION LAT/LONG 56.8747, -5.5835, NM 817 817, 34m, LR Map 40

Essan, from the Gaelic *easan* meaning 'waterfall' is a bit of an oddball. Set on the S side of Loch Eilt, part-way between Lochailort and Glenfinnan, the bothy is easy to spot from the A830 Fort William to Mallaig road, and almost within touching distance of the West Highland Line, yet because of the watery barrier manages to remain aloof and retain a homely, well-loved ambience. The bothy is well worth a visit, as well as offering useful back-up if your other plans have gone awry because of bad weather.

This former crofter's cottage, which predates the coming of the railway in the early 1900s, appears on the first 1in OS map of 1876. The track into the cottage ran along what is now the route of the railway. The number of ruined houses close by indicates a small community and there is a wide area of pasture towards the loch. The bothy is a classic *but and ben* with a large room at either end; another small chamber sandwiched between is used for storage. The RHR is the communal space and has an almost stately feel – original wood panelling, a high ceiling, a set of antlers mounted above the hearth, and pictures on the wall. There is a table under some shelving, a number of comfortable chairs, and even a small library. The LHR, where the hearth has been blocked up, is a designated dormitory and the substantial L-shaped bunk-bed platform constructed along two of the walls sleeps 12. Many come to Essan for the craic, but if you are feeling energetic, the walk round the rarely trodden slopes of the Corbetts S of the bothy makes a fine day out.

ROUTE 1

The easiest way into Essan is by boat. There are a couple of places to stop and launch on the main road, the most official-looking a little parking bay at NM 829 821, just before Loch Eilt narrows. From here it is a simple paddle across to the railway bridge over the Allt Easain, where, after ducking under the span, you can tie up on the riverbank.

DISTANCE 500 yds from launching
TIME 15 mins
TERRAIN Easy canoe across loch
PARKING Small bay (NM 829 821)

ROUTE 2

From the boathouse take the track which heads off L into the trees parallel to the main road, onto the embankment and then across the railway bridge at the head of Loch Eilt. Leave the line as it sweeps round the shore, hopping over a fence and onto a faint, undulating path uphill. Do not be tempted to continue along the railway, (technically this is trespassing). After a couple of miles the contours open out and the bothy comes into view.

DISTANCE 3 miles
TIME 1 to 1½ hours
TERRAIN Straightforward. Undulating path above railway track (cross with care)
PARKING Before the boat house (NM 787 830)

FUEL SUPPLY Some wood in the plantations. Best to bring supplies.

KEY ATTRACTIONS Spend a day climbing nearby Stob Coire nan Cearc (887m) and the Corbett, Streap (909m).

PUBLIC TRANSPORT Scotrail West Highland Line from Glasgow Queen St. to Mallaig, stops at Glenfinnan. Citylink coach service 915/916 Glasgow to Fort William. Daily bus from Fort William to Mallaig stops at Glenfinnan (Shiel Buses 01397 700 700) service 500, then 2-mile walk on A830 from Glenfinnan to start of track.

SPECIAL NOTES Open throughout the year. Contact Fassfern Estate during the stalking season (07767 267433 or 01397 722217 or 01397 772288) regarding access.

GLEANN DUBH-LIGHE

5-star, beautifully secluded accommodation (2005 / 2014)

SIZE Medium: 2 rooms, 1 with a 2-person platform bed
LOCATION LAT/LONG 56.8836, -5.3748, NM 944 819, 128m, LR Map 40

Held in great affection by its regulars, Gleann Dubh-lighe burned down to the ground in the summer of 2012 when gas escaping from a cylinder with a faulty seal was accidentally ignited by a candle. There was some debate about whether the bothy should be rebuilt, but the MBA's efforts, combined with the enthusiastic help of the Fassfern Estate, ensured that it rose from the ashes in spectacular fashion. In Gaelic, *Gleann an Lighiche dubh*, translates as 'black doctor' – perhaps dark forces were at play when the bothy caught fire or maybe benign magic secured its resurrection. Once the stonework was stabilised and a new roof attached, two internal rooms were reconstructed plus an entrance lobby. Boasting new pine panelling throughout, it is a far cry from the basic nature of the first incarnation. The RHR contains the original fireplace, chairs and a table, plus a sleeping platform tucked into a back alcove. The LHR is empty except for a new table. Both rooms have small skylights to add a little extra brightness. The restoration work, funded largely by his family, is dedicated to the memory of Nick Randall, an accomplished climber and hill-walker who perished in the Auch Forest in 2008.

Insight into life in the bothy came via a letter (received by the MBA) from Sheila Potter, a descendant of the McLennan family who lived in the cottage in the early 1900s. In these cramped confines 7 children were raised, their father combining work as a shepherd and forester with duties as a ghillie and stalker on the estate. A typical *but and ben*, its 2 narrow front doors opened into a small entry space with a kitchen/living area to the L. A shelf-bed with curtain across lay to the R of the fire, and to the L was a large chest – colloquially known as a girner – with flour on one side and oatmeal on the other. The sleeping room was to the R of the front door, with a small pantry facing it. When it finally fell vacant, the cottage became an open shelter under the custodianship of the Loch Eil Outward Bound Centre, before the MBA took over its maintenance. Hopefully the new bothy will survive intact long into the future.

ROUTE 1

From the small parking bay head up the forestry track which contours above the W side of the Gleann Dubh Lighe, parallel to the river, before rising steeply by Tom nam Fineachan where the track forks. Take the track on the R, which doubles back down to the river, across a bridge and up the opposite bank. Within about 200yds the trees start to thin out and the bothy quickly comes into view. Straightforward to mountain bike, with a bit of pushing.

DISTANCE 2 miles
TIME 45 minutes to 1 hour
TERRAIN Easy. Forestry track all the way to the bothy
PARKING Drochaid Sgainnir (NM 931 799)

GLENPEAN

Amazing views from this remote yet easily accessible bothy (1968)

SIZE Medium; 2-person sleeping platform plus attic space
LOCATION LAT/LONG 56.9579, -5.3957, NM 936 903, 106m, LR Map 33/40

Looking west from the bothy door at Glenpean through the interlocking ridges of the upper valley to the peak of An Stac at the head of Loch Morar, and S across the river to the towering peaks of the Corryhully Horseshoe, it seems remarkable that the view has been so easily earned. The cottage is only 3 miles along newly enlarged forestry access track from the end of the road that winds round Loch Arkaig to Strathan. The only catch is that the final 500yd stretch where the track abruptly stops becomes an obstacle course of twisted roots, boggy puddles, and thick grass tussocks. History weighs deeply in the valley, going back to the time of the Viking settlers. Glenpean is from the Gaelic *Gleann a' Pheiginn*. A *peighinn* or *pennyland* was a measure of land in the Norse system, and 20 pennylands, each with their own individual farm, made up an 'ounce land' – an acreage capable of producing an ounce of silver in rent. Peanmeanach Bothy near Arisaig

(p133) has a similar derivation. In the 18th century, the ruin across the river from the bothy was the home of the famed Donald Cameron of Glenpean, a local pathfinder who guided Bonnie Prince Charlie across the hills above Glen Dessary to Glen Shiel after the battle of Culloden in 1746. The bothy dates from about 1870 and was an estate cottage where a shepherd, his family and a helper lived. Irvine Butterfield pieced together a picture of life in Glen Pean through a series of interviews with Lexie Campbell, one of 5 siblings, who was born in the cottage just after the turn of the 20th century. She remembered her christening in the nearest church at Tarbert on Loch Nevis, the SS Rifle, a steamer that plied goods up and down Loch Arkaig before it sank in the 1930s, and a coming-of-age dance at the annual gathering of tenants at Achnacarry Castle hosted by Cameron of Loch Eil. Sadly, Lexie's 3 brothers lost their lives within 6 months of the start of World War I, which led her parents to leave the homestead after 45 years of service.

One of the first projects undertaken by the MBA, the bothy is now owned by the Bothy Trust, a charity set up after the forestry land on which the building sits was sold by the Balfour family in 2002. The bothy was excluded from the sale to ensure that it would remain an open shelter. Thick wooden panelling splits the ground floor into 2 sections, with stairs rising steeply into the attic just as you enter. The LHR is the communal area, with a large stove standing proud of the fireplace at the W gable end. A 2-person sleeping platform runs along the wall underneath the window, and there are shelves with various odds and ends. A table and a couple of chairs complete the scene. The larger RHR has a fireplace and an ancient iron bunk-bed; it is mainly used for wood sawing and storage. Neither room has any insulation, and the bothy can get pretty cold once the stove has gone out. Upstairs is a large area used for sleeping, and a little wood-panelled room at the E end with a small window.

ROUTE 1

From the large car park follow the main track and once beyond the ruins of the barracks, take a L at the junction where there is an impressive signpost, in the direction of Oban, Kinlocheil and Glenfinnan. Head down to a bridge before ascending a little. Ignore the track leading R, (to A' Chùil Bothy p111) and contour round the S slopes of Monadh Gorm. The bothy comes into view 2 miles later when you leave the plantation. Here the track stops and you must pick your way down to the river bank and round the meander. This final 500 yds is extremely heavy going, especially after prolonged rainfall.

DISTANCE 3½ miles

TIME 1 to 1½ hours

TERRAIN Easy. Unmetalled forest access road, then 500 yds on poorly maintained path

PARKING Car park at Strathan (NM 987 916)

ROUTE 2

The more adventurous may choose to make the 9-mile trek from the S, following part of the Cape Wrath Trail up from Glenfinnan. The first section is along a private metalled road on the W side of the River Finnan, signposted to Strathan, that heads up under the famous viaduct featured in the first Harry Potter film, and onto Corryhully Bothy. You can make an overnight stop here if it is getting late (see p113 for directions). Take the track that bears off R from the road as Corryhully comes into view, and follow this past the bothy and a new hydroelectric dam, climbing steadily to the bealach between Streap and Sgùrr Thuilm, topping out at 471m, before descending into Gleann Cuirnean. This stretch is notoriously boggy and a quick decision needs made as to which side of the Allt Cuirnean to travel down, as there is a faint path down the E side of the river as well as the one marked on the 1:50000 map. on the W bank. This is easier to follow but the bridge crossing the River Pean is on the E bank. In poor weather, the E bank path is a better bet. After crossing the River Pean, head up through the trees and then turn L onto the forestry track, which takes you to the bothy.

DISTANCE 8½ miles

TIME 4 to 5 hours

TERRAIN Challenging. Combination of metalled road, steep track and boggy path, then forestry access road

PARKING Glenfinnan (NM 906 808)

FUEL SUPPLY Abundant fallen timber in surrounding plantations.

KEY ATTRACTIONS Corryhully Horseshoe peaks Sgùrr nan Coirechan (956m) and Sgùrr Thuilm (963m) loom up above the river to S across from the bothy; Corbett Carn Mór (829m) is to the W. Lovely low-level walk up the glen to Lochan Leum an t-Sagairt.

PUBLIC TRANSPORT Scotrail West Highland Line from Glasgow Queen St. to Fort William and Mallaig, stops at Glenfinnan station. From here, start of walk in is ½ mile along A830. No public transport to Loch Arkaig.

SPECIAL NOTES Deer control takes place from 1 July to 16 February, with a critical period from 20 August to 20 October. A sign is fixed to gate at the road end at Strathan when stalking is happening. Please stick to the low-lying routes and ridges marked on noticeboard (Glendessary Estate 01397 712406). Major timber felling is also underway with removal of the entire plantation round into Glen Dessary by 2021. Expect some disturbance and heed any warning notices. Route 1 easy to mountain bike until the last section before the bothy.

FUEL SUPPLY Plenty of timber along river bank.

KEY ATTRACTIONS Admire Ben Nevis from Beinn Bhàn (796m), the Corbett to S. Visit Clan Cameron Museum at Achnacarry, former training centre for WWII commandos in main house; commando monument near Spean Bridge has a spectacular view of Ben Nevis.

PUBLIC TRANSPORT Scotrail West Highland Line from Glasgow Queen St. to Fort William, stops at Spean Bridge. Citylink coach service 915/916 Glasgow to Fort William. Daily bus from Fort William to Spean Bridge and Achnacarry, service 512 (Shiel Buses 01397 700 700).

SPECIAL NOTES Open all year round. Access restricted during the stalking season (contact Locheil Estate 01397 712608). In persistent rain, path and ground floor of bothy can flood; see noticeboard inside. River bridge marked on OS 1:50000 map now ½ mile upstream. New track and bridge appear on new OS 1:25000 and Google maps. Easy mountain bike.

⩕
INVERMALLIE

Large, popular bothy easily accessible from Fort William (1981)

SIZE Large; 4-person sleeping platform plus 3 attic rooms
LOCATION LAT/LONG 56.9529, -5.0668, NN 136 888, 45m, LR Map 34/41, Explorer Map 399

The remote mountain slopes that cradle Loch Arkaig were the training grounds for thousands of commandos during the dark days of World War II. Chosen for the secrecy of its location, the valley is a world away from the main Scottish artery of the Great Glen, barely 10 miles to the east, and is entered by an otherworldly cleft, *Mìle Dorcha*, the Dark Mile, a damp, deeply wooded trench of moss and ferns. The bothy is named after *Màillidh*, an early Christian monk and saint, and *inbhir* (or *inver*), refers to the mouth of the river where the estate house was built over 150 years ago. The lodge was home to a succession of families employed by the Loch Eil Estate as gamekeepers and ghillies, before finally being vacated in the 1960s. It was semi-derelict when Hamish Brown passed here on his odyssey round the Munros a decade later. Today the bothy still feels surprisingly off the beaten track considering how close it is to civilisation. The building is also remarkably intact given its popularity:

from fishing parties, to regulars who treat it as a de facto holiday home.

One of the largest MBA properties, the bothy comprises 4 ground-floor rooms and 3 self-contained attic bedrooms, plus a large external porch, and a wood store at the W gable end. From a wide hallway, the large RHR, originally the parlour, remains the main communal area, while the LHR is now a dormitory. There are 2 storage cubicles in-between. The main room has a comfortable, lived-in feel, with a well-drawing fireplace, shelves either side, a table, and a sideboard with worktop. The dormitory has a small stove and a raised platform sleeping 4. The upstairs rooms have been recently lined in tongue and groove and the floorboards replaced.

ROUTE 1

From the waterfall near the Forestry Commission car park (a location for the film *Rob Roy*), continue along the road for 300yds, before turning L onto a track just after the cattle grid, signed 'Locheil Estate - Private Road'. Cross

a wooden bridge at the head of the loch, and, at the next junction, turn R to follow a gently undulating forestry track leading off along the S side of the water. After a couple of miles, pass an estate lodge, and soon after emerge from the trees. Now, keep a close look out for a stony, overgrown path leading off to R (marked on OS 1:50,000 map). Do not take the main track up Glen Mallie. The bridge by the bothy was swept away in 2009, and the track continues to the new bridge, 500yds further upstream. Head along this R turn to the bothy. Alternatively, from the museum, walk to the end of the tarmac at Achnacarry House and on to the head of the loch to join the track from the waterfall.

> **DISTANCE** 3 miles
> **TIME** 1 to 1½ hours
> **TERRAIN** Easy. Track to within 500yds; path from this point occasionally waterlogged
> **PARKING** Eas Chia-aig waterfalls (NN 177 888) or Achnacarry museum (NN 176 877)

KINBREACK

A welcome refuge in a wild and rugged glen (1969)

SIZE Small; just attic space
LOCATION LAT/LONG 57.0127, -5.2924, NN 002 961, 370m, LR Map 33

Pressed into the hillside above a sweeping meander of the River Kingie, the loft at Kinbreack is very much an outlier to its sister shelters in the Rough Bounds. In this surprisingly remote glen just 15 miles NW of Fort William, you are immediately struck by the sense of peace and isolation, which is precisely what makes it so appealing. You are also likely to have the place to yourself because others head to more popular spots. The name derives from the Gaelic *Ceann Breac*, where *ceann* means the 'head' or 'end' (of the glen) and *breac* is 'speckled' and also (as a noun) 'trout'. The bothy is the byre to a ruined house that lies close by, once an outpost of a large sheep farm that operated as part of the Loch Eil Estate from the mid-19th century. The last inhabitants, the Camerons, moved to Strathan during World War II, yet sheep continued to graze in Glen Kingie until the 1990s. When guests came to the estate for stag shooting, they stayed in the house and were waited on by the family, who moved

out into the attic of the byre which is now the communal bothy space. Family life was documented in the diaries of Ronnie Burn, an eccentric hill-walker and the first to complete the full round of Munros in the 1920s. In her biography *Burn on the Hill: the Story of the First Compleat Munroist*, Elizabeth Allen includes his description of the shepherd going down Glen Kingie in his trap to fetch supplies from Invergarry. One of the steel rims from the trap is propped up against the bothy wall. At that time there was no road along Loch Arkaig so the community of Strathan was more remote than Kinbreack, and the path between the two was little used. Supplies were delivered to the community at Strathan twice a year by estate boat.

The bothy is one of just two MBA shelters where the communal area occupies only the attic space (the other is Luib Chonnal p155); the ground level is simply an empty shell with a cobbled floor. Access is via the new, very conspicuous staircase that

replaced a slightly precarious ladder up to a trap door. The room is slightly cramped but there is a big stone fireplace at one end, and with a fire going, it is very cosy. A worn chaise longue left in the house functions as a table, flanked by a couple of benches. Natural light filters through four clear perspex roof panels, but the winter months can be a little gloomy when the bothy is shaded by the hill and gets no direct sunlight.

ROUTE 1
The best way to get to Kinbreack is from the Loch Arkaig side. From the car park, follow the main track which starts up Glen Dessarry past the ruins of the barracks and at the junction where there is an impressive signpost, head R towards Tomdoun and Morar. After 300 yards, take a second signposted track to Tomdoun, heading steeply N up onto the hill just before a small bridge over the Dearg Allt. Initially, the route over the bealach is a well-trodden track, but becomes increasingly boggy as you head into Glen Kingie and can be hard to follow

if you walk in after dusk. Also, in wet conditions it is advisable to cross the Allt a' Chinn Bhric before you head too far down the glen; the burn can be difficult to ford closer to the bothy. All in all, the walk in can be a tough 3 miles.

DISTANCE 3 miles

TIME 1½ to 2 hours

TERRAIN Challenging. Steep track up to bealach, boggy trails into glen, then established path to bothy

PARKING Car park at Strathan (NM 987 916)

ROUTE 2

It is possible to travel in from Glen Garry, but it is a long and arduous trek. From the layby, cross the dam and follow the stalkers' path up to Gairich, skirt round Lochan an Fhigheadair, cross the ford by means of stepping stones, and proceed into the forestry plantation. At the meeting of paths head through the gate into the conifers and down to Glen Kingie past the ruin at Lochan. The path continues through the trees round the bottom of Gairich before heading out across the moor above the river. As the path starts up hill, head off along the bank following a faint trail until you pick up another stalkers' path close to the bothy. This is notoriously rough terrain, and you still have to cross the river.

DISTANCE 8 miles

TIME Up to 4 hours

TERRAIN Challenging. Stalkers' path into Glen Kingie, boggy in places. Faint trail along river bank. River crossing

PARKING At hydroelectric dam (NH 069 024)

FUEL SUPPLY Bring supplies.

KEY ATTRACTIONS From the bothy door enjoy stunning views of the mountain ridge extending from Corbett Sgùrr an Fhuarain (901m) to one of the most remote Munros, Sgùrr Mòr (1003m). To the NE, an excellent stalkers' path heads over to Gairich (919m).

PUBLIC TRANSPORT No public transport to Loch Arkaig or Loch Quoich.

SPECIAL NOTES Open throughout the year. Access to hills may be restricted during the stalking season from August to February. Check with the Loch Eil Estate (01397 712709) before your visit.

OBAN

Remote lochside bothy in spectacular location (1989)

SIZE Large bothy; 2 downstairs rooms plus open attic for sleeping
LOCATION LAT/LONG 56.9522, -5.5151, NM 863 901, 11m, LR Map 33/40, Explorer Map 398

Sheltering above the uncharted chasm of Loch Morar, Oban Bothy is one of the most remote MBA properties accessible on foot. You could easily run out of superlatives for this breathtaking spot, where the deepest loch in the UK is set among wild, isolated hills. Among seasoned bothy-goers, a pilgrimage to Oban has quietly earned a reputation as an unmissable experience. For a long time there was a real pressure to keep the shelter's whereabouts under your hat, its location only passed on by word of mouth. And up to the late 1990s, the bothy's owners requested that the grid reference be withheld from the MBA membership book. Those days are gone, but access is now restricted by the estate, which chooses to close the bothy for up to 6 months from August.

Oban sits close to a small sandy inlet at the end of Loch Morar. Its Gaelic name, like that of its more illustrious namesake, means 'white' or 'fair bay'. Small communities still existed here

in the early 19th century, despite the pressures of the Clearances, and over at Kinlochmorar, the ruins of a township are visible (complete with threadbare furniture and iron bedsteads as late as the 1970s). The bothy has a country-cottage feel, with its whitewashed exterior and 2 dormer windows, but still follows the typical *but and ben* template, with an additional tumbledown extension at the W gable end. A small porch protects the entrance and there is a wood store tacked onto the E end, left unlocked and used as an emergency shelter. Through the small hallway, the RHR is the most welcoming: the walls and floor wood panelled and a stone fireplace jutting out from the original mantelpiece. There is a table in the N-facing window and a few chairs. The LHR is a little soulless, the floor concrete and the walls bare stone, though there is a small inset hearth. Some water damage, awaiting attention, is also apparent here. Upstairs in the attic space, left as one single room, there are 2 iron

bed frames, but without mattresses, and a table. The light from the dormer windows brightens the space, which doubles up as a second communal area if there is more than one group in the bothy.

ROUTE 1

This is the most obvious approach to Oban, starting from the road end at Strathan and walking in via the head of Glen Pean. Although of no great length and reaching only modest altitude, this is one of the most remote and rugged glens in Scotland. Take the track through the forestry plantation to Glenpean Bothy (p119), pass by it and follow a path up the glen. Before you reach Lochan Leum an t-Sagairt, cross the river and follow a narrow exposed path on the S side of the lochan. This should not be attempted if the river is in spate. There is also no path on the N side as marked on some old maps. The lochan's name, the 'Priest's Leap', refers to an incident in clan days when a priest pursued by his enemies found his way blocked and jumped into the loch to escape.

Bonnie Prince Charlie also passed through here on 18 April 1746 when escaping from Culloden. Continue on to the watershed, scrambling up a boulder field to the smaller Lochan Dubh, and pass it on the S side. A little further on pick up the stalkers' path descending from the W ridge of Sgùrr nan Coireachan that continues up Gleann an Obain Bhig, but before you can finally relax, you must cross the ford below the waterfall of the Allt an Toll Gainmhich, which can be a serious obstacle when in spate. After this the trail becomes clearer as you head towards Loch Morar, and after a another mile or so the bothy finally comes into view.

DISTANCE 8 miles

TIME 4 to 5 hours

TERRAIN Challenging. Track to Glenpean bothy, then path and faint trails to Loch Morar. River crossings

PARKING Strathan (NM 987 916)

ROUTE 2

This alternative route, from the S, starts from a layby on the A830 Fort William to Mallaig road (or a 1-mile walk from the station at Lochailort). Requiring expert navigation skills in poor weather, it is physically and psychologically challenging and should not be undertaken lightly. The route involves the ascent of 2 passes, one at 330m, the other 400m, and a tough section through the wild terrain of the Slaite Coire. From the bend of the A830 by Craiglea Farm , take the path signposted to Meoble. Duck under the low railway bridge and walk up the course of the Allt na Criche, over the bealach and down through some woodland, passing Prince Charlie's Cave, into the River Meoble valley. Crossing a footbridge, head up the glen and a few hundred yards before the estate cottage, strike up E past some farm buildings onto the Slaite Coire. Make your way on a faint path across the wild, remote moor before reaching the protection of Gleann Taodhail. Before you pick up the stalkers' path that descends to the loch, you need to cross the Abhainn Taodhail, which can be a serious obstacle when in spate. Once down by the shore, contour round to the bothy and give yourself a big pat on the back.

DISTANCE 8 miles; 9 miles from Lochailort station

TIME 4 to 5 hours

TERRAIN Very tough. Combination of tracks, established paths and faint trails. River crossings

PARKING Layby on A830 (NM 784 832)

FUEL SUPPLY Some driftwood where the river slows to enter Loch Morar. Best to bring supplies.

KEY ATTRACTIONS Just getting here! Prized remote Grahams An Stac (718m) and Meith Bheinn (710m) lie S of the bothy.

PUBLIC TRANSPORT Scotrail West Highland Line from Glasgow Queen St. to Fort William and Mallaig, stops at Lochailort station. 1 mile walk along A 830 to start of path. No public transport to Loch Arkaig.

SPECIAL NOTES Locked from 12 August to end February. Further information from the Meoble Estate (01687 470326).

FUEL SUPPLY Some fallen branches and driftwood; best to bring supplies.

KEY ATTRACTIONS Mussel-picking on the flats below bothy at low tide. One mile west magical beach known locally as 'singing sands'. Great for kayaking.

PUBLIC TRANSPORT Scotrail West Highland Line from Glasgow Queen St. to Mallaig. Nearest stop Lochailort. Citylink coach service 915/916 Glasgow to Fort William. Daily bus from Fort William to Mallaig stops on request (Shiel Buses 01397 700 700).

SPECIAL NOTES Open throughout the year. Access to the hills is restricted during stag stalking, 15 August to 20 October and the hind cull from 21 October to 15 February. Please comply with notices posted in the vicinity when out walking. Be prepared to camp.

PEANMEANACH

Bothy perfection in a serene and beautiful coastal setting (1975)

SIZE Medium; 2 rooms, 1 with 4-person bunk-bed plus large attic
LOCATION LAT/LONG 56.8595, -5.7542, NM 712 805, 8m, LR Map 40

It is easy to see why people fall instantly in love with Peanmeanach. Its location, above a raised beach on the rugged headland of Ardnish with fine views over to Ardnamurchan and Eigg, is a delight and this whole peninsula between Lochailort and Arisaig seems lost in time. The small bay's rich history goes back to the Viking settlers and the bothy's name reflects the Norse system of land division. Pean derives from *peighinn* meaning 'pennyland': 20 of these, each with a farm, made up an 'ounce land', an acreage capable of producing an ounce of silver in rent. *Meanach* simply means 'middle'. At its height, the small community here had a population of over 150 . The bothy was built in the mid-19th century and sits in a line of ruined 'black houses' reminiscent of the classic crescent of cottages on St. Kilda. At this time, when the principal means of travel along the W coast was by boat, Peanmeanach was a bustling fishing village. In the late 19th century the bothy was the post office for the whole area round the Sound of Arisaig. The village's demise followed the completion of the railway in 1901, which bypassed the peninsula and focused trade on Mallaig.

The building is a typical *but and ben* – 2 downstairs rooms and an extensive loft area above. Both ground-floor rooms have fireplaces and the RHR has a bunk-bed platform sleeping 4. The walls are whitewashed stone and the floor exposed concrete, so the bothy does feel a little chilly before a fire is lit. Upstairs, the open attic space is lit by 3 clear roof panels. By the end of the summer you may pick up some fallen wood from the trees back inland, but the beach is usually stripped and the MBA recommends you bring in your own fuel. Peanmeanach has a varied patronage. One weekend it can be full of party-goers, on another a family group can have the place to themselves. You just have to take your chances as this wonderful spot makes a very good introduction to the charms and randomness of bothying.

ROUTE 1

From the layby close to the houses at Polnish, take the gravel path signposted to Peanmeanach, ignoring a L turn. After a short, steep descent, go under the railway line, then steeply up the hill, earning increasingly impressive views of Loch Nan Uamh, where Bonnie Prince Charlie landed in the aftermath of the 1745 Jacobite rebellion. Soon the path levels out onto moorland surrounding Loch Doire a' Ghearrain. Pass the loch on your L, crossing a stream at its head on some steeping stones. Heading a little way inland, walk down through enchanting birch woodland. Continue out onto flat marshland, flanked by reed beds, and the bothy comes into view on the coast. Head straight down a streamside path and breathe in the sea air.

DISTANCE 3½ miles
TIME 1½ to 2 hours
TERRAIN Straightforward. Stalkers' path to the bothy, boggy in parts
PARKING Layby on A830 at Polnish (NM 742 835)

SOURLIES

Wonderful, wild lochside setting; very popular in summer (1977)

SIZE Small; single room with raised platforms, sleeping 8
LOCATION LAT/LONG 56.9974, -5.5127, NM 869 951, 24m, LR Map 33/40

Tucked into the hillside, Sourlies sits on the edge of a grassy field above the stone beach and mudflats at the head of Loch Nevis. After the hard-earned walk in, there is a real sense of satisfaction as you soak in the stunning fjord-like landscape reminiscent of Norway or New Zealand. Unfortunately over recent years, the shelter has gained in popularity, perhaps a little to its cost. There are few days in the summer months when a tent is not pitched within view of the bothy door, and the accumulation of rubbish is a continual problem. Although you are unlikely to get the place to yourself, Sourlies' particular brand of west-coast magic is irresistible and will draw you in time and again. Try to visit out of season, when spending time here feels like a real privilege.

Recorded history of the area dates back to the 1750s, and evidence of habitation is clear from the ruined farmsteads, rusting fence posts, and cleared areas. The once orderly landscape of hayfields and neat ridge-and-furrow beds of corn, potatoes and oats is reflected in the Gaelic name, which suggests an enclosed garden in a swampy place. Despite the effects of the Clearances, a small community still eked out a living here well into the 1900s, serviced by boat from Mallaig and Inverie. There were even enough young men in Finiskaig, across the bay from the bothy, to field a shinty team. Once the byre to the original croft – the ruin sits near by – the bothy comprises a single, low-slung room with an open hearth at one end and a sleeping platform at the other, accommodating 6 people at a squeeze. Another sleeping platform runs along the length of the far wall, fashioned into a bunk bed at the fireplace end. This doubles up as seating if the bothy is not too crowded. There is a long solid table, a few plastic chairs, and someone has rather optimistically slung a netting hammock across the roof beams that hardly looks comfortable enough to sit in, let alone sleep in. Light is provided by 2 transparent roofing panels, and a small window at the W gable end, as well as perspex window panes in the door frames. The fireplace has a reputation for being very smoky so lay your fire as far back as possible. The bothy's construction was part-funded by the Scottish Rights of Way Society, which also raised money to repair the Allt Coire na Ciche bridge, a once-notorious river crossing ½ mile above the bothy.

Walking into Sourlies requires concentration and commitment, with some steady ascents and descents to negotiate. The route from Inverie is slightly shorter but goes over the bealach at Màm Meadail, an energy-sapping climb up to 550m from a sea-level start. The walk in from Glen Dessarry is a mile longer with a lower highpoint – still a respectable 330m.

ROUTE 1

From the pier, head through the village and turn L just before Inverie House, then quickly L again, following a track signposted to Strathan and Kinloch

Hourn. As you contour round the hillside parallel to the Inverie River, ignore the first junction R but take the second, following a track that heads down to a bridge across the river, and up into Gleann Meadail. Climb steadily to the bealach and down the steep zigzags leading to the ruin at Carnoch. A little further on you must cross the still-intact but rickety wire bridge (NM 866965), which is a little unnerving, then there is a ½ mile stretch of wetland to negotiate before you reach Loch Nevis. From here it is best to follow the meanders of the river rather than march straight across the bog, where drainage channels can catch you unawares. There is a small path to the L over the point for the final scenic stretch to the bothy, though at low tide you can pick your way along the shore.

DISTANCE 7½ miles

TIME 3 to 4 hours

TERRAIN Challenging. Well-maintained track climbs to (550m) then faint path down to loch and bothy. Very rickety bridge to be traversed

PARKING Inverie pier (NG 764 001)

ROUTE 2

From the large car park beyond Loch Arkaig, follow the main track signposted to Tomdoun and Morar, which starts up Glen Dessarry, past the farm and on to the house at Upper Glendessary. This section of the route forms part of the Cape Wrath Trail. Continue on a well-established path along the forestry boundary fence and up onto the moor to the Bealach an Lagain Duibh where there is a large cairn. Contour round the crags to the ribbon-like Lochan a' Mhaim and continue on its S side. The key obstacle from here is fording the Finiskaig River, which can be difficult to cross in times of spate. The best place to cross to the N bank is approx. 500yds beyond the end of the lochan at NM 890 944.

Be aware that you could very easily miss the crossing in the dark and find yourself much further along the S bank and forced to cross the burn further downstream, which can be hazardous. As the path skirts down the slope to the mudflats at Finiskaig, the bothy comes into view and the final stretch is a pleasant relief. One option for those arriving at the road head late in the day is to stop off at A' Chùil Bothy for the night (p111).

DISTANCE 8½ miles

TIME 3 to 4 hours

TERRAIN Challenging. Vehicle track to Upper Glendessarry.Well-maintained path to bothy from here. River crossing

PARKING Loch Arkaig, Strathan (NM 987 916)

FUEL SUPPLY Some driftwood by the shore; best to take supplies.

KEY ATTRACTIONS Munro- and Corbett-baggers can choose from Sgùrr a Ciche (1040m), Garbh Choire Mhor (1013m) to E, Meall Buidhe (946m), Luinne Bheinn ((939m) and Beinn an Aodainn (887m) to N, and Bidein à Chabair (867m) to S. Stop at the Forge in Inverie, UK's most remote mainland pub. Spectacular trip by kayak up Loch Nevis from Inverie.

PUBLIC TRANSPORT Scotrail West Highland Line from Glasgow Queen St. to Fort William and Mallaig. Knoydart Seabridge Ferry from Mallaig to Inverie, regular daily service (01687 462916). No public transport to Loch Arkaig.

SPECIAL NOTES Small bothy in popular area. Be prepared to camp on large, flat field close by when full. During stalking in September and October the Camusrory Estate (01687 462342) requests that visitors keep to main paths. No rubbish collection so please take your litter home. Using the footbridge at Carnoch, signed 'in dangerous condition', is at your own risk. Open all year round.

CENTRAL
HIGHLANDS

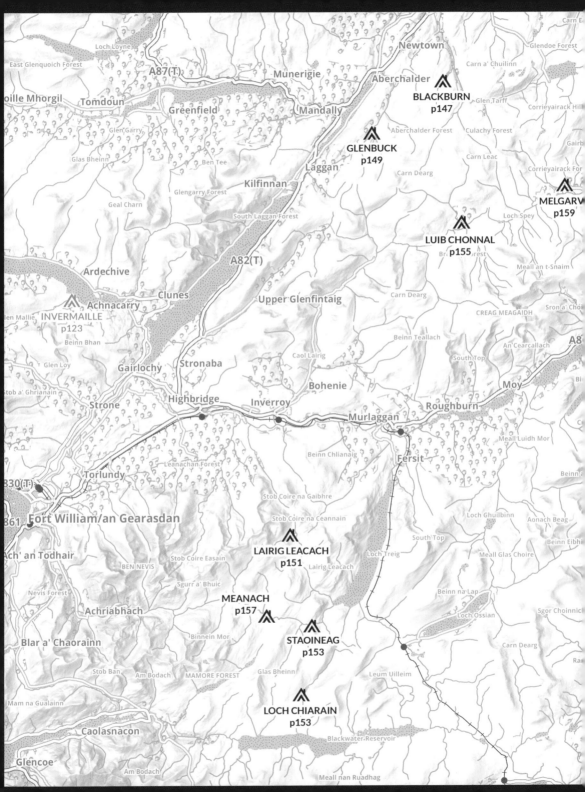

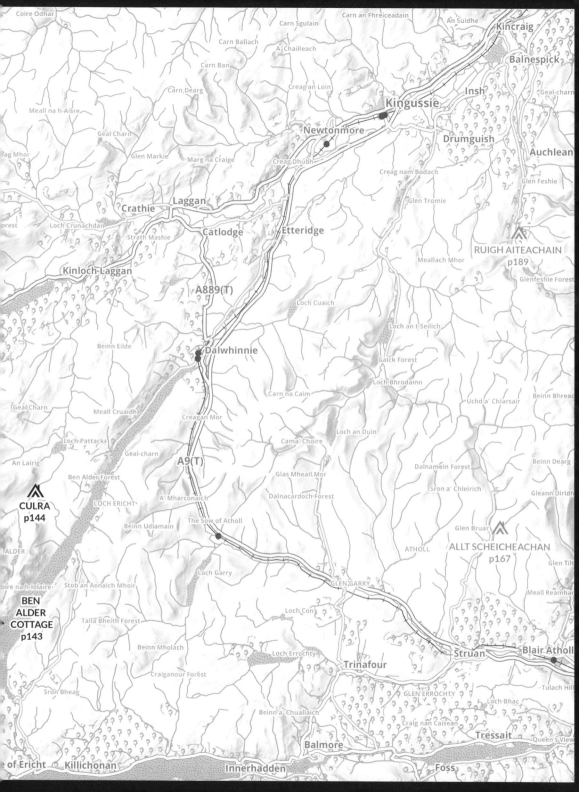

BEN ALDER COTTAGE

Classic bothy expedition (1969)

SIZE Medium; 3 rooms; raised platform sleeps 2, bunk bed sleeps 4
LOCATION LAT/LONG 56.7790, -4.4592, NN 499 680, 373m, LR Map 42

A trip to remote, atmospheric Ben Alder Cottage (aka McCook's Cottage) is not for the faint-hearted but there is a tremendous sense of achievement when you arrive. Tucked beneath the shadow of the Ben Alder massif, above a small bay on the shores of Loch Ericht, the bothy has a rich history and is the source of much anecdote and myth. Among the hill-walking fraternity, it is one of the most well-known bothies in Scotland, not only because its remoteness is a testing challenge and an opportunity for adventure, but also because it is reputedly haunted. The present Ben Alder Cottage dates back to 1871 but stories persist of an earlier hideout called Cluny's Cage, where Bonnie Prince Charlie took refuge for a time after the Battle of Culloden. A jumble of boulders above the cottage may well mark the spot. The name McCook's Cottage refers to Joseph McCook, a deer stalker and forester who finally left the cottage for Newtonmore after World War I,

following a tenancy of 40 years. The building was then used by various ghillies and stalkers, and by increasing numbers of tramps, walkers, fishermen and poachers. By the end of the 1920s, it was a bunkhouse for navvies employed on the construction of the new dams on Loch Rannoch, Loch Tummel and Loch Ericht.

During this time rumours about the bothy being haunted, including the blatant untruth that McCook had hanged himself there, were spread by head stalker Finlay MacIntosh and novelist Ian Macpherson in an attempt to frighten away unwelcome visitors. Over the years the anecdotes were embellished, with various accounts of a poltergeist moving furniture and the mysterious heavy tramp of hob-nailed boots outside the bothy. In *Undiscovered Scotland*, WH Murray vouches for a companion's story of a disturbed night in the bothy, and then describes his own feelings of apprehension when disturbed by strange noises in the night. These

later turned out to be the shenanigans of a party of youths out on a covert poaching expedition. But ghost stories tend to fire the imagination and many who visit the bothy become spooked.

The Ben Alder Estate came under new ownership in 2011 and its infrastructure has been greatly improved, including renovation work on the bothy, which now sports a new roof and windows. The building consists of 3 rooms accessed by a natty little porch. A fair-sized stove has been installed in the LHR, along with a sleeping platform and new wood panelling. The RHR is a little scruffier but still has its own stone fireplace, a table and some chairs, while the small room sandwiched in-between has an integral bunk bed. The W end of the building, which has been newly clad, is not open to visitors and is kept locked.

ROUTE 1

From the car park by the sawmill at Bridge of Gaur, head up the track, through the forestry plantation and out onto the moor. At the corner of the next plantation, either continue along the track through the conifers, or follow a path along the boundary fence which meets the track further towards Loch Ericht. At the S end of the loch continue up its W shoreline until you arrive at the Alder Burn. Cross the burn on a funky bridge and arrive at the bothy, which is just ahead, after fording the stream outside it.

DISTANCE 7½ miles

TIME 2½ to 3 hours

TERRAIN Challenging. Track and well-established paths. Boggy in places, less distinct on final stretch

PARKING By sawmill at Bridge of Gaur (NN 506 577)

ROUTE 2

From Rannoch power station take the metalled access road that runs parallel to the river from Bridge of Ericht up to the dam. Continue W along the shoreline to meet the track described in Route 1 at the SE corner of the loch. This is a mile or so shorter but the section along the forested shoreline after the dam can be heavier going.

DISTANCE 7 miles

TIME 2½ to 3 hours

TERRAIN Challenging. Metalled access road, then heavier going to SE corner of Loch Ericht to join Route 1

PARKING By Rannoch Power Station (NN533 582)

An alternative walk in along the western shore of Loch Ericht to the bothy from the north is possible but is not recommended. The route starts at a signposted path just beyond Ben Alder Lodge (NN 596 787). This meets a track heading to the heliport by the waterside, which continues on to the Allt Camas nan Cnàmh. From here you pick your way along a faint trail with many fording points, with the last mile or so particularly hard going.

FOOTNOTE ON CULRA BOTHY

LAT/LONG 56.8537,-4.4239, NN 523 762, 460m, LR Map 42

Located 6 miles NE of Ben Alder Cottage, Culra Bothy enjoys a fantastic location at the foot of Càrn Dearg and can sleep more than 20. Sadly closed since March 2014, it is awaiting demolition owing to the presence of asbestos. Although much of the asbestos had been replaced, a survey undertaken by the MBA advised that the structure was unsafe for public use. The bothy was closed with immediate effect yet remains unlocked. It should not be used except in a real emergency. It is hoped that a new bothy can be built on the site, and the MBA is encouraged by the co-operation shown by the Ben Alder Estate over a number of years.

FUEL SUPPLY Some timber on headland S of the River Alder, ½ mile away. Best to bring supplies.

KEY ATTRACTIONS Perfect base for an ascent of Ben Alder (1148m) and Beinn Bheòil (1019m). A traverse of Corbetts Beinn a' Chumhainn (903m), and Sgòr Choinnich (929m) and Sgòr Gaibhre (955m) is another fine round. Multi-day possibilities include camping at the old bothy at Culra, or a station-to-station trip from Rannoch to Corrour as described in *Classic Walks*.

PUBLIC TRANSPORT Scotrail West Highland Line from Glasgow Queen St. to Fort William. Nearest station: Rannoch then the best option is Dial-a-bus service (01882 632418) from the station to Kinloch, Rannoch, and on to Pitlochry. Walking the whole way involves a challenging trek through to the end of Loch Ericht via Lochan Sròn Smeur and Lochan Lòin nan Donnlaich.

SPECIAL NOTES Open all year round. Deer control takes place during stag stalking from 15 August to 20 October, and during the hind cull from 21 October to 15 February. Please contact the Ben Alder Estate (01540 672000) regarding hill access.

FUEL SUPPLY Bring supplies.

KEY ATTRACTIONS Take a trip to celebrated Loch Ness (but don't expect to see any monsters). Enjoy lunch in the Bothy pub or Lock Inn by the gates of the Caledonian Canal in Fort Augustus.

PUBLIC TRANSPORT Citylink bus service 919 from Inverness to Fort William, stops in Fort Augustus. Scotrail service from Perth to Inverness, stops at Dalwhinnie. Fishers Tours service 226/242 Fort William–Dalwhinnie–Arbroath/Forfar stops at Laggan.

SPECIAL NOTES Open throughout the year. Both routes straightforward to mountain bike.

BLACKBURN OF CORRIEYAIRACK

Simple shelter on the route of a high mountain pass (1998)

SIZE Small; single room, no sleeping platform
LOCATION LAT/LONG 57.0880, -4.6721, NH 382 029, 344m, LR Map 34

High above the deep gorge of the River Tarff on the route of General Wade's Military Road through the Corrieyairack Pass, Blackburn Bothy is a slightly unexpected sight, tucked away in a small fold in the hillside just off the main highway. The Military Road is part of a network of routes through the Highlands that were built after the Jacobite rebellion of 1715 to allow rapid deployment of British government forces. Ironically, it was used by Bonnie Prince Charlie in the 1745 uprising, as he prepared to battle against the British Army over the pass. The confrontation did not actually take place as the soldiers loyal to the crown retreated.

The bothy is thought to be a former stalkers' hut and comprises just one small, plywood-lined room. Besides a rudimentary fireplace, which has no proper hearth and lacks a grate, there is just a table and a few plastic chairs. A large S-facing window helps illuminate the space, and an internal porch keeps out the worst of the weather. The track is popular with mountain bikers, and the route of the annual Corrieyairack Challenge, a tough mountain duathlon involving running and biking, goes through the pass. Although Blackburn has a few dedicated devotees, the bothies of Glen Buck (p149) and Melgarve (p159) hold much more appeal.

ROUTE 1

The easiest way into the bothy is from the N. From the layby go through a gate marked 'Corrieyairack Pass Fort Augustus to Laggan', then head steeply up the hill, past Culachy House. Contour round above the falls and pass the small lochans at Coille Craige Duibhe. At a junction of paths just beyond them, turn L across an old bridge, before following a zigzag route up the slope. The track levels off as it contours round Liath Dhoire and the shelter's roof appears on your R as you arrive at the bridge across the Black Burn. Take a small path along the bank of the stream to reach the bothy door.

DISTANCE 4 miles

TIME 1½ to 2 hours

TERRAIN Easy. Track all the way; steep in places, until last 200 yards where path is marked by a cairn

PARKING Small layby before Ardachy House (NH 373 072)

ROUTE 2

This approaches from the Laggan side. Head up the Military Road past Melgarve bothy (p159), over the ford of the Allt a' Mhill Ghairbh (NN452 964) and up into Corrie Yairack. Ford crossing difficult in times of spate. Once into the coire, the path zigzags steeply to the bealach before descending into Glen Tarff. Cross 2 bridges. Path contours above the valley to the Black Burn with the bothy on the L.

DISTANCE 8 miles

TIME 3 to 4 hours

TERRAIN Straightforward. Track over the pass (770m) until last 200 yards where path is marked by a cairn. River crossing

PARKING Road end beyond Garva Bridge (NN 467959)

FUEL SUPPLY Plenty of fallen wood in surrounding woodland.

KEY ATTRACTIONS Climb the twin Corbetts, both named Carn Dearg (815m and 768m) or explore the Caledonian Canal from Aberchalder N to Fort Augustus. This section of the new Great Glen Way is also a great cycle route.

PUBLIC TRANSPORT Citylink bus service 919 from Inverness to Fort William, stops at Aberchalder on request.

SPECIAL NOTES Closed during stag stalking, 15 September to 20 October. Permission is required during the hind cull, 21 October to 15 February (Steven McKenzie 07920 757737 or Aberchalder estate 01828 640000). Crossing the Calder Burn when in spate is a serious obstacle (check with estate). Possible to mountain bike but approach is initially very steep.

GLENBUCK

Exclusive getaway in a secluded, wooded glen (1981)

SIZE Large; plenty of sleeping space plus attic
LOCATION LAT/LONG 57.0568, -4.7455, NN 336 996, 283m, LR Map 34

Gleann a'Bhuic, simply 'glen of the buck', is an old estate house perched high above a secluded, tree-lined valley, in the cleave of two tributaries of the Calder Burn, and commands a fine view north to the hills above Fort Augustus and the Great Glen. While the Military Road over the Corrieyairack Pass is an obvious draw, this quiet glen remains largely overlooked and the bothy receives few visitors. The Aberchalder Estate keeps the building in very good order and once you are settled by the fire, the world of work seems miles away. The only real drawback is the hydroelectric dam currently being constructed on the Caochan a' Bhrudhaiste Burn (NN 329 996) on the hillside 500 yards above the bothy. It remains to be seen how much visual impact the scheme will have in the long term, though there is a commitment to keep this to a minimum.

The bothy is a typical *but and ben* with a byre extending from the N-facing gable and a small storm porch protecting the doorway. The interior retains much of its former character, and all the old wood panelling is intact. From the porch you enter a dark hallway, and straight ahead, the original staircase leads up to 2 self-contained attic rooms that make fine sleeping quarters. The LHR communal room has a very comfortable sofa and armchair, positioned in front of a large, well-drawing hearth, and there is a small wooden table under the window. The RHR is a little more spartan, but still has 2 sofas, an armchair, and a table and bench, where you can prepare food. There is another working fireplace, and the panelling has been whitewashed, making it a brighter space. Tucked away at the back is a small box room with a mattress.

ROUTE 1

After parking, beware of traffic as you walk across the swing bridge, continuing on the A82 for 500 yds before turning R up a track signposted to Aderchalder Farm and Laiter Fearn House. Pass through the farm and over a bridge before heading L up a steep slope onto the hillside before dipping down into Glen Buck proper. Continue for another couple of miles through lovely birch and oak woodland dropping down to the ford on the Calder Burn, the only real obstacle on the route. Some concentration is required even if the water level is quite low and you will probably get your feet wet. Best avoided when the river is in spate. Once across, push on up the hill and the bothy soon appears.

> **DISTANCE** 3½ miles
> **TIME** 1½ to 2 hours
> **TERRAIN** Straightforward. Short roadside walk, then track, initially steep, to the bothy. River crossing
> **PARKING** At Bridge of Oich (NH 338 035)

Note: Once the dam is completed, the glen should return to its peaceful self although it will take time for the obvious signs of construction work to disappear. There are also plans to add a water supply to the bothy.

FUEL SUPPLY Bring supplies.

KEY ATTRACTIONS Munro baggers are spoilt for choice. Both Stob Ban (981m) and the Eassians, Stob Coire Easain (1115m) and Stob a' Choire Mheadhoin (1105m), are straight out of the door while the Grey Corries ridge is further W.

PUBLIC TRANSPORT Scotrail West Highland Line from Glasgow Queen St. to Fort William, stops at Corrour and Spean Bridge.

SPECIAL NOTES Open throughout the year but access to the hills may be restricted during the stag-stalking season from 15 August to 20 October, and the hind cull from 21 October to 15 February. Contact the Killiechonate and Mamores Estate (01855 831 337) for information. Route 1 straightforward to mountain bike.

LAIRIG LEACACH

Tiny, basic bothy very popular throughout the year (1977)

SIZE Small; bunk-bed sleeping platform for 8
LOCATION LAT/LONG 56.8227, -4.8158, NN 283 736, 467m, LR Map 41

Lairig Leacach, the 'pass of the flagstones' is a very handy place to know. Found in a tight V-shaped cleft between the Grey Corries and the Eassians, on the high point an old droving road that used to run from Great Glen to the Kingshouse, the bothy is surrounded by high peaks that cannot help but whet your appetite. Consequently the shelter is very popular. A bunk-bed platform sleeping 8 at a push dominates the interior and there is also limited space on the floor to accommodate latecomers. But there have been rare incidents when the bothy has been deemed 'full', and people directed on to Meanach or Staoineag further S. Although this is strictly against the MBA code, come prepared with a tent although there is limited potential to camp close to the shelter. Inside there is long shelf for cooking on, and a petite Dowling stove.

ROUTE 1

After driving up the unmetalled road from Corriechoille, park by the old 'Puggy Line', a dismantled narrow-gauge railway. Head up the track and give a nod to the Wee Minster, a cedar statue said to bestow luck on climbers and walkers. Go through a small forestry plantation and then on to the hillside above, following the line of the Allt Leachdach. Cross a bridge to the E bank of the burn and continue up the bealach, where the path trends back to the W slope and on to the bothy. You can cycle this route, though it is steep in a couple of places. If using public transport, it is an additional 5-mile walk: 3 from Spean Bridge along the road to Corriechoille, and 2 up the track to the plantation.

DISTANCE 4 miles

TIME 1½ to 2 hours

TERRAIN Straightforward. Track all the way, steep in places

PARKING By the old tramway (NN 256 788)

ROUTE 2

Heading in from the S from Corrour station, take the path signposted to Spean Bridge that runs NE and parallel to the railway line, then pick up a wide unmetalled road leading down to a new hydro scheme on the short S side of Loch Treig. Continue on round the loch, crossing the bridge at Creaguaineach Lodge (NN 309689) – where the paths to both Staoineag (p161) and Meanach (p157) head off L on either bank of the Abhainn Rath – and up into the Lairig Leacach. Ignore another bridge and a path on the R, then pass through a narrow gorge before following the L bank of the Allt na Lairige up into the glen. As the path starts its climb towards the bealach it meets a track which continues up the hill to just before the fording point of the Allt a' Chùil Choirean and the bothy. There are a number of streams on the route to be aware of, but this final obstacle is the one to be most wary of if it is in spate.

DISTANCE 7½ miles

TIME 4 hours

TERRAIN Challenging. Track plus well-defined path, boggy in places

PARKING Corrour station (NN 356 664)

FUEL SUPPLY Bring supplies.

KEY ATTRACTIONS Prime Corbett-bagging country. Leum Uilleim (909m) and Corbett top Beinn a' Bhric (876m) lie to the E, Glas Bheinn (792m) to the W. Ice Factor, Kinlochleven Indoor ice climbing wall and café.

PUBLIC TRANSPORT Scotrail West Highland Line from Glasgow Queen St. to Fort William, stops at Corrour Station. Regular bus service from Fort William to Kinlochleven. Stagecoach service 44.

SPECIAL NOTES Open all year but hill access restricted in stag-stalking season from 15 August to 20 October and during the hind cull from 21 October to 15 February. Please contact the Killiechonate and Mamores Estate (01855 831 337) for information.

⩔
LOCH CHIARAIN

Remote moorland bothy that you may have all to yourself (1977)

SIZE Large; 2 attic rooms, single sleeping platform
LOCATION LAT/LONG 56.7307, -4.7983, NN 289 634, 370m, LR Map 41

Loch Chiarain, a proud old estate house, lies next to a gentle little lochan in remote moorland hills. To the N and 7 miles E of Kinlochleven, is Blackwater Reservoir, the first major hydroelectric project in Britain, built to supply power to smelters at Kinlochleven and later Fort William. On completion in 1910, the scheme turned Kinlochleven into the 'Electric Village', the first in the world with every house connected to the electricity supply. An account of the harsh conditions faced by the Irish navvies employed on the dam's construction is told in *Children of the Dead End* by Patrick MacGill.

As a consequence of the flooding of the glen, the property was referred to as New Chiarain, as the old homestead was drowned by the rising water. From the outside the bothy looks substantial, but in practice only the 2 upstairs attic rooms are regularly used. The ground level is a stone shell partitioned using sterling board sections, and recently wood panelling

was added. One rough-looking fireplace is open; the other blocked up. Fortunately, the LHR upstairs has retained its original hearth and wood panelling, and a lovely little dormer window has a fine view. Before a major renovation by the MBA in 2004, this was the only serviceable room and accessed by a rickety ladder. The RHR is larger than its neighbour but not as well insulated. The bothy lacks ambience, so receives far fewer visitors than its 2 near neighbours Staoineag (p161) and Meanach (p157).

ROUTE 1
After parking at Kinlochmore, follow the path through the woodland on the N bank of the River Leven and out onto the moor, passing the imposing dam at the end of Blackwater. Continuing on the N shore, the path becomes very boggy and indistinct for a mile or so before you head up alongside the flooded gorge of the Allt an Inbhir. On the other side of the burn is a monument to Reverend Alexander Mackonochie, who lost his way and died at this spot in 1887.

DISTANCE 6 miles
TIME 2½ to 3 hours
TERRAIN Straightforward. Signposted path, boggy in places. Initial steep ascent
PARKING Kinlochmore (NN188 622)

ROUTE 2
From Corrour station, take the signed Spean Bridge path NE, parallel to the railway line. Then pick up a wide unmetalled road leading down to a new hydroelectric scheme on the S side of Loch Treig. Continue around the loch, taking a path on L heading S up Glen Lolairean, signposted to Kinlochleven (NN 320 687). The path climbs steeply to a wide bealach at 400m before descending gently to the bothy. It is possible to mountain bike this route, though it is boggy in places.

DISTANCE 7 miles
TIME 2½ to 3 hours
TERRAIN Straightforward. Track and signposted paths, 1 steep ascent
PARKING Corrour station (NN 356 664)

FUEL SUPPLY Wood occasionally donated. Best to bring supplies.

KEY ATTRACTIONS Explore the rarely-visited N side of the Creag Meagaidh massif and walk to Drochaid na Saobhaide, an unusual natural bridge (NN 368 918). The Lochaber Geopark visitors' centre is in nearby Roybridge.

PUBLIC TRANSPORT Scotrail West Highland Line from Glasgow Queen St. to Fort William, stops at Roybridge. Stagecoach bus service 411 from Fort William to Roybridge. No public transport up Glen Roy.

SPECIAL NOTES Open all year but hill access is restricted in stag-stalking season from 15 August to 20 October, and during the hind cull from 21 October to 15 February. Please contact the Braeroy Estate (01397 712587) for information. Route 1 straightforward to mountain bike with some pushing.

LUIB CHONNAL

A place of solitude north of the Creag Meagaidh plateau (1971)

SIZE Small; just the attic space
LOCATION LAT/LONG 57.0059, -4.6461, NN 394 936, 331m, LR Map 34

As you climb up the steep track from Glen Roy and see the tiny dot of the bothy at Luib Chonnal, it brings into perspective the vastness of this neglected stretch of desolate moorland between Creag Meagaidh and the Corrieyairack pass. For some cynical bothy folk, the area epitomises MAMBA (miles and miles of bugger all). For others, this lonely, windswept land has a raw beauty all of its own. An old droving road, the 'Soft road of the Hoggs', ran through here because the terrain was well suited to young sheep. The farmstead itself, first recorded in the census of 1861, was occupied by 2 different families over the next 30 years. Its name derives from *lùb*, a 'bend', referring to the meandering river, and *Conall*, an ancient name in Celtic mythology meaning wolf. Finally vacated in the late 1950s, it fell into disrepair before being rescued by the MBA.

The original house was one of half a dozen on the Glenshero and Sherramore Estate and had a byre, now demolished, at the W gable end. The whole bothy space is contained in just the attic, which has been partitioned into 2 with a sleeping area at the W gable end and a small Dowling stove at the other. A low table and some comfortable chairs add a homely touch and 4 Velux windows provide much-needed light. A purpose-built staircase leads up from the ground floor. Despite its open, exposed position, the bothy is very cosy once the fire is lit.

ROUTE 1

Park by the cattle grid then follow the road past the estate buildings, where it becomes a well-maintained track. Once over the 18th-century Turret Bridge, the track turns E following the River Roy into the upper reaches of the glen, past the picturesque Falls of Roy. The track undulates then climbs steadily before levelling off about a mile from the bothy. There are a number of fords to cross, with the Allt na Glas Bheinne (NN 383 929) the most difficult when in spate. From here follow a boggy path just after a meander and arrive at Luib Chonnal.

DISTANCE 5 miles
TIME 2 to 2½ hours
TERRAIN Straightforward. Track all the way, steep in places. River crossings
PARKING Near Brae Roy Lodge at end of tarmac (NN 334912)

ROUTE 2

Head up the Military Road to Melgarve Bothy (p159). Turn L here and down past the estate house, over a bridge on the plantation edge, and continue on, following the meandering River Spey to Shesgnan, where the track finishes. (This is a locked estate bothy). Take the boggy path round the slopes of Meall Clach a' Cheannaiche, past Loch Spey. Walk through forestry then cross the Allt Chonnal, which could be a hazard when in spate.

DISTANCE 6 miles
TIME 3 to 3½ hours
TERRAIN Straightforward. Track and boggy path all the way. River crossing
PARKING Beyond Garva Bridge, (NN467959)

FUEL SUPPLY Bring supplies.

KEY ATTRACTIONS A challenging round of Munros lies to the N encompassing Stob Ban (977m), and a traverse of the Grey Corries Ridge – Stob Coire an Laoigh (1111m), Stob Choire Claurigh (1177m). To the S, another big walk leads round from Binnein Beag (943m), Binnein Mor 1130m and on to Sgurr Eilde Mor (1010m).

PUBLIC TRANSPORT Scotrail West Highland Line from Glasgow Queen St. to Fort William, stops at Corrour station. Regular Stagecoach bus service 44 from Fort William to Kinlochleven.

SPECIAL NOTES Open throughout the year but hill access may be restricted during the stag-stalking season from 15 August to 20 October, and the hind cull from 21 October to 15 February. Please contact the Killiechonate and Mamores Estate (01855 831 337).

MEANACH

Surprisingly remote bothy with a fantastic view (1977)

SIZE Small; 2 rooms, 1 with sleeping platform for 3
LOCATION LAT/LONG 56.7754, -4.8390, NN 266 685, 345m, LR Map 41

If some things in life are worth a little extra effort, then getting to Meanach is an example where you reap a rich reward. The great little bothy out in the middle, *meadhan*, of the surprisingly remote sweep of moorland between Fort William and Loch Treig, has an amazing view of the Grey Corries ridge and over to Binnein Beag and Sgùrr Eilde Mòr. The bothy is an old shepherd's hut which sits across the Abhainn Rath from a larger house, Lùibeilt, now a ghostly ruin and guarded by a distinctive stand of conifers. The building is an intimate *but and ben*, its 2 small, sparsely furnished rooms separated by a tight vestibule. Both have working fireplaces but the RHR's does not draw well – unfortunate because this room has an alcove with a neat sleeping platform for 3 people. A table and some chairs add domesticity, but the bothy is a little spartan. Renovation work in 2012, including the installation of wood panelling and new ceilings, has greatly improved the insulation.

ROUTE 1

From the station take the path signposted to Spean Bridge that runs NE, parallel to the railway line, and pick up a wide unmetalled road to arrive at a recently constructed hydroelectric scheme on the short S side of Loch Treig. Continue on round the loch, crossing the bridge at Creaguaineach Lodge (NN 309689), and taking the track heading L. A small path before the bridge heads to Staoineag bothy (p161). Then simply follow the N bank of the Abhainn Rath all the way the bothy, giving a wave to Staoineag as you pass. The last section is a bit of a plod and the meadow area just before the cottage is notoriously boggy. You could cross the river using the stepping stones at Staoineag but the water level quickly rises after any rain so this crossing is not reliable.

DISTANCE 8 miles
TIME 3 to 4 hours
TERRAIN Straightforward. Track and signposted path, boggy in places
PARKING Corrour station (NN 356 664)

ROUTE 2

From Mamore Lodge take the track from the hotel. Walk a short distance up the Allt Coire na Bà then round to the N shoreline of Loch Eilde Mòr. Persevere on past Loch Eilde Beag and about a mile before Lùibeilt the terrain opens out and you can see the bothy on the far bank of the Abhainn Rath. Even in benign conditions take care crossing the river. The best place is just down from the bothy (NN264 684), but there is also a fording point by the mouth of the Allt nam Fang. Do not attempt to cross when the river is in spate. The bothy is a short trudge over the frequently saturated meadow.

DISTANCE 7½ miles
TIME 3 to 3½ hours
TERRAIN Challenging. Track to Luibeilt, including serious river crossing, then path
PARKING Mamore Lodge Hotel (NN186 630)

FUEL SUPPLY Bring supplies.

KEY ATTRACTIONS Corbett Gairbeinn (896m) and Corrieyairack Hill (891m, now downgraded) are close by while from Carn Leac (884m) at the top of the pass there are wonderful views. Melgarve makes a great base for an onward trek up over the Corrieyairack Pass to Blackburn Bothy (p147) and Fort Augustus. You could also head across the watershed to Luib Chonnal (p155) and Glen Roy.

PUBLIC TRANSPORT Scotrail service from Perth to Inverness stops at Dalwhinnie. Fishers Tours service 226/242 Fort William–Dalwhinnie–Arbroath/Forfar stops at Laggan.

SPECIAL NOTES Open throughout the year and made available for walkers courtesy of the Glenshero and Sherramore Estate, owned by British Alcan.

MELGARVE

First-class accommodation, easily accessible by car (1996)

SIZE Medium; single room downstairs, 2 attic rooms above
LOCATION LAT/LONG 57.0303, -4.5336, NN 463 960, 350m, LR Map 34

Melgarve or *Meall Garbh*, 'rough rounded hill', is an old estate cottage on the S side of General Wade's Military Road – the route through the Corrieyairack Pass in the upper reaches of the River Spey. In spring and early summer this expanse of open meadow is a breeding ground for oystercatchers and other wading birds. On the flip side, the glen is dominated by a controversial line of electricity pylons, which runs all the way from Beauly near Inverness to Denny in Fife. Fortunately, once in the bothy you quickly forget about human impact as you survey the beautiful vista of the wide floodplain and moorland to the S, with the Creag Meagaidh plateau looming on the horizon. And reassuringly, although it is possible to drive almost to the bothy door, Melgarve manages to avoid being prone to either vandalism or excessive revelry.

The cottage is extremely well looked after by the Corrieyairack Club. This group of like-minded folk restored the shelter in 1996 in memory of 3 members of the Mayo family who perished in a climbing accident. A commemorative plaque on the stairwell wall ends with a quote from the opening line of *Rocky Acres* by Robert Graves: 'This is a wild land, country of my choice'. Entering from the S side, the bright-blue door opens into a tight hallway, with stairs leading to the attic where there is ample sleeping space in 3 separate wood-panelled rooms, one sporting the rather stately title of Tweeddale. On the R is a door into the main communal area – generally kept very tidy and with a patriotic blue-and-white colour theme. All the woodwork is painted blue as well as the lower portion of the walls. There are 2 comfortable sofas, an easy chair, a large open hearth, and even a ceiling-mounted drying rack operated by a pulley. A solid table sits at the window, and there is a press with some kitchenware. At the back, a box-room with its own small window could sleep 3 additional people at a squeeze. The other half of the building is a locked stables, accessed from a door on the N side that is visible from the track and emblazoned with a fire danger sign.

ROUTE 1
Heading up from Laggan, there is a parking layby just before the Garva Bridge, but it is possible to drive on to the end of the tarmac stopping at a small bridge over the Allt Fèith a' Mhoraire (NN 468 959). A 'road closed' sign indicates the end of public vehicle access. Park carefully to avoid blocking the track. A simple saunter up the track, round a hefty road closed barrier, brings you to the bothy door. A bridge built under General Wade's supervision, close to the cottage, is now bypassed by a modern culvert just upstream.

DISTANCE 500 yards
TIME 10 minutes
TERRAIN Easy. Track to the door
PARKING At end of single-track road from Laggan (NN 468 959)

FUEL SUPPLY Fallen branches are often found on the meander just under a mile S of the bothy, but best to bring supplies.

KEY ATTRACTIONS Munros Stob Coire Easain (1115m) and Stob a' Choire Mheadhoin (1105m) are within reach. Glas Bheinn (792m), a Corbett to S is a more leisurely objective. Wild swim in the river pools above the bothy and picnic at picturesque waterfall Eilean a' Ghiubhais on the way to Meanach. Station House restaurant/café (01397 732236) March–October.

PUBLIC TRANSPORT Scotrail West Highland Line from Glasgow Queen St. to Fort William, stops at Corrour station.

SPECIAL NOTES Open throughout the year, but hill access may be restricted during stag stalking from 15 August to 20 October, and the hind cull from 21 October to 15 February. Contact the Killiechonate and Mamores Estate (01855 831 337) for information. Stepping stones outside the bothy may be submerged after rain.

STAOINEAG

Welcoming bothy held in great affection; accessible by train (1966)

SIZE Large; plenty of sleeping space, plus attic
LOCATION LAT/LONG 56.7708, -4.7905, NN 296 678, 293m, LR Map 41

Staoineag is a special place. Set on a rocky pinnacle above the meandering Abhainn Rath, this large welcoming bothy is most accessible by train, a characteristic that widens its appeal. As well as archetypal outdoor enthusiasts, it attracts those who have no car and are eager to enjoy a slice of wilderness with relatively straightforward access. The name derives from the Old Norse 'stein' meaning stone, and John Matheson, one of the last stalkers to live in the cottage until his death in 1922, referred to it as 'Stoniag'. John's grandson, Angus Montgomery, recalls spending childhood holidays there. These included visits to the extended family over the hill at what is now Loch Chiarain Bothy (p153), as well as regular gatherings at the Elliots', who lived at Luibeilt (Meanach, p157). Remarkably, the postman walked the length of Glen Nevis and the Abhainn Rath to deliver mail to Staoineag, which was inhabited well into the 20th century. The two cottages at Steall, the house at Luibeilt and Creaguaineach

Lodge (occupied into the 1980s) were also on his delivery route. The building is a typical *but and ben*, with 2 downstairs rooms and a large open attic space. There is wood panelling throughout, sound floors, and well-drawing fireplaces. The LHR has a large alcove at the back and a N-facing window overlooking the river but no sleeping platforms. Clear corrugated sections allow some light into the attic, which can accommodate a fair number if the bothy has filled up.

ROUTE 1

Starting from Corrour station, take the path signposted to Spean Bridge that runs NE, parallel to the railway line, and pick up a wide unmetalled road to arrive at a recently constructed hydroelectric scheme on the short S side of Loch Treig. Continue on round the loch to until you see Creaguaineach Lodge, and just before the bridge take a small path to the L which runs along the S side of the Abhainn Rath. A new signpost here adds an element of doubt, as it only directs you over the bridge to Spean

Bridge, back the way you have come and on to Rannoch. The path to Meanach (p157) follows the northern bank of the river. After just over ½ mile the path rises above the river along a steep bank lined with birches. It then crosses the Allt Cam nan Aighean, the only stream you need to negotiate on the walk in, which is not normally an obstacle, even when in spate. The trail gently rises past some impressive rapids, and onto the flats just before the bothy. Although straightforward in daylight, the path around the long meander can be elusive in the dark. If arriving late, look out for the old iron estate fence posts that lead W parallel to the river bank.

DISTANCE 6 miles

TIME 2½ to 3 hours

TERRAIN Straightforward. Track and signposted path

PARKING Corrour station (NN 356 664)

EASTERN
HIGHLANDS

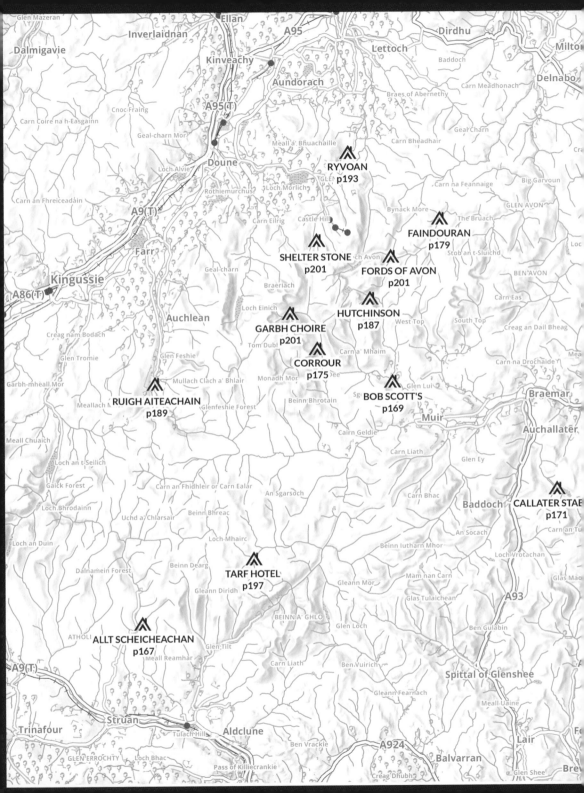

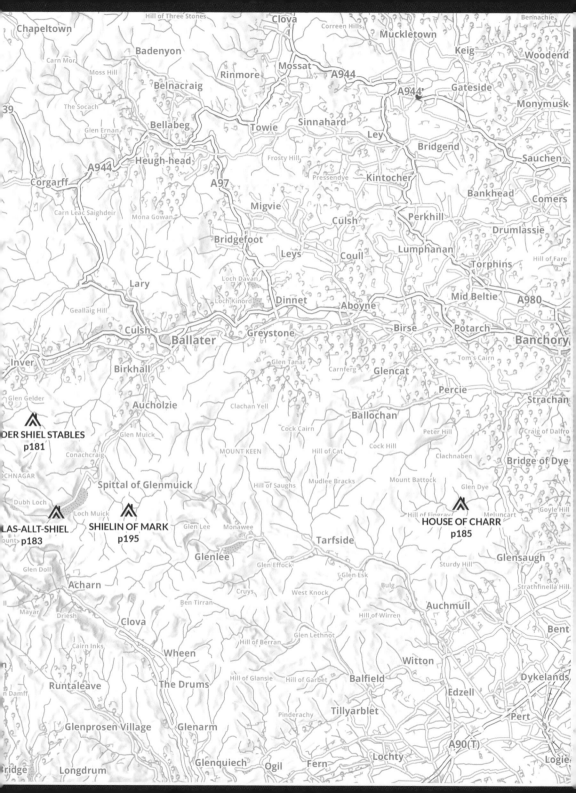

FUEL SUPPLY Bring supplies.

KEY ATTRACTIONS Beinn Dearg (1008m). A perfect base for an ascent of Beinn Bhreac (912m) lies to the E. For a less energetic alternative, soak up some history at Blair Castle and gardens.

PUBLIC TRANSPORT Scotrail Service from Glasgow/Edinburgh–Perth–Inverness, stops at Blair Atholl as does the Citylink coach service M90/M91 Glasgow/Edinburgh–Perth–Inverness.

SPECIAL NOTES Open throughout the year. Check www.outdooraccess-scotland.com during the stalking season from 1 September to 20 October if you intend to venture into the hills. Easy to mountain bike.

ALLT SCHEICHEACHAN

One-roomed shelter; ideal for a brief, solitary escape (1974)

SIZE Small; 1 room with 2 single sleeping platforms
LOCATION LAT/LONG 56.8399, -3.9118, NN 835 738, 487m, LR Map 43

Sheltered in a small fold beneath the sprawling bulk of Beinn Dearg, Allt Scheicheachan lies on the edge of the remote expanse of peat, heather and moss that now sits within the Cairngorms National Park. Walking up through the pines lining the Banvie Burn, high above the impressive white façade of Blair Castle, the busy A9 is forgotten and there is no movement save the fluttering of disturbed grouse and the ever-watchful red deer.

The bothy, an old stables for the stalkers on the Atholl Estate, may also have been used to wash, cure and tan deer skins. *Scheicheachan* (pronounced 'shee-cha-chan' with the 'ch' as in loch) translates as 'animal hides' in Gaelic. The shell of the building has been divided into 2 rooms, each with a separate entrance. There is also a rather claustrophobic attic space accessed by ladder; this serves as a dormitory in the unlikely event of the bothy being busy. The LHR, the main accommodation area,

has whitewashed stonework, an inset hearth, and windows front and back. A large picnic table takes up much of the available space, with wooden benches wide enough to sleep on set along 2 walls. There is also a small table and a couple of chairs. The estate uses the RHR for storage. The bothy is particularly cold in the winter, owing to the stone floor and lack of insulation, so don't forget the coal!

Passing climbers, off to bag Beinn Dearg (1008m), may stop at the bothy. There is a second picnic table outside, making it a tempting lunch spot. You may also see the occasional walker in search of the old drove road that heads over the Minigaig Pass and eventually ends at Kingussie.

ROUTE 1

From the Glen Tilt car park off the B8079, turn L onto the metalled road and take the R fork away from the Blair Castle grounds before heading over a crossroads. Follow a track leading up into the woodland above the Banvie Burn, which continues

parallel and above the river bank. Ignore 2 paths descending steeply to the water. Continue out of the forestry onto the moor. The track gently gains altitude, and passes a large drystone cairn dedicated to Lady March, a former duchess of Atholl, before heading onto a low bealach at 515m. The final ½ mile is all downhill and the bothy is just before the burn, coming into view in the last 100yds. From the station and bus stop it is a mile-long walk along the road to the car park at Old Bridge of Tilt.

DISTANCE 5 miles
TIME 2 to 3 hours
TERRAIN Easy. Well-maintained track all the way
PARKING Glen Tilt car park (NN 872 663)

FUEL SUPPLIES Bring Supplies. Fallen timber an important habit for insects.

KEY ATTRACTIONS Wander through the ancient Caledonian pines around Derry Lodge and Glen Derry, a renowned Cairngorms beauty spot. Great walk up Munros Derry Cairngorm (1155m) via Carn Crom and onto Ben Macdui (1309m), Beinn Breac (931m) and Carn a' Mhaim if you have strong legs. The 'Bothy' in Braemar, a climbing shop and café, serves excellent cakes and scones.

PUBLIC TRANSPORT Stagecoach Bluebird service 201 from Aberdeen to Braemar. Bus from Braemar to Linn of Dee runs July to September, Thursday to Monday.

SPECIAL NOTES Open throughout the year. Be prepared to camp at popular times: alternative unofficial campsite beyond Derry Lodge by the Derry Burn at NO 041 935. Easy to mountain bike.

BOB SCOTT'S

Haunt of climbers past and staging post for Cairngorms expeditions

SIZE Small; single room with platform sleeping 6
LOCATION LAT/LONG 57.0190, -3.5795, NO 042931, 421m, LR Map 43/36

Obscured by pines on a meander of the Lui River, a few hundred yards from Derry Lodge, Bob Scott's has had a chequered history. The eponymous gamekeeper for the Mar Lodge Estate lived with his wife and daughter at Luibeg Cottage (on the opposite bank), from 1947. The wooden shed beside his house had long served as a make-do shelter and Bob, known for his sharp wit and storytelling skills, continued the tradition. Many Aberdonian climbers, among them pioneer Tom Patey, Malcolm Smith (author of the first *Cairngorms Climbing Guide*) and ecologist and author Adam Watson. A chapter of *Mountain Days and Bothy Nights* is devoted to the bothy and its characters, and there is another snapshot in Tom Patey's own *Cairngorm Commentary*.

Following Bob's retirement in 1973, the new keeper had little time for outdoor enthusiasts but a group of regulars looked after the bothy and persuaded the estate to keep it open.

In the winter of 1986 the shelter was accidentally burnt down and was rebuilt further down the Glen. Unfortunately, this structure also went up in flames in 2003. Through the determination and fundraising skills of the 'Friends of Bob Scott's', bothy Mark III was constructed on the same spot, a stove replacing the original open fireplace. The present bothy, a well-insulated wooden structure, is clad in stone and painted black so it blends into its surroundings. Inside there is a single room with a large, handsome stove to sit round and, in a back alcove, a neat worktop for food preparation. A sleeping platform constructed across the far gable end can sleep 6 at a push, and a space beneath can accommodate a similar number. One whole wall is a dedicated noticeboard, featuring a picture of Bob Scott himself decked out in plus fours. The bothy also has a small outhouse with a septic toilet, flushed with a bucket filled from the river. Some regulars regard Bob Scott's as their unofficial clubhouse and on

occasion it is wise to bring a tent and either camp on the flat by the bothy or in the unofficial site N of the Mountain Rescue Post at Derry Lodge. There is a proposal for a new bunkhouse here.

ROUTE 1

Take the path signposted to Glen Lui through the forestry onto the main track from the Linn of Dee. Turn L, and after a short while the track curves to the R and you arrive at Black Bridge. Cross the bridge and immediately turn L to start the walk up Glen Lui. There is a shelterbelt of pines surrounding Derry Lodge up ahead but you need to keep a look out for a cairn marking a small path heading off L to the river bank. Turn here and the bothy comes quickly into view. If you reach Derry Lodge you have gone too far.

DISTANCE 3 miles
TIME 1 to 1½ hours
TERRAIN Easy. Vehicle track to within 500yds of the bothy; well-trodden path for the final stretch
PARKING Linn of Dee car park (NO 063 898)

⩕

CALLATER STABLES

Basic shelter in beautiful, out-of-the-way glen (1993)

SIZE Small; 2 rooms, one a dormitory with 4 bunk beds sleeping 8
LOCATION LAT/LONG 56.9435, -3.3527, NO 178 844 , 514m, LR Map 43

Standing in the quiet, reflective confines of Glen Callater, Lochcallater Lodge and its stables lie on the once-busy route of an old droving road. From nearby Braemar, herders drove sheep along 'Jock's Road' over the Tolmount plateau to the market at Cullow, near the foot of Glen Clova. Callater, derived from the Gaelic *caladair* meaning 'hard water' was known at one time as 'miracle glen' after a local clergyman's prayers for help were answered. When an exceptionally cold winter left those living around Braemar without any water, Patrick (aka 'Peter the Priest') went down to the lochside below the lodge's boundary fence and prayed for a thaw. Miraculously, the ice began to melt and a large stone commemorates the site of 'Peter's Well', which is marked on the large-scale OS map (NO 179 843). The glen is also reputed to be a favourite haunt of Prince Charles because it has far fewer visitors than neighbouring Glen Shee, and further W into the heart of the Cairngorms National Park. In August, when the

Royal Family decamp to Balmoral, the prince is occasionally seen wandering the plateau above the glen. Charles is said to have sought sanctuary at Lochallater Lodge after the Queen Mother's death in 2002, sharing a dram with members of the mountain rescue team who use it as a training base.

The bothy is a small stone outbuilding beside the lodge owned by the vast Invercauld Estate. A recent work party has split the interior into 2 rooms, one a dedicated dormitory with four bunk beds. The reduced size of the living area means that is not as cold, as crucially, there is no fireplace. So although the bothy makes a great lunch spot, it is still not particularly conducive to an overnight stay, especially in the winter. At one time it was still occasionally used as a stables and described in a chapter of *Mountain Days and Bothy Nights* as a 'dreadful doss' and 'unfit for human habitation'. Fortunately, through the efforts of its dedicated maintenance officers, the bothy is now in good

condition. The neighbouring lodge is still used occasionally by shooting parties, and the loch is well known for its pike fishing. A dry toilet was built on the end of the wooden shed beside the bothy in 2016.

Jock's Road played a key role in the history of public access to the Scottish countryside. In 1885 the Glen Doll estate was bought by Duncan MacPherson, who made his fortune sheep-farming in Australia, and he immediately tried to ban all access to the land. Jock's Road was one of a number of access routes across the Grampians that were under threat and the newly formed Scottish Rights of Way Society decided to contest their closure. Macpherson brought the issue to the Court of Session in 1886-87, and the dispute eventually went all the way to the House of Lords. By the time the judiciary found in favour of the Society, it was bankrupt – a fate that also befell MacPherson. This judgement led to the passing of the Scottish Rights of Way Act in 1894, which was the most important piece of legislation for walkers until the 2003 Land Reform Act further clarified public rights of access. Jock's Road is said to be named after John (Jock) Winter, one of those who testified against McPherson, though some believe the name pre-dates the court case. In more recent times, 5 lives were lost on this route – one of the worst tragedies to befall the Scottish hill-walking community. The men, all members of a Glasgow club, were attempting to walk over Jock's Road on Hogmanay 1959. They were caught in a vicious 2-day storm and were not able to stumble back to the relative safety of Glen Clova. In 1966, following the disaster, a small rough shelter known as 'Davie's Bourach' (NO 232 778) was built on the Glen Doll side of the plateau. Maintained by Forfar and District Hillwalking Club, the shelter has been instrumental in saving quite a few lives over the years.

ROUTE 1

The small parking area just off the A93 at Auchallater has a notice suggesting the donation of a voluntary contribution for the upkeep of the estate. The path is signposted to Glen Doll via Jock's Road and a Scottish Rights of Way Society sign points the direction. After parking, follow the track through a gate as it winds its way up the valley, above the waters of the Callater Burn, crossing a bridge over to the E bank after a mile or so. Continue, ignoring a track that heads off to the R back down to the river (and up towards the Bealach Buidhe), and keep going until eventually the lodge comes into view. Just before you reach the outer fence, there is a path off to the L. This is an old stalkers' path that leads eventually to Lochnagar.

DISTANCE 3 miles

TIME 1 to 1½ hours

TERRAIN Easy. Vehicle track all the way

PARKING Auchallater (NO 156 822)

ROUTE 2

From the layby take a small path up the steep-sided valley of the Allt a' Mhaide. As you ascend, cross the stream by some shielings, and continue on up to the Bealach Buidhe. The path becomes a little more difficult to follow as it skirts around some grouse butts, before joining a wider track that heads down into Glen Callater. As the track begins to contour round the slope, strike off down to the R on a faint path that leads to a footbridge a few hundred yards from the lodge and the head of the loch.

FUEL SUPPLY No fireplace or stove.

KEY ATTRACTIONS Make an expedition up the Munros – Tolmount (958m), Tom Bhuidhe (957m) and Carn an Tuirc (1019m) – that lie beyond the head of the glen or walk to the dramatic coire above Loch Kander. In nearby Braemar, the 'Bothy', a climbing shop and café, serves delicious tea and cakes.

PUBLIC TRANSPORT Stagecoach Bluebird service 200/201 from Aberdeen to Braemar.

SPECIAL NOTES Open all year. round. Easy to mountain bike.

Cross a second, larger bridge over the Callater Burn and head up the river bank to the lodge.

DISTANCE 3 miles

TIME 1½ to 2 hours

TERRAIN Straightforward. Small path over a bealach (656m) then descent. River crossings

PARKING Layby on A93 (NO 140 835)

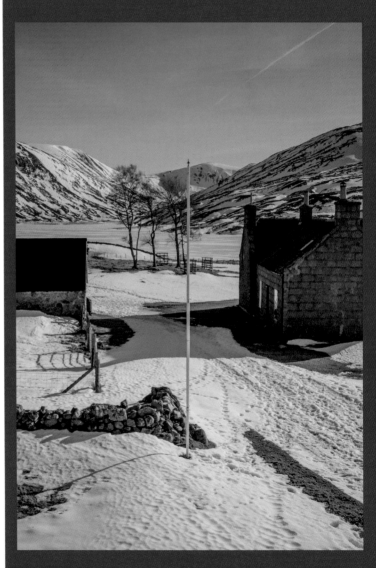

⩓ CORROUR

Very well-known and popular bothy below the Lairig Ghru (1967)

SIZE Small; single room with sleeping platform for 3
LOCATION LAT/LONG 57.0418, -3.6810, NN 981 958, 564m, LR Map 36

Standing resolute beneath the steep slabs of The Devil's Point in the strath of the meandering River Dee, Corrour Bothy is one of the most famous and popular of all Scotland's open shelters. Over the best part of a hundred years, it has been a refuge for generations of hill-walkers and climbers, and is referenced in numerous dispatches, articles and books such as Gordon Seton's *The Charm of the Hills* and Adam Watson's *It's a Fine Day for the Hill*. Consequently, the bothy can be busy during the summer months so it is best to take a tent, especially at weekends. But in the quieter winter months, the shelter really comes into its own and if you are prepared to venture out here under a covering of snow, the true sense of the majesty of the Cairngorms' inner sanctum reveals itself.

The bothy is a simple granite dwelling, built in the latter part of the 1870s as a deer-watcher's hut – one of a number on the Mar Lodge Estate. Gamekeepers would stay here to observe the movements of the deer for the benefit of the paying guests who came stalking. They also had to stop anyone roaming the hills from disturbing the deer and guard against poachers. One local character who served his time there, Charlie Robertson, was himself regularly observed pedalling down to Braemar for chapel on Sunday, and then meandering his way back in the gloaming fortified with a 'drop of whisky'. In the 1920s the estate closed the hut, but the lock was soon forced and it became well known as an unofficial 'open' bothy. Over the years the wooden internal fixtures were stripped out and burnt, and the external stonework slowly deteriorated. In his memoir *Always a Little Further*, Alistair Borthwick described the shelter as 'absurdly lonely, no more than a small shed with an earth floor and a leaky roof'. It was only through the initiative of members of the Cairngorm Club in 1949 that it was rescued from total ruin, after they made a successful public appeal for funds.

After the MBA took over maintenance in the late 1960s, the bothy remained a simple shelter until major renovation over 2006-7 transformed it into a snug, comfortable abode. Upgrading included the construction of a wooden extension with a dry long-drop toilet at the S gable end, which solved the ongoing problem of 'human pollution'. An enclosed porch opens into a single room with a small sleeping platform in an alcove to the L of the entrance and a fireplace. The platform can comfortably sleep 2 people with space below it for 2 more. A wooden floor, panelling and insulation has made the bothy cosier and the whitewashed stonework on the hearth wall reflects more light. There is a table and a couple of plastic chairs to draw up to the fire.

ROUTE 1

From the car park, take the path signposted to Glen Lui through the forestry, past a lookout area and onto

a section of boardwalk which curves round to the R and soon emerges onto the main track up to Glen Derry. Turn L along the track, which keeps to the L-hand side of the fenced forest. Soon the track curves to the R and you reach Black Bridge. After crossing, turn L to start the walk up Glen Lui, keeping on the track as it passes more fenced forestry on the R. Continue on to Derry Lodge and the Rescue Station, past the path that leads down to Bob Scott's Bothy (p169). From here, head round to the footbridge that spans the Derry Burn, cross and turn immediately L onto a boggy path across the heather. You then join the vehicle track from the cottage at Luibeg. Continue along the N bank of the Luibeg Burn, through the pines and round to the plantation enclosing the burn. Here the track comes to a halt. To continue on towards Corrour, you can ford the burn over some large boulders but the best option is to head up to nearby Luibeg Bridge and back down the main path. Continue on this path, climbing the slope above the Allt Preas nam Meirleach and contouring round into the upper reaches of Glen Dee. Soon the bothy comes into view, and it is simply a case of heading down to the bank of the river, turning L over the footbridge and on to the bothy.

DISTANCE 7 miles

TIME 2½ to 3 hours

TERRAIN Straightforward. Vehicle track to Derry Lodge then track and very well maintained path

PARKING Linn of Dee car park (NO 063898)

ROUTE 2

Approaching from the Aviemore side, park at the lower Cairngorm Ski-Centre car park and head down across Utsi's footbridge over the Allt Mòr. Following the wide path onto the terrace above the N bank of the burn, wind your way steadily up to the Chalamain Gap, clearly visible on the horizon. Take care when crossing the boulder field, then contour round the edge of Lurcher's Crag and down to join the main Lairig Ghru path from Rothiemurchus. Climbing up into the pass, the path now becomes less distinct in places and the summit's location is hard to pinpoint because several stony moraines run across it. Once past the atmospheric Pools of Dee, the path improves and the bothy is clearly visible in the distance, on the far bank of the Lairig Ghru snaking down the glen. Continue down to Clach nan Taillear, the 'Stone of the Tailors'. According to local legend, this marks the spot where a group of tailors died in a blizzard. Pass the stone and take the obvious path R that crosses a bridge over the River Dee and on to the bothy.

DISTANCE 7½ miles

TIME 3 to 3½ hours

TERRAIN Challenging. Follows well-established path, plus traverse of a boulder field and less distinct section through the Lairig Ghru (835m)

PARKING Lower Cairngorm Ski Centre car park 'The Sugar Bowl' (NH 985 074)

FUEL SUPPLY Bring supplies.

KEY ATTRACTIONS Wonderful walking country. The round of Munros to the W: The Devils Point (1004m), Cairn Toul (1291m) and Braeriach (1296m) is a classic outing, while a longer trek brings you to Beinn Bhothair (1157m) and Monadh Mòr (1113m). A wander up to the Lairig Ghru and Pools of Dee, or round to Garbh Choire refuge (p201) are good wet weather options.Public Transport Stagecoach Bluebird service 201 from Aberdeen to Braemar. Bus from Braemar to Linn of Dee runs July to September, Thursday to Monday. Daily shuttle bus from Aviemore to the Ski Centre stops on request.

SPECIAL NOTES Open throughout the year. Small bothy, which is often crowded, so be prepared to camp. Local contacts: NTS Ranger Service (01339 741669); Mar Lodge Estate (01339 741669). Possible to mountain bike but with obstacles to negotiate.

FUEL SUPPLY Bring supplies.

KEY ATTRACTIONS The round of Beinn a Bhuird (1179m) and Ben Avon (1171m) makes a fine expedition, access to the hills via footbridge at NJ 099 061.

A wander to the Fords of Avon refuge (p201) is a far easier proposition.

PUBLIC TRANSPORT No public transport further than Granton on Spey to the N and Ballater to the S.

SPECIAL NOTES Open throughout the year. Before visiting the bothy between 1 September and 20 October, please contact the Inchrory Estate (01807 580256) to check where stalking is taking place.

FAINDOURAN

Distant mountain sanctuary by the River Avon (1966)

SIZE Small; single room plus attic
LOCATION LAT/LONG 57.1370, -3.5189, NJ 081 062, 603m, LR Map 36

Lying beneath the looming presence of Beinn à Bhuird and the distinctive granite tors of Ben Avon, Faindouran Bothy overlooks the crystal-clear waters once proclaimed the purest in all Scotland. This wild expanse of heather, moss and grit is one of the remotest corners of the Cairngorms National Park, and the bothy is certainly among the most isolated in the country.

A safe haven in bad weather, the bothy rose from the ruins of a former Victorian hunting lodge on the Glen Avon Estate and was one of the first projects the fledgling MBA took on in the late 1960s. Following extensive damage by extreme winds in February 2013, the gable end was reconstructed, the fireplace blocked up, and a stove installed. The bothy's structure occupies only the W gable end of the original footprint, and consists of a ground-floor room with an attic above, accessed by steep stairs. The communal area is bright and airy, with whitewashed walls and a large S-facing window, and there is a 2-person sleeping platform to the R of the doorway. Opposite the bothy is the old stables, which is used as storage by the estate but left open to provide extra sleeping accommodation. Walking into Faindouran, either from the E or N, is no small undertaking. Cycling is the best option because the track from each direction is maintained for vehicle access.

ROUTE 1

From Corgarff Castle, set off up the metalled road as far as Badochurn. Continue along a well-maintained track that winds up to the watershed of the River Don, (ignoring a track L at Inchmore) and continue on to Inchrory Lodge, where the track descends steeply. From here, follow Route 2.

DISTANCE 13½ miles
TIME 5 to 7 hours
TERRAIN Straightforward. Long, unmetalled vehicle track with short steep sections in the last 6 miles
PARKING Corgarff Castle car park, Cock Bridge (NJ 254 089)

ROUTE 2

From car park take a turning to the L and cut down to the E side of Glen Avon floodplain. Pass the bridge at Delavorar, following a tarmac road to Dalestie, then on to Inchrory Lodge. Continue up the S side of the valley, before crossing a bridge (ignoring track on L) and climb steeply above the river before dropping down again. Follow the meandering river to the bothy. Along the way, you pass a small shelter called the Ponyman's Hut (NJ 126 059) and 2 bridges where tracks head up to Ben Avon and Beinn a Bhuird. There are tracks to Faindouran from Glen Derry and Loch Avon, but these are best left to the more intrepid, or those on a multi-day trip from Bob Scott's (p169) or Hutchinson (p187) bothies.

DISTANCE 15 miles
TIME 5 to 7 hours
TERRAIN Straightforward. Long, unmetalled vehicle track with short steep sections in the last 6 miles
PARKING Queen's View car park, Tomintoul (NJ 165 176)

FUEL SUPPLY Bring supplies.

KEY ATTRACTIONS Head up Lochnagar (1150m) and the Munros of the White Mounth or make the short walk from Easter Balmoral up to Prince Albert's Cairn on Creag an Lurachain. Stop for lunch at the excellent 'Bothy'

café in Ballater or call in at Royal Lochnagar distillery.

PUBLIC TRANSPORT Stagecoach Bluebird service 201 from Aberdeen to Braemar stops at Crathie

SPECIAL NOTES Open throughout the year. Contact the Balmoral

Estate (01339 742534) before planning a trip between 1 September and 20 October. Access made be denied when the Royal Family is in residence during August. Camping is not encouraged outside the bothy. Easy to mountain bike.

GELDER SHIEL STABLES

Bothy by royal appointment (1983)

SIZE Small; 3 bunk-beds, sleeping 6
LOCATION LAT/LONG 56.9945, -3.2244, NO 257 900, 444m, LR Map 44

After a glorious walk up through the perimeter grounds of Balmoral Castle and onto the moorland under Lochnagar, you come to Gelder Shiel Stables in a stand of Caledonian pines. Set directly across from a royal hunting lodge commissioned by Queen Victoria in 1865, the bothy lies beside the Gelder Burn, which gives its Gaelic name 'white water', on the path leading up to Lochnagar's impressive coire. Gelder Shiel now offers 5-star accommodation, as befits its royal association, but it was once reputed to be a cold, draughty, uninviting doss. In the chapter devoted to the shelter in *Mountain Days and Bothy Nights*, climbers from Aberdeen bedded down on its stone cobbles, apprehensive that water would start trickling across the floor, and bemoaning the whistling and cold draughts from the prevailing westerlies. Although bunk beds and a concrete floor were added, improvements were kept to a minimum given the estate's understandable reluctance to encourage overnight stays in a secluded location so close to the Royal Family's summer residence. However, after years of careful negotiations assent was finally given for a complete overhaul of the building.

The Ballater Chiels, a charitable group of local tradespeople and business owners funded and carried out the renovations over a weekend, dedicating the finished work to Ernie Rattray, former president and long-standing member of Braemar Mountain Rescue. An enclosed porch now keeps out draughts, there is a new wooden floor, walls and ceiling are insulated and lined, and Velux windows in the roof have increased light levels. A new multi-fuel stove keeps the bothy warm and to the R are 2 bunk beds, with another tucked into an alcove by the door. Drainage ditches have also been dug to stop water penetration in wet weather and a lean-to shed at the back houses a long-drop toilet flushed by a bucket of water. Prince Charles officially opened the refurbished bothy in the autumn of 2015, and signed the bothy book for good measure.

ROUTE 1

Leave Easter Balmoral village from the old Post Office building (NO 264942), heading SW on a tarmac road which quickly changes into a well-maintained vehicle track, up past several houses and a 'sentry box'. At the next junction (NO 256935) keep L heading S and continue up out of the woods for about 1½ miles to arrive at another junction (NO 258908) where you turn R. About ½ mile from here the stand of pines is visible, and the bothy lies hidden within.

DISTANCE 3 miles
TIME 1 to 1½ hours
TERRAIN Easy. Vehicle track all the way to the bothy door
PARKING E of road junction at Easter Balmoral (NO 265 941)

FUEL SUPPLY Wood collection discouraged. Bring your own supplies.

KEY ATTRACTIONS Excellent base for an ascent of Lochnagar (1150m) and there is an impressive waterfall en route to the summit from the bothy. For eager baggers there is the incentive to complete the round of the White Mounth (1051m) and Broad Cairn (998m).

PUBLIC TRANSPORT Stagecoach Bluebird service 200/201 from Aberdeen to Braemar, stops at Ballater.

SPECIAL NOTES Open throughout the year. Toilet in a separate building behind the bothy.

GLAS-ALLT-SHIEL

Hidden quarters in the back of a Royal Estate lodge

SIZE Small; attic space sleeping 6
LOCATION LAT/LONG 56.9272, -3.1903, NO 276 824, 400m, LR Map 44

Glas-Allt-Shiel is a quirky wee bothy tucked away in an outbuilding at the back of a large granite house on the Balmoral Estate, built by Queen Victoria in 1860 after the death of Prince Albert. In her later years the Queen spent much time living here as a virtual recluse. Originally a storage room, the bothy went on to become a well-established doss for those either walking or climbing up Lochnagar and Creag an Dubh-loch. The Dundee University Rucksack Club renovated the shelter as a memorial to Graham Leaver, a fellow member who died in a climbing accident on Askival, one of the summits on the Rùm Cuillin, in 1988. The club has maintained it since 1991.

As you approach from Spittal of Glenmuick, head to the back of the house, which has a small courtyard, and leading off it, a narrow passageway. The bothy is on the L-hand side and takes a little finding, especially in the dark. The entrance is the furthest in a line of doors and has a brass memorial plaque, put up by the new custodians after the restoration was complete. Inside the rather large but rather dark room, there is a sturdy table, a scattering of chairs, and a bizarre candelabra hanging from the ceiling. In 2012 the Friends of Bob Scott's donated a stove – a very welcome addition. A steep wooden ladder leads up to an attic space. There is also a toilet in another outbuilding behind the bothy, flushed using a bucket filled from the stream. The shelter is a useful place to know, although maybe not the most inspiring place to spend more than a night or two. One for a quiet winter evening perhaps.

ROUTE 1

From the Cairngorm Outdoor Access Trust car park walk down past the Balmoral Estate visitors' centre, and on through the junction of paths towards the S side of Loch Muick (ignoring the track on the L). Just before a small conifer plantation, take a well-established path on the R down to the lochside, and cross a sturdy footbridge, before heading to on a small boat house at the most N point of the shore. Turn L here onto a wide vehicle track heading to Glas-allt-Shiel (from Allt-na-giubsaich), which follows a contour 20m or so above the water line. After an easy mile's walk, the plantation of trees surrounding the granite lodge comes into view. Easy to mountain bike.

DISTANCE 2 miles
TIME 1 hour maximum
TERRAIN Easy. Well maintained track all the way
PARKING Loch Muick car park, Spittal of Glenmuick (NO 310 851)

Note: The fence running along the L side of the track protects the woodland above the shore from red deer, and is key to the successful regeneration of the remaining area of birch woodland. The enclosure is temporary and will be taken down once new saplings grow high enough to withstand deer browsing.

FUEL SUPPLY No fireplace or stove.

KEY ATTRACTIONS Cairn o' Mount (455m) on the B974 is on a challenging cycling route from Strathmore over into Lower Deeside – there is a brilliant view from the summit cairn.

Clachnaben (589m), a distinctive local hill topped by a granite tor is a popular Sunday afternoon jaunt, and easily accessible from the bothy. Mount Battock, (778m) the most easterly Corbett, is a little further but a fine walk.

PUBLIC TRANSPORT None

SPECIAL NOTES Open throughout the year. No fires outside the bothy. Easy to mountain bike.

HOUSE OF CHARR

Well-kept bothy and ideal lunch spot (1992)

SIZE Medium; 3 rooms, 2 with sleeping platforms
LOCATION LAT/LONG 56.9376, -2.6332, NO 616831, 264m, LR Map 45

On the northern side of the heather clad, pink granite hills of the Mounth, breached at the Cairn o' Mount by the old military road into Deeside lies House of Charr, the most easterly MBA bothy. This is a quiet spot, bypassed by the summer crowds funnelled from Aberdeen into the tourist villages of Banchory, Ballater and Braemar. At one time, unescorted travellers were vulnerable to attack by robbers and bandits on this isolated throughfare. Thieves' Bush strikes a warning note on the large-scale Ordnance Survey map as you sweep down from the bealach to the beautiful 17th-century Bridge of Dye. The ruined cottage on the Spital Burn, on the far bank as you walk in to the bothy, was a notorious haunt of unscrupulous folk, belying its Gaelic name, *Spideal* meaning hospice.

The bothy lies at the confluence of the Waters of Dye and Charr, from the Gaelic *car*, meaning winding and describing the meandering channel, and occupies one side of a long, single-storey property; the other side is kept locked for private use. From a small lobby you enter the large, communal space where your eye is immediately caught by the mortar between the stonework and a blocked-up fireplace, all painted a vivid red. To the R is a cupboard and opposite, a wide alcove with a single-person sleeping platform. A table sits under the S-facing window, and there is a low bench and a couple of white plastic chairs. At the back are 2 more rooms, each with their own window: one a kitchen area with shelves and a worktop; the other a dormitory with a 2-person platform bed. There was talk of putting in a stove but the Fasque Estate, which owns the cottage, has concerns about the bothy's proximity to the road, making it an easy target for those not necessarily conversant with the MBA bothy code. The interior is clean and well kept, but a little lacking in atmosphere. It makes a good lunch stop, and there is a good network of tracks up to the surrounding hills.

ROUTE 1

From parking just S of the Spital Burn bridge (being careful not to block access), follow the track down to the bridge over the Water of Dye, before turning L at the junction immediately after crossing. Continue as the track contours gently around the meanders of the river on the E side of the glen. At about halfway there are a number of crumbling stone dykes, and off to the L, a solitary pine. According to an Aberdeenshire folk tale, the tree was the home of Colin Massie, a warlock who consorted with a coven of witches. As the bothy comes into view, the track forks; take the R fork, heading up the slope a short way before continuing on to the bothy.

DISTANCE 2 miles
TIME 1 hour
TERRAIN Easy. Vehicle track all the way
PARKING By gate S of Spital Burn bridge on B974 (NO 647 845)

FUEL SUPPLY Bring supplies.

KEY ATTRACTIONS A gentle walk takes you up to Loch Etchachan or you can plan an assault on the surrounding Munro summits: Ben Macdui (1309m), Beinn Mheadhoin (1182m), Derry Cairngorm (1155m) and Beinn a'Chaorainn (1082m). Coire Etchachan and Loch Avon are classic rock- and winter-climbing spots.

PUBLIC TRANSPORT Stagecoach Bluebird service 201 from Aberdeen to Braemar.

SPECIAL NOTES Open throughout the year. Local contacts: NTS Ranger Service (01339 741669) and Mar Lodge Estate (01339 741669). Popular bothy so be prepared to camp. Straightforward to mountain bike: some obstacles to negotiate.

HUTCHISON MEMORIAL HUT

Tiny shelter in the wild heart of the Cairngorms (1967)

SIZE Very small; 1 room with platform sleeping 2, plus floor space for 4
LOCATION LAT/LONG 57.0783, -3.6133, NO 023998, 747m, LR Map 36/43

High on the northern flank of Derry Cairngorm, next to the path to Ben Macdui that runs beneath the steep slabs of Creag a' choire Etchachan, lies the small, understated 'Hutchie' hut. One of the very few purpose-built shelters in the Highlands, it was once renowned as a very uninviting place, described in *Cold Climbs* as having 'dubious comforts', with steel poles forming an open porch which used to whistle disturbingly in high winds, the accompanying percussion provided by the persistently rattling front door. Thankfully those days are now past, a major renovation having been undertaken by the MBA in 2012, turning an uninspiring doss into minimalist boutique accommodation, which has so grown in popularity that it is wise to take a tent.

The shelter was constructed in 1954 in memory of geologist Dr Arthur Gilbertson Hutchison, a keen outdoor enthusiast from Aberdeen who died in a climbing accident in 1949. After funds were raised by his many friends, the building materials were transported to the site by a team from the city's climbing clubs, with the assistance of Bob Scott and some of the estate's ponies. The shelter proved an instant hit with unfussy climbers scaling the crags of Coire Etchachan, Coire Sputan Dearg and the Loch Avon basin, at a time before the Cairngorm ski road was constructed from Aviemore. The hut's original stone shell is now wood-lined and insulated, the open porch is enclosed, and on the new external door a sign reads 'please remove your crampons'. Once through the original paint-chipped door into the communal space, there is a 2-person sleeping platform/bench, a multi-fuel stove in the far corner, and hanging rails for wet clothes. Fortunately, the old perspex panels have been replaced with a single E-facing window, which even has curtains. The room is so snug once the stove is lit that one party boasted that they got the ambient temperature up to over 30C!

ROUTE 1

Take the path signposted to Glen Lui through the forest onto the main track from the Linn of Dee. Turn L, the track curves to the R and you arrive at Black Bridge. Cross, and turn L up Glen Lui. Once past the turning to Bob Scott's Bothy (p169) and Derry Lodge, head up to the temporary bridge over the Derry Burn, but instead of crossing keep walking along the E side, where a well-made path leads all the way up the glen. Pay attention when fording the Glas Allt Mòr via the stepping stones particularly when in spate. A little further on, the path splits and you take the L fork, crossing the Coire Etchachan Burn by a footbridge before the bothy comes into view.

DISTANCE 8 miles
TIME 3 to 4 hours
TERRAIN Straightforward. Vehicle track to Derry Lodge then well-maintained path. River crossing
PARKING Linn of Dee pay and display car park (NO 063898)

RUIGH AITEACHAIN

One of the best – a great introduction to bothying (1969)

SIZE Large; 2 rooms, both with raised platforms, sleeping 10, plus attic
LOCATION LAT/LONG 57.0118, -3.9004, NN 847927, 389m, LR Map 43/35

Carved and smoothed by glaciers and carpeted with moss and heather, Glen Feshie is crowned by a patchwork of beautifully shaped trees interspersed with spiky green knots of juniper. This wide valley, the 'jewel in the crown of the Cairngorms', is the stunning setting for Ruigh Aiteachain, the 'shieling of the juniper bush'. The bothy has a particular association with the 19th-century English landscape painter Sir Edwin Landseer, whose most famous work, the instantly recognisable *Monarch of the Glen*, was inspired by the time he spent here, and the bothy is often mistaken for the cottage where he stayed. This stood close by though, owned by the Duchess of Bedford, Landseer's patron and long-time lover. Over the years the artist painted a number of frescoes of stags on the interior walls, including a fabled work above the fireplace. Sadly, the building was left to deteriorate after Landseer's death, and all that remains is a lone chimney stack, with its fireplace and hearth still intact.

The 'Feshie' as it is affectionately known, was one of 3 houses recorded in the 1841 census, an estate house that fell into disrepair before World War II, when it was used as an army training base. By the early 1950s, anything of value had long since disappeared, and there was barely a habitable room. The only door had been jammed shut, so you had to enter through the remains of a window opening, covered at night by a sheet of corrugated iron placed across the gap. Once the MBA took over maintenance, the place was transformed into one of the best-kept bothies in Scotland. Danish businessman Anders Povlsen, the new owner of the Glen Feshie Estate, has not only supported the bothy's upkeep but begun a major refurbishment. An external porch has been constructed, with stairs leading to the attic, which has become an additional sleeping space. New windows and doors and a second wood-burning stove have also been installed. Povlsen has also

prioritised the regeneration of the natural habitat, aiming to double the area of native woodland, investing heavily in stalking to drive down the numbers of deer browsing the ancient Caledonian pine. This strategy, together with some re-seeding, has resulted in young pines, birches, and rowans flourishing on the forest floor, while the high woodland edge has started to extend back towards Rothiemurchus. Today the changes in the landscape are clearly visible, and wildlife has also started to return in high numbers. Capercaillie have been seen in the glen again and blackcock numbers are rising; crested tits and tree pipits nest in the canopy, and common sandpipers in burrows in the riverside shingle beds. Red squirrels are welcome visitors, and there have even been sightings of badgers and pine martens.

The ground floor of the bothy consists of 2 well-proportioned rooms, one leading into the other. The first room has a boxy, 3-storey wooden bunk-bed extending up to the ceiling at the E gable end, sleeping up to 10 people. The second has a small dining table and chairs. The exposed stone walls have been whitewashed, and large S-facing windows provide fine views up the glen. The two stoves share a central flue. A toilet is in a separate outbuilding a few yards away from the bothy. If you are looking for an authentic bothy experience which is not too arduous, without the obligation of carrying in fuel, you should look no further than here. The bothy is generally kept clean and tidy, and the composting toilet is a real bonus. Best of all, the estate usually supplies a generous wood pile, a rare thing indeed, but it serves a practical purpose, discouraging people from cutting down live wood or burning dead branches, in this precious nature conservation area. As you might expect, this is a popular bothy, and although occupied most weekends, it is spacious enough to accommodate plenty of people.

ROUTE 1

Turn off the B970 at Feshiebridge and stop at the car park ½ mile before Auchlean. A 5-minute walk brings you to the end of the road. Here the path leads up through the glen, passing large pockets of Caledonian pines at various points. There are 2 stream crossings to be wary of after heavy rain, the first close to the start of the path and the second, across the Allt Garbhlach, a more serious obstacle. Note: Be wary of a small section of the path at the top of the riverside moraine, washed away in the floods of 2015.

DISTANCE 3½ miles

TIME 1½ to 2 hours

TERRAIN Straightforward. Vehicle track all the way. River crossings

PARKING near end of single-track road out of Feshiebridge (NN 851 984)

FUEL SUPPLY Fuel provided by the estate.

KEY ATTRACTIONS Munros Mullach Clach a' Bhlàir (1119m) and Sgòr Gaoith (1118m) are within easy reach or, if you are feeling less energetic, there is a beautiful walk up the glen through the pines to Creag na Caillich. Feshie Bridge and Inshriach both have popular forest trails.

PUBLIC TRANSPORT Scotrail Service from Glasgow/Edinburgh–Perth–Inverness, stops at Kingussie and Aviemore. Citylink coach service M90/M91 Glasgow/Edinburgh–Perth– Inverness also stops at both places. Stagecoach Highlands service 38a Aviemore–Kincraig–Kingussie.

SPECIAL NOTES Open throughout the year. Please contact the Glen Feshie Estate (01540 651212) if you plan to use the bothy during stalking season, between 1 September and 20 October. The Carnachuin Bridge near the bothy (NN 845 937) was swept away and Pony Bridge (NN850 964) is currently the last crossing in upper Glen Feshie. There is no access to the bothy via the track on the W bank. Straightforward to mountain bike: need to carry bike across the Allt Garbhlach.

FUEL SUPPLY Fallen branches provide habitat so bring supplies.

KEY ATTRACTIONS An Lochan Uaine 'Little Green Loch', an idyllic kettle hole between Glenmore and Ryvoan is a tranquil spot. For a great day out walk up Corbett Meall a' Bhuachaille (810m) and enjoy marvellous views over the Cairngorm plateau. In Aviemore The Old Bridge Inn and the Winking Owl are recommended.

PUBLIC TRANSPORT Scotrail Service from Glasgow/Edinburgh-Perth–Inverness, stops at Aviemore. Citylink coach service M90/M91 Glasgow/Edinburgh–Perth–Inverness stops at Aviemore. Stagecoach Highlands service 31 Aviemore to Cairngorm Ski Centre.

SPECIAL NOTES Open throughout the year. The bothy sits in an RSPB nature reserve so abide by restrictions during nesting time. Only take water 500 yards S of the bothy, due to reports of human waste closer by. Popular bothy, be prepared to camp. Easy to mountain bike.

RYVOAN

Small popular bothy with easy access from Glenmore (1967)

SIZE Small; single room with 4-person sleeping platform
LOCATION LAT/LONG 57.1837, -3.6458, NJ 006 115, 394m, LR Map 36

Out above the pines between Glen More and Abernethy, the ever-popular Ryvoan lies on a route once used to run stolen cattle S to Glen Feshie and beyond. The Grants, a crofting family, lived here until they moved out permanently in 1877. The cottage was abandoned, and the traditional *but and ben* quickly became established as an open shelter. In his *Cairngorm Diary* of 1932, James Henderson describes his relief on arriving around 10pm, after walking with companions from Corrour Bothy over Ben Macdui and Cairn Gorm: 'never was 'home' in the hills more appreciated!' Yet by the time mountaineer and historian Affleck Grey, author of *The Legends of the Cairngorms*, visited the bothy in the late 1950s, only one wood-lined room remained habitable. Over the years the gable end and byre collapsed, but the place was saved from total ruin by the Creag Dhu Climbing Club, who undertook temporary repairs before the MBA's involvement in the late 1960s. The bothy was reconstructed as a single room, a storm porch added, and a clear panel set into the roof to allow more light into the interior. The main body of the shelter is quite spacious, with a long platform sleeping 4 running under the single S-facing window. The inset fireplace burns fuel efficiently and warms the space, which has homely touches such as coat hooks and a mirror.

ROUTE 1

From the parking bay just before the end of the public road, follow the forest trail with its blue and orange waymarks up a steady slope NE through the Scots pines to An Lochan Uaine, before heading out onto the moor. When the track forks, take the L-hand path and after about 500yds you arrive at the bothy.

DISTANCE 2 miles
TIME 45 mins to an hour
TERRAIN Easy. Track all the way
PARKING Just beyond Glenmore Lodge (NH 988 095)

POEM BY AM LAWRENCE

I shall leave tonight from Euston
By the seven-thirty train
And from Perth in early morning
I shall see the hills again.
From the top of Ben Macdhui
I shall watch the gathering storm,
And see the crisp snow lying
At the back of Cairngorm.
I shall feel the mist from Bhrotain
And pass by the Lairig Ghru
To look down on dark Loch Einich
From the heights of Sgoran Dubh.
From the broken burns of Bynack
I shall see the sunrise gleam
On the foreheads of Ben Rinnes,
And Strathspey awake from dream.
And again in the dusk of evening
I shall find once more alone
The dark waters of the Green Loch
And the pass beyond Ryvoan.
For tonight I leave from Euston
And leave the world behind
Who has the hills as lover
Will find them wondrous kind.

FUEL SUPPLY Bring supplies.

KEY ATTRACTIONS Mount Keen (939m), the most easterly Munro, is a fair old trek yet within view of the bothy door. A shorter walk (Route 2 passes close by) takes you to the scenic Falls of Unich and Damff under the steep crags of Craig Maskeldie.

PUBLIC TRANSPORT Stagecoach Bluebird service 200/201 from Aberdeen to Braemar stops at Ballater. No public transport up Glen Esk.

SPECIAL NOTES Open throughout the year. Access from Glen Lee is discouraged during the stalking season from 1 September to 20 October.

⋀
SHIELIN OF MARK

Place of retreat on high, trackless moorland (1991)

SIZE Small; single room with 2-person raised platform bed
LOCATION LAT/LONG 56.9299, -3.0923, NO 337 827, 644m, LR Map 44

A solitary stone cottage in a trackless landscape of peat bogs, heather and marsh, Shielin of Mark sits on the banks of a tumbling burn that feeds the Water of Mark. Trudging across the empty moor towards it as the light fades, weighed down by a sack of fuel, you might despair of ever finding the place. But once settled inside with the stove glowing, there is nothing to disturb the silence. As the word shielin suggests, it was probably a summer residence for the tenants who tended the flocks of sheep on these high pastures. The shelter is a solid, single-roomed stone cottage with a small stove at one gable end, and a single sleeping platform at the other. Besides a table, bench and a couple of chairs, there is a wee desk with a drawer containing useful bits and bobs, including a set of dominoes. Over a busy couple of days in May, people doing the annual TGO challenge pass through, but for the rest of the year visitors are few and far between, and you will probably have this wild corner to yourself.

ROUTE 1

The most direct route is from the large car park at Spittal of Glenmuick. Make for the visitors' centre, and just beyond a junction of tracks, take the L-hand path that climbs up the valley side, following the steep cleft of the Allt Darrarie. Three quarters of the way up, cross to the NE bank of the burn via a footbridge and continue up and out onto the moor. The path peters out before the top and it is wise to take a bearing SE from here. The bothy is tucked away on the S slope of the hill, by the bank of a small tributary of the Water of Mark. A good tactic is to head to the S of your bearing, so you can follow the burn downstream to the bothy.

DISTANCE 2½ miles

TIME 1 to 1½ hours

TERRAIN Challenging. Follows track, small path, then open moor. Navigation required

PARKING Loch Muick car park, Spittal of Glenmuick (NO 310 851)

ROUTE 2

From the car park head along the road past the church and across the bridge. At the junction turn L onto the vehicle track, past the impressive castle ruins and along the valley floor beside Loch Lee. Ignore the track L to Inchgrundle and continue up Glen Lee also ignoring the next path L. After the Stables of Lee take the R fork and walk on to the N shoulder of Muckle Cairn. The track stops at a grouse butt and you continue up on a faint path then down the other side through peat bogs. The bothy should now be in view. Follow the marshy bank of the Water of Mark, crossing a couple of small burns and arrive at the channel opposite the cottage. Fording it is straightforward but can be challenging in times of spate.

DISTANCE 8 miles

TIME 3 to 4 hours

TERRAIN Challenging. Track, path, then open moor. Navigation required. River crossing

PARKING Just before road end at Invermark (NO 447 804)

THE TARF HOTEL
FÈITH UAINE

Renowned refuge in high, remote wilderness (1992)

SIZE Large: 4 rooms, 3 with multiple sleeping platforms
LOCATION LAT/LONG 56.8888, -3.7632, NN 926 789, 566m, LR Map 43

Flung, almost wilfully, into one of the most isolated areas in the Cairngorms National Park, Fèith Uaine is famed for its welcoming yellow AA hotel sign. A first glimpse of the front door of the Tarf Hotel, as it is better known, comes as something of a relief as there is nothing casual about an expedition to this wild, intoxicating spot. Nestled in the expanse of grassy flats at the confluence of the Fèith Uaine Mhòr ('the gully of the large Green River'), and the wide, sinuous artery of Tarf Water, this former shooting lodge sits in high moorland NE of Blair Atholl. It was constructed by the 7th Duke of Atholl from the ruins of a traditional black house that had been occupied as far back as the 1680s. Boasting piped hot water and a tin bath, the lodge was a favourite retreat of the Duke, who made regular visits over the course of 30 years. A fire broke out in 1909 and although the lodge was subsequently rebuilt, it had fallen into disuse by the 1930s. By the time it was mentioned in *Mountain Days*

and Bothy Nights among the 'Dreadful Dosses', the bothy had only one usable room, and it was not until 1992 that Fèith Uaine was given a new lease of life by the MBA. A second, extensive renovation, undertaken in 2012 and dedicated to Flight Lt. Jeffrey Jenkins and his trusty hound Xyrion, included roof repairs, new floors and improved drainage, giving the notoriously damp building a chance to dry out.

The building has an unusual layout, with 3 rooms accessed from the main entrance and an E wing, which used to be an open terrace, accessed via a rear door. Pushing open the door with the distinctive sign, said to have been hung there by Dundee climber Graham Hunter in 1966, you enter a long corridor with a door to the L and another round a corner to the R. The LHR is a slightly gloomy communal space lit only by a N-facing window. It has a table in the centre and benches on 3 sides, each one wide enough to double as a bed for the night. Through a doorway, the second room

is a designated dormitory, with a large 2-person sleeping platform and windows front and back. The RHR may well have been the kitchen, and has a concrete floor, whitewashed wood panelling and a bench, while the back room is an airy, slightly unfinished-looking space with a table and two single-person sleeping platforms. There is also a locked storeroom on the N side of the building. Each of the 3 rooms has its own fireplace, yet the bothy is widely reputed to be an ice-box in winter. So although the walk in is a long haul, it is essential to bring in fuel if you plan to enjoy your stay during the colder months.

Getting to the bothy is a serious undertaking and is generally approached from the S. There is, however, a path all the way there through Glen Tilt to the Linn of Dee via Bynack Lodge and White Bridge, which is one of the great historical rights of way in Scotland. From the junction of paths just beyond Forest Lodge (NN 935 744) you must decide whether to take the shorter high-level route over Carn a' Chlamain (963m) or the longer low-level route ascending to 600m that follows the contours of the landscape round to Tarf Water. Some choose to cycle as far as Forest Lodge before abadoning their bikes. Alternatively, go as far as the junction of paths at NN 971 776, leaving your bike before the track heads up the slope. It is a mile-long walk from the station and bus stop to the car park at Old Bridge of Tilt.

ROUTE 1

High level. From the large car park beyond Old Bridge of Tilt, head up the vehicle track just to the right of East Lodge, signposted to Marble Lodge (5 miles) and Forest Lodge (8 miles). Go up through the tree-lined terrace above the River Tilt, before heading down to cross Cumhann-leum Bridge onto the E bank of the river. Continue on a gentle ascent, ignoring the turn to Gilbert's Bridge, go round the farm at Auchgobhal and arrive at Marble Lodge. Beyond the lodge, as the trees begin to thin out, cross Gaw's Bridge back to the W bank. The glen narrows and you pass Clachghlas before the conifers at Forest Lodge come into view. At the end of the plantation, turn L onto the old stalkers' path that zigzags steeply up the daunting slope to Creag Loisgte and on towards Carn a' Chlamain. At this point, use your judgement as to weather and conditions underfoot and decide whether to continue on the path to the summit and pick out a faint trail N down to the Fèith Uaine Beag. The alternative is to contour across the heather to Conlach Mhòr and descend

to the burn. The bothy finally comes into view as you reach the lower slopes, where, thankfully, a small wooden footbridge across the Fèith Uaine Mhòr opposite the building saves getting your feet wet.

> **DISTANCE** 13 miles
>
> **TIME** 6 to 7 hours
>
> **TERRAIN** Challenging. Vehicle track then steep climb on good path to summit (963m), then faint trail down
>
> **PARKING** East Lodge close to Old Bridge of Tilt (NN 874 663)

ROUTE 2

Low level. From Forest Lodge continue along the track parallel to the river as the glen continues to narrow and take the 4 x 4 track L at NN 971 776, heading up over the wide bealach.

Descend to the old stables on Tarf Water, where the track ends. Ignoring the new track on the far bank, which does not reach the bothy, continue on the S bank of the river on a boggy path as it meanders upstream, and before too long the bothy comes into view. On the final stretch leave the river and head L up the Feith Uaine Mhòr, crossing the footbridge over to the bothy.

> **DISTANCE** 15 miles
>
> **TIME** 6 to 7 hours
>
> **TERRAIN** Challenging. From Forest Lodge 4 x 4 track, then obvious path, boggy in places
>
> **PARKING** East Lodge close to Old Bridge of Tilt (NN 874 663)

FUEL SUPPLY Essential to bring supplies.

KEY ATTRACTIONS Popular with Munro baggers for its proximity to An Sgarsoch (1006m) and Carn an Fhidhleir (994m) to the N. The high-level walk in takes you up to the stony summit of Carn a' Chlamain (963m). From early autumn, walk back to beautiful Glen Tilt to watch the salmon run at the waterfalls 500yds beyond the conifers at Forest Lodge.

PUBLIC TRANSPORT Scotrail Service from Glasgow/Edinburgh–Perth–Inverness, stops at Blair Atholl. Citylink coach service M90/M91 Glasgow/Edinburgh–Perth–Inverness also stops there.

SPECIAL NOTES Open throughout the year. During the stalking season from 1 August to 20 October a daily notice of activity is posted on the visitors' information board at East Lodge car park. No vehicle access to Forest Lodge. Contact Atholl Estate Office (01796 481355) for information.

The Secret Howff

ADDITIONAL CAIRNGORMS SHELTERS

THE SECRET HOWFF
LOCATION UNPUBLISHED

Remarkably, the whereabouts of this establishment are still a closely guarded secret, even though it was featured on 'Bothy Life', a BBC Scotland documentary broadcast to coincide with the the MBA's 50th anniversary in 2015. Built in 1953 by a group of climbers based in Aberdeen, including Jim Robertson, a monumental mason, the bothy is watertight, well maintained and regularly used. There is a logbook to sign if you happen to stumble across it.

SHELTER STONE
LAT/LONG 57.0945, -3.6489,
NJ 001 015, 750m, LR Map 36

The location of the Shelter Stone, another celebrated howff in the National Park, is no secret, marked as it is on OS maps, even up to 1:250,000 scale. Sitting in a chaotic boulder field below the steep coire headwall of the Loch Avon Basin, and W of the main body of water, the Shelter Stone itself is by far the largest rock and usually has a small hand-built cairn on its flat top. The cavity underneath, just high enough to duck into, can comfortably sleep 4 and a low drystone wall built across the entrance keeps out the worst of the elements. In the 1950s a plaque above the entrance read 'Shelter Stone Guest House – Prop. Larry Gru'.

GARBH CHOIRE
LAT/LONG 57.0664, -3.7188,
NN 959 986, 710m, LR Map 36

Garbh Choire is a remote but well-known refuge lying between Cairn Toul and Braeriach. Aberdeen University Lairig Club built the shelter in 1966 as a base for their pioneering ascent up the icy slopes of the imposing coires that lie above the shelter. Consisting of a rectangular steel frame covered by tarpaulin and topped with boulders and turf, there is room inside for 4 to sleep in relative comfort. At the time of writing, however, the refuge is no longer watertight and its future is uncertain.

FORDS OF AVON REFUGE
LAT/LONG 57.1097, -3.5837,
NJ 041 032, 689m, LR Map 36

This basic emergency shelter lies in the lonely heart of the Cairngorms National Park, on the N bank of the River Avon and has been a lifesaver over the years. It is on the route of one of the 3 main drove roads through the plateau, which crosses the river by way of stepping stones. The refuge was constructed by the Royal Navy Fleet Air Arm as a training exercise in June 1970. In 2011 the landowner, the RSPB, the MBA and the Mountaineering Council of Scotland joined forces to rebuild it on condition that the structure retained its simplicity. Encased by boulders, this fairly watertight, windowless shed has a wooden floor but no sleeping platform or seating.

SOUTH WESTERN
HIGHLANDS

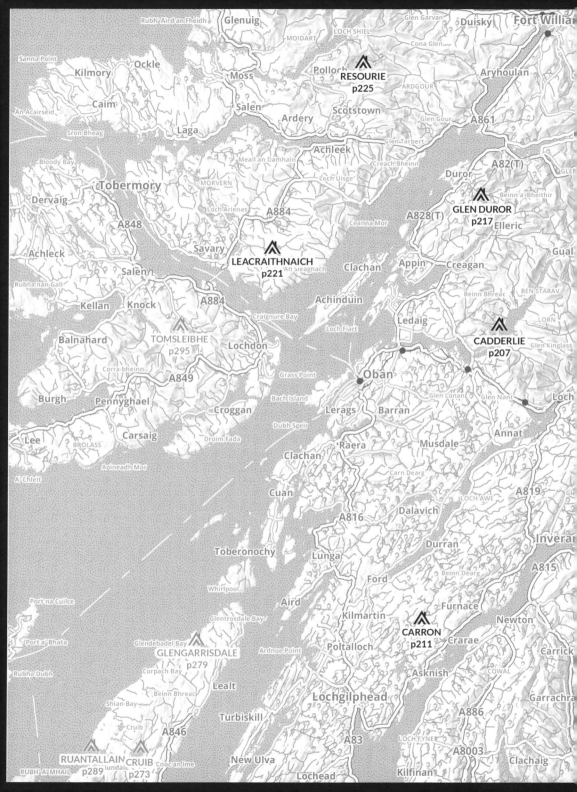

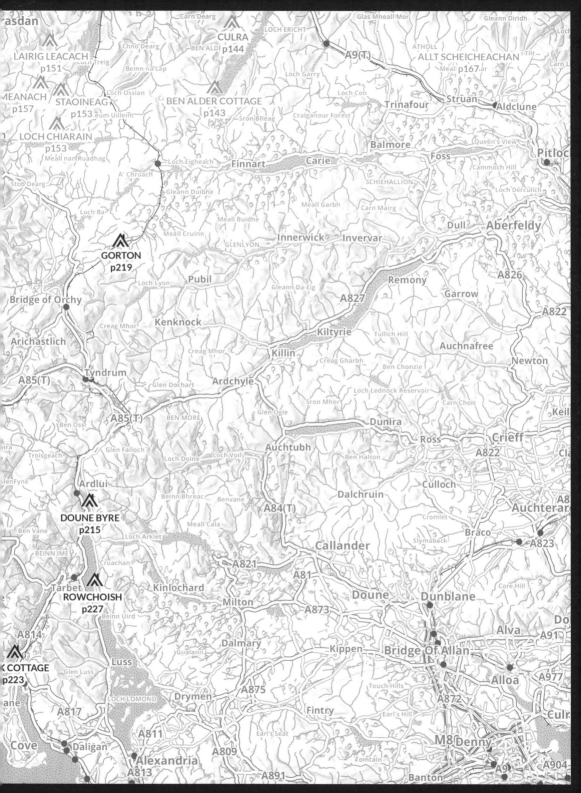

CADDERLIE

Exquisite views from this comfortable lochside bothy (1994)

SIZE Medium; 3 rooms, 1 with bunk bed sleeping 4
LOCATION LAT/LONG 56.4846, -5.1750, NN 046 370, 14m, LR Map 50

Cadderlie is one of those places, where, within 5 minutes of arriving you are already planning your next visit. Set a little way above Loch Etive's W shore, in a ribbon of birch and sessile oak, the bothy offers stunning lochside views across to Ben Cruachan and Ben Starav. Its beautiful location even inspired a song by Scottish folk singer Dougie Maclean, whose grandfather was brought up in the cottage. The history of the area dates back to at least the 13th century when Ardchattan Priory was built above the loch to provide a sanctuary for pilgrims on their way to the abbey on Iona. Along with the priory, Cadderlie lies within territory held by the Campbells from the early 14th century. The origins of the name are thought to derive from the Gaelic for 'the Burn at Deirdre's Garden', *lois* meaning 'garden' from an early spelling Cal-der-lys. An orchard stood on the site until the early 16th century, when it was hit by an excessively high storm tide. Until the

mid-1700s there was a good-sized crofting community here, which dwindled following the Clearances and the subsequent turning over of the land to sheep farming. The last recorded inhabitants of the tumbledown ruin just down from Cadderlie were the McLaurin family. After their children emigrated to the United States, the McLaurins lived out their days here. The present bothy, a relatively recent building dating back to the turn of the last century, housed shepherds and their families before the last permanent tenant moved to Glen Etive in 1948. From this point it was used as seasonal accommodation for estate workers, before it was handed over to the MBA in 1994.

There is something slightly amiss about the footprint of the bothy, which stands 30 degrees askew to the loch, and is forced a little close to the streamside trees. However, you can immediately see why when you are inside, as the view out of the

windows and doorway is superb, with Ben Cruchan peeking up directly towards you above the canopy. The building has retained its original wood panelling, and has a very comfortable feel. Its typical *but and ben* layout consists of 2 rooms, with a small chamber sandwiched between, accessed from a small vestibule. The RHR is the main communal area, with a fireplace, coffee table, chairs and even a small library. The LHR is sparser but does have another working hearth. The central room is a dormitory with a large bunk bed sleeping 4.

ROUTE 1

Park 300yds before the end of the minor road and follow the clearly signposted track, which initially skirts round a spoil heap before heading up the lochside, continuing past the house at Craig and on to the Cadderlie Burn. The bothy is a short distance down from the track towards the shore. Cross over a small bridge and the bothy is just beyond .

DISTANCE 3½ miles

TIME 1 to 1½ hours

TERRAIN Easy. Track all the way except for last 200 yds

PARKING Bonawe (NN 011334)

ROUTE 2

From the car park at the road end just beyond Gualachulain, continue on the wide track along the lochside to a new pier. From here the path winds its way past the point at Àird Trilleachan. Ignore the path heading R up to the famous climbing venue Etive Slabs, and a mile beyond the point take a turning R that ascends steeply for a short section before continuing to contour above the loch, eventually joining a forestry track. After walking round to a bridge over the Allt Easach you briefly leave the woods but soon enter the next plantation. Cross a second bridge over the Abhainn Dalach, and then arc round and down. Ignore the turning to the farm at Dail, and follow the track that heads R, and on to the edge of the conifers. The Cadderlie Burn and the bothy are now in sight.

DISTANCE 7 miles

TIME 2½ to 3 hours

TERRAIN Straightforward. Track all the way except for last 200 yds

PARKING Gualachulain (NN 112453)

FUEL SUPPLY Plenty of fallen timber in the surrounding woodland.

KEY ATTRACTIONS Although there are no Munros within range of the bothy, the Grahams Beinn Mheadhonach (715m), Beinn Mòlurgainn (690m) and Màm Hael are all close by. A little further, Corbett Creach Bheinn (810m) has many false summits to negotiate. Excellent kayaking on the loch.

PUBLIC TRANSPORT Scotrail train service from Glasgow Queen St or Citylink coach service 975/976 from Glasgow Buchanan Street to Oban, stops at Connel Bridge. West Coach Motors service 408 Oban–Connel Bridge–Bonawe.

SPECIAL NOTES Closed during the stalking season, 20 September to 20 October. Please keep dogs on a lead, especially during the lambing season. No vehicles beyond entrance to Bonawe quarry. Both routes are easy to mountain bike.

'Standing here on Cadderlie, between the burn and the turning sea, I gaze across at these golden hills, I'm looking all the way to eternity'. From Indigenous (1991/2), Dougie Maclean, Limetree Arts and Music

⋀
CARRON

Tranquil moorland bothy between forest and river (1997)

SIZE Small; 1 room with sleeping platform for 2, plus limited floor space
LOCATION LAT/LONG 56.1448, -5.3108, NR 944 996, 188m, LR Map 55

Folded into the gently undulating moorland that separates Loch Fyne and Loch Awe, the bothy at Carron sits above the River Add, which gives the shelter its Gaelic name *Car Abhuinn*, meaning 'winding river'. The cottage rests between two large expanses of forestry, and a new line of wind turbines that poke their heads above the tree line to the W. Despite these encroachments, this is a tranquil spot, where red-throated divers and black grouse share their moorland home with sheep, which are left to roam the hills, only corralled every spring in the gathering pens close by. The bothy serves as a waymarker on an old cattle droving road running from Auchindrain to Kilneuair and on to the inn at Ford (formerly known as Ford of the Hazels), a crossing point below the S end of Loch Awe. The most obvious remnant of the route is the fine old stone bridge that spans the River Add upstream from the bothy, a well-engineered curiosity startlingly out of place in this lonely glen. The fascinating 12th-century ruined church and holy

well hidden in woods by Kilneuair, named after St Columba, indicate that the route was once used by pilgrims bound for the abbey at Iona. When sheep farming became widespread and cattle were no longer driven on the road, charcoal was transported along it by pack horses to the iron smelter at Furnace, built in 1755.

Protected by a large sycamore, the bothy has been constructed from the remains of 2 terraced houses. Inside, the main feature of the single room is the 2-person sleeping platform squeezed in the space between the small brick fireplace and the far wall. A long table runs along the R-hand side and another sits under the S-facing window in the front façade. Another window opposite the entrance helps to reduce the gloom. The 2 low benches can be edged towards the hearth, but there is a strange absence of chairs. As is the case with many outlying bothies, visitors have donated books over the years and there is a small collection to peruse.

Carron can be approached from all sides but the route from Leckuary (W) is not recommended because of ongoing forestry operations. The easiest of the routes are from Auchindrain (E), or from Minard (S).

ROUTE 1
A new forest drive linking Loch Fyne and Loch Awe begins at Auchindrain and ends at a Forestry Commission car park by the lochside at Ardray (NM 933 062), open between 1 April and 31 October. If you are happy to drive on this unmetalled road, there is a large layby below the crags at Tom Soilleir (NM 960 005), which shortens the walk in from 4½ to 1½ miles. From the road end at Brenchoillie, take the track that steadily climbs the slope parallel to the electricity pylons. After just over a mile ignore a R turn and continue on to the layby below Tom Soilleir, where the track curves round to the N. From here, take a new path down through the cleared plantation, trending (though it may seem counter-intuitive) E before heading back W to join the original route of the drove road. This

has been ploughed up back towards the track as marked on the 1:50,000 OS map. Follow the path as it heads back into the trees, eventually leaving the forestry by the ruin of Creag an Iubhair. After crossing the old stone bridge over the River Add, and passing the gathering pens, the bothy quickly comes into view just up the slope.

DISTANCE 4½ miles

TIME 2 to 2½ hours

TERRAIN Easy. Track and then well-defined path all the way

PARKING Beyond Brenchoillie turning (NN 016 023)

ROUTE 2

At Minard, park by the boathouse in the centre of the village, not by the post office and shop. Head up the lane (a cul de sac) to the L of the post office, past the fire station and a row of houses. To the R of the last house, take the footpath through the trees, over the burn and L up a track signposted to Feorlin Loch and Steading via Garvachy, then head up through a conifer plantation to a line of electricity pylons. A little further on, ignore a track leading R and at the next junction, turn sharply L back towards Garvachy Farm. Before the farm buildings, take the track heading onto the moor, round a 90 degree bend, and then strike up the slope following the fence line up to the trig pillar on Sìdhean Beag (261m). From the summit pick your way through the rocky knolls and down to the River Add. The bothy is in clear view between the plantations above the far bank. The best place to cross is at the confluence of the main channel

with the Abhainn Bhuidhe just down from the ruin of Creag an Iubhair, and over the old stone bridge. Fording the river is not advisable especially when in spate.

DISTANCE 3 miles

TIME 1½ to 2 hours

TERRAIN Straightforward. Track and faint path across open moor

PARKING Minard, Loch Fyne (NR 978 961)

ROUTE 3

From Kilneuair at the W end of Loch Awe, park at the start of the track where there is space for a couple of cars without blocking access. Follow the track E ignoring a junction R, and carry on to a meeting of paths above the ruined church of St. Columba. Turn

R onto the route of the old drove road and wind your way uphill towards Loch Gainmheach, which has been recently dammed. After ½ mile, pick up a new unmetalled access road to the hydroelectric scheme. When this ends at a bridge at the head of the loch, continue up to the Bealach Gaoithe, the 'Pass of the Winds', and across the open moor, skirting 2 small lochans and round the shoulder of A' Chruach to the boundary fence of a conifer plantation. The track cuts down the slope following the line of this fence and the bothy is soon in view.

DISTANCE 4½ miles

TIME 2 to 2½ hours

TERRAIN Straightforward. Track

PARKING Kilneuair (NM 884 037)

FUEL SUPPLY Some wood in the surrounding plantation.

KEY ATTRACTIONS Mid-Argyll is bursting with archaeological sites. Visit the mystical hillfort at Dunadd on the Mòine Mhòr, Neolithic burial chambers in Kilmartin Glen, or the standing stones, crumbling castle and crannogs by Loch Awe. See a restored Highland township at the Auchindrain Folk Museum, and stop at Inveraray Castle, which has gardens and an infamous jail.

PUBLIC TRANSPORT West Coast Motors coach service 926 from Glasgow Buchanan Street to Campbeltown, stops on request at Auchindrain and Minard.

SPECIAL NOTES Open throughout the year. Stag stalking takes place between 20 September and 20 October to the S and W of the bothy. The Ederline Estate discourages dogs, especially during the lambing season. Straightforward to mountain bike.

FUEL SUPPLY Some timber in the surrounding woods.

KEY ATTRACTIONS The Drovers Inn at Inverarnan is a celebrated pub with a stuffed bear in the lobby. Spend a day climbing Ben Glas and Munro Beinn Chabhar (933m) or just walk as far as the Ben Glas Burn waterfall.

PUBLIC TRANSPORT Scotrail service from Glasgow Queen St. to Fort William, stops at Ardlui. Ferry connection from Ardlui to Ardleish, ½ mile N of the bothy. Citylink coach services 914/5/6 and 976 from Glasgow to Oban or Fort William, stop at Inverarnan, for Beinglas campsite.

SPECIAL NOTES Open throughout the year. Nearby cottage has been fenced off. No dogs. Campsite at Beinglas has a shop, café/bar and showers. Rubbish accumulation is a problem; please burn or take it with you. The WHW is only suitable for skilled mountain bikers due to its short steep slopes and many stone drainage channels.

DOUNE BYRE

Iconic lochside shelter on the West Highland Way (1980)

SIZE Small; 1 room with 2 platform beds sleeping 4
LOCATION LAT/LONG 56.2931, -4.6959, NN 332 144, 71m, LR Map 56

In stunning surroundings high above the E shore of Loch Lomond on the West Highland Way (WHW), Doune Byre Bothy has a very distinctive slit window in its front façade. Little is known about its history, but the byre was most probably used to house livestock or grain. The bothy is fairly rudimentary, and little has changed since the MBA took over its maintenance. The door opens straight into a big, bright stone room with 2 small windows, whitewashed walls and ceiling and contrasting black roof beams. At either side of the large brick fireplace, 2 raised sleeping platforms double up as fireside seating, and there is another sleeping area at the opposite end. The only other furniture is a metal shelving unit and a couple of battered chairs. Although basic, the shelter is very accessible, making it popular with walkers and weekenders, and also with first-time bothy-goers. For intoxicating scenery it takes some beating, and you may see wild goats as well as osprey.

ROUTE 1

From the campsite at Beinglas follow the WHW S, immediately crossing a footbridge over the Ben Glas Burn before winding up through the birch and oak woodland lining the slopes above the River Falloch. Continue past the ruin at Blarstainge before the path levels out by Dubh Lochan, where you suddenly catch sight of Loch Lomond. Just beyond the old croft at Ardleish, the path heads down to the shore, passing close to the Ardlui ferry stop. After another mile, you leave the lochside, climb a small rise past another abandoned croft, and the bothy appears next to the path. Arriving by ferry shortens the walk by 2 miles.

DISTANCE 3 miles
TIME 1 to 1½ hours
TERRAIN Easy. Well maintained path all the way
PARKING Beinglas campsite (NN 321 187)

ROUTE 2

From the car park at Inversnaid, head N along the WHW past a boathouse and up the side of the loch. The initial section is along a track that soon becomes a well-managed path and undulates above the rocky shore. Before the point at Sroin Uaidh you pass a signpost to Rob Roy's Cave, the alleged hideout of the famous outlaw, close to the water's edge. It's hard to miss, especially as the word 'CAVE' has been painted in large white letters on a boulder above the entrance. Continue past the ruin at Pollochro and a little further on look out for the small island, *Eilean I Vow* ('Island of the Cow'), where a crumbling 16th-century castle is enclosed by trees. After another mile or so of slow ascent and descent, you reach the top of a small rise where the bothy comes into view.

DISTANCE 4 miles
TIME 1½ to 2 hours
TERRAIN Easy. Track and well maintained path all the way
PARKING Inversnaid (NN 337 089)

FUEL SUPPLY Some wood in the surrounding plantations.

KEY ATTRACTIONS Climbing the summits of Beinn a' Bheithir (the Ballachulish Horseshoe) Munros Sgorr Dhearg (1024m) and Sgorr Dhonuill (1001m) is a great day out. At nearby Cuil Bay there are lovely views down Loch Linnhe.

From the A828 as you pass Duror, look out for the impressive Bronze Age Achara Stone (NM 987 546). National Cycle Network route 78 from Oban to Ballachulish passes the turning to the bothy.

PUBLIC TRANSPORT Citylink bus service 918 Oban to Fort William, stops in Duror.

SPECIAL NOTES Open throughout the year. Fire risk in the surrounding plantation. Avoid lighting fires outside the bothy. Do not drive on forestry roads. Easy to mountain bike.

GLEN DUROR
TAIGH SEUMAS A' GHLINNE

Bothy in a forest maze with a compelling tale to tell (1994)

SIZE Medium; long single room, platform bed sleeps 4
LOCATION LAT/LONG 56.6350, -5.2268, NN 022 539, 203m, LR Map 41

The 'House of James of the Glen' lies deep in the Glen Duror woods beneath the imposing curve of Beinn a' Bheithir. This quiet backwater between the W periphery of Glen Coe and the Appin Peninsula was the birthplace of James Stewart (James of the Glen), who was framed for the murder of Colin Campbell and hung at nearby Ballachulish in 1752. Campbell, the 'Red Fox', was a government agent who collected taxes from the local rebel clan leaders and evicted tenants who could not or were unwilling to pay rent. The Stewarts of Appin, veterans of the rebellion, sworn enemies of the law enforcer and about to be evicted themselves, were easy targets. Although the conviction amounted to a serious miscarriage of justice, James Stewart's family never received a pardon. These events are woven into the plot of Robert Louis Stevenson's classic novel *Kidnapped*.

The bothy was once slightly off the beaten track, but a number of the locations associated with what is now referred to as the 'Appin Murder', have been identified and marked with a distinctive Scottish Saltire of blue and yellow. Waymarkers now line the track and there is a board outside the shelter giving more historical details, as well as a picnic table. Inside, the bothy has a comfortable, uncluttered feel. A long, low-ceilinged room has a wood burning stove at one gable end and a U-shaped sleeping platform at the other, which can comfortably accommodate 4. A chair and a low settee have been pushed towards the fireplace, there is a large table underneath the N-facing window and additional light filters through transparent roof panels. The present bothy replaced the former Glen Duror Hut situated close by, which had been maintained by the MBA since 1978.

ROUTE 1

From the A828, take the turn-off to Auchindarroch then follow the single-track road past a small housing estate to a forestry commission car park. Then follow the lower of the 2 tracks down towards the river signed 'Birthplace of James of the Glen'. Continue along this waymarked track as it curves round the slope above the River Duror and then runs parallel to it. After a mile or so, ignore a track coming down at a sharp angle L and then almost immediately after this take a smaller stony track to the L. This track is also waymarked and leads straight up the hillside. After a short distance, pass a concrete bridge with a 3-tonne weight-limit sign before the path levels out and then descends for a short stretch to the clearing where you will see the bothy.

DISTANCE 2 miles
TIME 45 minutes to 1 hour
TERRAIN Easy. Forestry track all the way
PARKING Achindarroch (Achadh nan Darach, NN 004 552)

FUEL SUPPLY Bring supplies.

KEY ATTRACTIONS Ideally situated to tackle Beinn Achaladair (1036m) and Beinn a' Chreachain (1081m). For refreshment, call in at the Bridge of Orchy Hotel, which has a fine bar and restaurant.

PUBLIC TRANSPORT Scotrail West Highland Line from Glasgow Queen St. to Fort William, stops at Bridge of Orchy. Citylink coach service 915/916 Glasgow–Fort William, stops on request at the turn-off to Achallader farm.

SPECIAL NOTES Not officially available during stag stalking from 12 August to 20 October but in practice it is left unlocked. Please contact the Blackmount Estate (01838 400 255). Easy to mountain bike.

GORTON

A peaceful refuge in high, wild moorland (1978)

SIZE Medium; 2 rooms, sleeping restricted to the floor
LOCATION LAT/LONG 56.5970, -4.6485, NN 375 481, 299m, LR Map 50

In this land of massive skies, steep slopes and wild moorland crossed by the West Highland Line, Gorton Bothy is a welcome refuge. The topography was formed by meltwater following last Ice Age, when the vast expanse of Rannoch Moor to the N was covered by a large ice cap. The bothy's name derives from the Gaelic *goirtean*, referring to a small field or enclosure, implying agricultural use, and records dating back to the 16th century show that an old droving road passed through to Glen Lyon. The strategic tower house of Achallader Castle at the head of Loch Tulla, a stronghold of the Campbells, was built in the late 1590s, partly to protect the route from cattle rustlers, only to be burnt down by the Jacobite army a century later in the aftermath of the Glen Coe Massacre. Following the Clearances, when the land was given over to sheep-farming, Gorton farmstead was built to house a shepherd and his family. With the coming of the West Highland Line in the 1890s, a small halt was built opposite and Gorton became a

meeting-point. Shepherds from all the outlying farming communities gathered here, bringing sheep to be transported to the Moray coast for winter grazing. A siding and island platform were built, as well as a signal box, and the local school established itself in a single railway carriage. Gorton was occupied well into the 1950s and has survived intact, in contrast to the station, of which only a few bricks survive.

Considering its proximity to Scotland's main population centres, Gorton has somehow retained its original character. Fortunately the bothy is highly regarded by those who frequent it, and its location is just far enough from the popular West Highland Way to keep visitor numbers manageable. The bothy is a typical *but and ben*, with a slightly outsized byre (used for storage) still intact on the E gable end. Leading off a large corrugated porch, there are 2 equal-sized rooms, one with a large open fireplace. The wood panelling has survived and there are windows front

and back. Both rooms are sparsely furnished with just a table and some chairs and you must bed down on the floors. Evenings here are simple affairs, very much focused on the fire.

ROUTE 1

From the parking area follow the track past the farm outbuildings and the ruined tower. Keeping to the drystone wall that runs along the edge of an open field, you soon come to the Allt Coire Achaladair which crosses the track, and could be an obstacle after heavy rain. Once over, continue on across the fields and then go over the Water of Tulla by Barravourich (NN 338453), on a rather rickety bridge. From here you head upstream passing the beautiful Caledonian pines of Crannach Wood on the way.

DISTANCE 5 miles
TIME 2 to 2½ hours
TERRAIN Straightforward. Forestry track all the way. River crossing
PARKING Off the A82 before Achallader Farm (NN 314 438)

FUEL SUPPLY Wood occasionally provided; best to bring supplies.

KEY ATTRACTIONS Explore charming Ardtornish Gardens on the estate or visit Aoineadh Mór by Loch Arienas, a ruined crofting township. From Ardtornish Point you can walk along the coast to Inninmore Bay. The bar at the Lochaline Hotel has great views across to Mull.

PUBLIC TRANSPORT Scotrail train service from Glasgow Queen St or Citylink coach service 915/916 from Glasgow Buchanan Street to Fort William. Daily bus from Fort William to Lochaline, service 507 (Shiel Buses 01397 700 700). Calmac ferry from Fishnish (on Mull) to Lochaline.

SPECIAL NOTES Not available during stag stalking, 1 September to 20 October. From then until 15 February access usually restricted to track from Ardtornish. Contact Ardtornish Estate (01967 421292). Permit required for loch fishing. Easy to mountain bike.

⌂ LEACRAITHNAICH

Basic bothy by a loch on an ancient site (1983)

SIZE Medium; 2 rooms , sleeping platform for 4
LOCATION LAT/LONG 56.5619, -5.6764, NM 742 471, 148m, LR Map 49

When you approach the bothy at Leacraithnaich after the steady pull up from Ardtornish and spy the loch that lies just beyond, your eye is immediately drawn to a solitary tree close to the far shallows. This is all that remains of a medieval *crannag*, a fortified island stronghold that was reputedly used as a sanctuary for suspected criminals from Lismore or Mull. This resonates with *Teàrnait*, the Gaelic name of the Loch, which means 'place of safety'. According to local folklore, if those accused of crimes could obtain permission from the clan chief of Ardtornish to spend 48 hours on the island, they were spared any further punishment. *Leacraithnaich*, the 'place of the wheat-milling stone', or, alternatively, 'wheat slope', was built as an estate lodge for fishing parties in the 19th century on an even older site – a late Iron Age settlement catalogued by a 1968 archaeological survey. A monastic community is also said to have been established here.

The shelter is basically a large stone carcass split into two by a partition. The main room, which is quite large and airy, has been made a little cosier by lowering the ceiling, while the addition of a small porch helps to keep out the draughts. There is a well-appointed stone fireplace, a couple of sturdy tables, and chairs that have seen better days. The corner press is well-stocked with books, unfortunately now somewhat mildewed on account of damp seeping in at the gable end. The second room contains a low raised platform sleeping 4, but the chimney has been blocked up. A hydroelectric scheme on the loch, completed in 2011, does detract from the wilderness feel, and you cannot quite escape the presence of the Glen Sanda super-quarry, which you can see out of the corner of your eye from the bothy door. Despite these intrusions, the bothy manages to retain its authenticity and atmosphere. It has also benefited from the benevolent attitude of the landowner.

ROUTE 1

From the Ardtornish estate office car park, head up the wide unmetalled road that ascends steeply and then winds round Lochan Lub an Arbhair. Follow the route as it contours across and over the Allt na Claise Brice to where it turns L down to the hydroelectric scheme 'powerhouse'. Ignore this turning and keep straight on. After ½ mile the bothy comes into view on the L shore of the loch.

> **DISTANCE** 3 miles
> **TIME** 1 to 1½ hours
> **TERRAIN** Easy. Well-maintained track all the way
> **PARKING** Ardtornish, end of minor road off A884 (NM 704473)

A *crannag* is a man-made island that housed a round, thatched dwelling. Usually located close to the loch side, it was an easily defended refuge. Several dotted about Scotland date back to the Iron Age. A unique reconstruction has been built at the Crannog Centre on Loch Tay.

FUEL SUPPLY Plenty of dead wood in the surrounding plantation.

KEY ATTRACTIONS Although there are no hills of note close to the bothy, a stay could easily be combined with a trip up The Cobbler (884m) or Beinn Narnain (926m) if you are travelling by car. A short stroll along the shore takes you to the navigation beacon at Cnap. Loch Long and Loch Goil are both good for kayaking.

PUBLIC TRANSPORT Scotrail train service from Glasgow Queen St. to Fort William, stops at Arrochar. West Coast Motors coach service 926 from Glasgow Buchanan Street to Campbeltown; request a stop at Ardgartan information centre.

SPECIAL NOTES Open throughout the year. Beware of fire risk in the area around the bothy. Easy to mountain bike.

MARK COTTAGE

Peaceful city escape by woods and water (2010)

SIZE Medium; 2 rooms, 1 with bunk-beds, sleeping 6
LOCATION LAT/LONG 56.1164,-4.8492, NS 229 952, 9m, LR Map 56

Relaxing on the bench outside Mark Cottage, it is hard to believe that the start of the walk in to this tranquil sanctuary is less than an hour's drive from Glasgow. The bothy sits above the W shore of Loch Long, near the foot of the Ardgartan Peninsula and on the edge of an extensive forestry plantation which stretches down from Arrochar and round to Lochgoilhead. On the opposite bank there is a gas storage facility and pier, and high above this trains trundle by on the West Highland Line, but this a surprisingly isolated spot. Apart from the occasional tanker docking, little else disturbs the peace. Mark was once served by ferry from Portincaple, and the track over to Lochgoilhead was one of the main routes N in the Highlands well into the early 20th century. The bothy was once the home of James Grieve, Scotland's oldest man, who lived to be 110. There is a photo of him above the fireplace in the cottage taken in 1906. Standing next to him is his son, also looking quite elderly,

who was often mistaken for his father by curious visitors who came calling from Glasgow. Apparently, the family supplemented their income by charging day trippers to have their photo taken with the record holder.

The MBA took possession of the bothy from the Forestry Commission in 2008 and partitioned the space to create 2 rooms. The comfortable communal area has 2 long benches at either side of a fireplace, a large alcove at the back with a good-sized work top, a table, chairs and even a small library. In the RHR are 3 red bunk-beds sleeping 6, though, alas, no mattresses. The whole place has been liberally whitewashed, which, in combination with the large windows front and back, gives it a bright, welcoming feel.

ROUTE 1
The only direct land access to the bothy is from the N. Turn off the A83 at the Forest Enterprise Information Centre (NN 269 037), signposted to the Ardgartan Hotel, and head along

a single track road to a large parking area at Coilessan Glen. From the bus stop at Ardgartan it is a 2-mile walk to Coilessan Glen following the route of the Cowal Way. From Arrochar station, the walk takes an additional 4 miles. From the car park pass by the locked gate and ignore the immediate L turn. Instead, take a track which traces a line between the 100m and 150m contour above the shore of the loch. Ignoring 2 more paths that come in from the R, loop round the Allt a' Guanan, and take care to avoid the immediate L turn leading down to Guanan. After another mile or so, ignore a turn to the R and, soon afterwards, the track finally descends steeply down and round to the bothy, which is hidden among conifers.

DISTANCE 4½ miles
TIME 1½ to 2 hours
TERRAIN Easy. Track all the way
PARKING Ardgartan Forest, Coilessan Glen (NN 258 012)

FUEL SUPPLY Fallen timber in conifer plantations.

KEY ATTRACTIONS Land of prized remote Corbetts Bhealach an Sgriòdain (Meall Mòr) (770m) and Carn na Nathrach (786m).

The nearby village of Strontian (where the element strontium was discovered) has a campsite, forest walks and a fine hotel, with an appropriately named Bothy Bar.

PUBLIC TRANSPORT None.

SPECIAL NOTES Fire risk to surrounding plantation. Do not light fires outside the bothy or drive on forestry roads. Open all year round. Easy to mountain bike until you reach the final section through the plantation.

RESOURIE

A place to meditate, deep in spruce forest (1978)

SIZE Medium; 3 rooms, all with bunk-bed platforms; sleeps 10
LOCATION LAT/LONG 56.7808, -5.5023, NM 862 709, 139m, LR Map 40

Resourie is a mysterious, almost fabled bothy hidden away in the deep blanket of regimented conifers that line the slopes of Glen Hurich, in the rarely visited back country between Strontian and Glenfinnan, SE of Loch Shiel. The cottage's Gaelic name *Ruighe Samhraidh*, 'the summer shieling', harks back to a time when sheep roamed the hills, and the property was once home to a tenant shepherd and his family. Now the shelter has been engulfed by silence and trees, which will certainly appeal to those just happy to meditate, read from the well-stocked library and sit by the fire. The more adventurous may be tempted to fight through the forestry and numerous deer fences in an attempt to reach one of the surrounding summits. The bothy is a classic *but and ben* with 2 main rooms and a small cubbyhole with a 2-person bunk-bed sandwiched between. The LHR contains a Dowling stove and a basic sleeping platform for 4 running the length of the back wall. A table sits under the S-facing window, there is a low bench, a couple of chairs, and a shelving unit with the well-thumbed books of the bothy library. The RHR has a brick fireplace, a smaller bunk-bed platform sleeping 2, and another table under the window. In contrast to the bare stone interior of the LHR, the walls have been whitewashed and a couple of fading, framed landscapes add a homely touch. To the L of the grate is a *swee* – a pot stand on a swinging arm that can be turned to the grate. Both rooms benefit from the light coming through transparent roofing panels.

ROUTE 1

The walk in is unusual because there are 3 signs en route that point the way 'to the bothy'. In bothy culture, it is very rare that locations are so clearly advertised, and an illustration of just how out of the way Resourie is. However, at the time of writing, the second signpost at (NM 858 708), directing you into the woods from the forestry track has been dismantled, leaving only the stumps visible. After parking by the houses at Glenhurich, follow the track down to the River Hurich. Just before the bridge, take a L turn onto a forestry access road, signposted to the bothy, that slowly winds its way up the W bank of the river. From here it is a straightforward 1½ miles up a gentle slope. After passing a Scottish Rights of Way sign (NM 849 699), keep a very close lookout for the bothy turning, which is marked by the stumps of the vandalised second signpost. Once into the gloom and across a stream, the third sign points reassuringly L. After another 300 yds you see the bothy in a small clearing.

DISTANCE 2½ miles

TIME 1 to 1½ hours

TERRAIN Easy. Forest access road all the way until the last 500yds. From here, path through conifers

PARKING Glenhurich (NM 834 683)

ROWCHOISH

Popular shelter by Loch Lomond on the West Highland Way (1977)

SIZE Medium; 1 long room with raised area sleeping 12
LOCATION LAT/LONG 56.2021, -4.6839, NN 336 044, 41m, LR Map 56

Enclosed within the tightly packed pines that weave a mesh above the eastern side of Loch Lomond, across the water from the hum of traffic passing through the popular tourist haunt of Tarbert, lies the small basic hut that is Rowchoish bothy. The shelter is a natural stopping-off point on the West Highland Way (WHW), and over the years it has provided a welcome refuge to thousands of hardy walkers making the long trek to Fort William and the shadow of Ben Nevis. Rowchoish is also a popular weekend destination for those escaping the towns and cities of Scotland's central belt and beyond. It even has its own postcode (Glasgow G63 0AR), though I suspect it does not get much mail! In the summer months, after negotiating slow-moving cars, BBQ's and bathers, the walk in through peaceful woodland comes as a blessed relief, though the bothy suffers a little from overuse.

The refuge is the former stone byre of the nearby ruined cottage, which was still occupied well into the 1930s. A rough pen-and-ink sketch on the bothy wall, dating from 1929, shows the property in a wide fenced field with a fine view of the loch – long before the slopes were engulfed by conifers. The name derives from the Gaelic *ruighe* and *coise*, meaning 'shieling' and 'foot' respectively, which may denote its position below Ben Lomond. A community of 9 families lived in the vicinity of Rowchoish as far back as the mid-18th century and along with the cottage, there are at least 3 more settlements in the undergrowth along the shore up to Inversnaid. The byre fell into disrepair but was rescued in 1965, through an initiative of the Scottish Rights of Way Society, and renovated with the consent of the Forestry Commission. The MBA took on maintenance in 1977.

The bothy door opens straight into a single windowless room lit by 6 large transparent panels in the roof. There is a stone fireplace at one end and a high sleeping area at the other reached by 3 steps. A rather functional arrangement of scaffolding poles and wire separates this space from the communal area where a stone worktop with some kitchen equipment runs along the wall. A rickety table and a few plastic chairs complete the scene. The only source of water is from the nearby loch, reached by a path from the bothy to the shore. From the small pebble beach there is a wonderful view of the mountains at the head of the loch and W to Beinn Narnain and Arrochar. The bothy recently gained notoriety as one of the locations used in *Under the Skin*, an independent feature film starring Scarlett Johansson, released in 2013. Public access was denied during shooting, and (just in case you were wondering) , she did not leave a note in the bothy book.

ROUTE 1
From the large visitors' car park 200 yards beyond the Rowardennan Hotel, follow the minor road which ends at the youth hostel, passing the start of the main path up Ben Lomond. Bear L

at the next fork to pass through some oak woods, and then R at the entrance to Ptarmigan Lodge where there is a metal gate. As the track climbs the slope, turn L down a path, which eventually leads to the bothy. This was the original route of the WHW before deterioration led to its upgrading by the Forestry Commission in 2014, with the help of a £750,000 grant from the Scottish Government. The path hugs the shoreline of the loch, negotiating rocks by means of steps and sections of boardwalk. About ½ mile from the bothy, ignore a track ascending steeply (back to the new route of the WHW) and continue on to a boggy path that leads off to the L. The shelter is in a clearing 100 yds from the main path and can take a little finding in the dark.

DISTANCE 4 miles
TIME 1½ to 2 hours
TERRAIN Easy. Track and well maintained path all the way
PARKING Rowardennan (NS 359 986)

ROUTE 2

Reach the large car park across from the Inversnaid Hotel by ferry from Inveruglas or by driving round from Aberfoyle and Loch Arklet. From here, head S across a footbridge over Arklet Water on the WHW, just below a picturesque waterfall. Continue down a well-made path, winding your way just above the shore until you pass a distinctive cottage at Cailness. Cross a footbridge over Cailness Burn and after 1½ miles the path becomes a track. Very soon turn R to the boggy path described in Route 1, this time heading R to the bothy.

DISTANCE 3 miles
TIME 1 to 1½ hours
TERRAIN Easy. Track and good path
PARKING Inversnaid (NN 337 089)

CAMPING NEAR THE BOTHY

In response to years of unofficial camping, partying and people thoughtlessly leaving rubbish on the E side of Loch Lomond, restrictions are now in place. There are 3 official sites further S at Milarrochy, Cashel and Sallochy where you can pitch a tent between 1 March and 31 October – camping anywhere else incurs a £500 fine. The restrictions end 2 miles S of the bothy just beyond Ptarmigan Lodge. Walkers not using the bothy for an overnight stay are able to camp responsibly from here up to Inversnaid and on to Ardlui.

Scotttish hero and outlaw Rob Roy was born by Loch Katrine and fought in the first Jacobite Rebellion of 1719, becoming a cattle rustler when his

FUEL SUPPLY Some fallen timber in surrounding woods.

KEY ATTRACTIONS Combine your stay with the ascent of Ben Lomond (974m) from Rowardennan – a rite of passage. For refreshment, try the popular Rowardennan Hotel (busy at the weekends) and stop at the memorial dedicated to armed forces personnel killed in action. Visit Rob Roy's prison, just off the path into the bothy from the south (NN 338 028). If you have plenty of time, continue along the West Highland Way to Doune Byre Bothy (p215) and beyond.

PUBLIC TRANSPORT Scotrail train service from Glasgow Queen St. to Fort William stops at Arrochar and Tarbert. Citylink coach services 914/5/6 and 976 from Glasgow to Oban or Fort William, stop at Luss, Tarbert and Sloy Power Station (for Inveruglas). Waterbus service run by Loch Lomond and the Trossachs National Park from Luss or Tarbert to Rowardennan and Inveruglas to Inversnaid (01389 722600).

SPECIAL NOTES Open throughout the year. Boil water from the loch before use. No fires outside the bothy and do not drive on forestry roads. Please burn or take away your rubbish – it is an ongoing problem at this bothy. Easy to mountain bike from either route, though if you are cycling to the bothy from Rowardennan, you need to continue up the WHW track and down to the junction on the N side (Route 2).

lands were seized. The 'prison' is a snook (cave) in the rocks just above Loch Lomond, about a mile S of the bothy. Rob Roy allegedly used the cave as a hide-out and held the Deputy Sherriff Dunbartonshire hostage here before his eventual capture. When a fictionalised account of Rob Roy's travails, The Highland Rogue, found favour with the public, he was released. Sir Walter Scott's famous novel Rob Roy is based on his life.

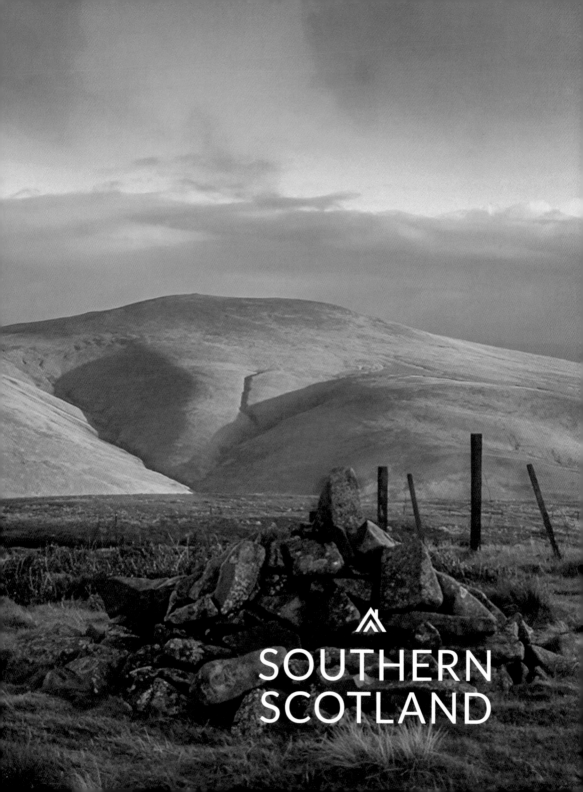

SOUTHERN
SCOTLAND

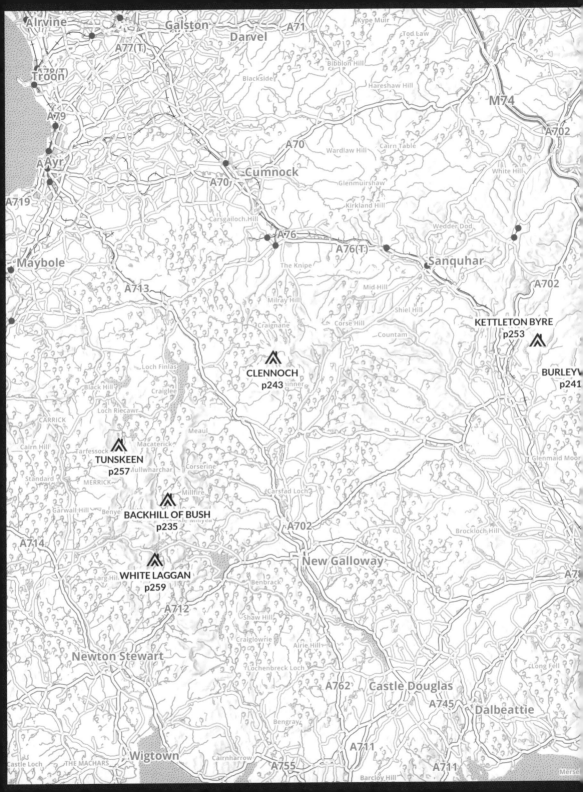

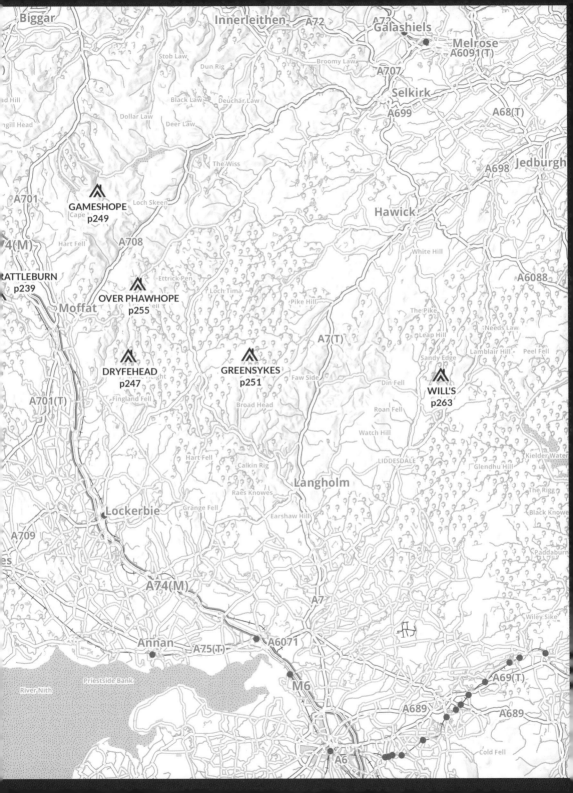

BACKHILL OF BUSH

Place that sowed the seed of bothy restoration

SIZE Medium; sleeping platform for 4
LOCATION LAT/LONG 55.1296, -4.3846, NX 481 843, 270m, LR Map 77

Celebrated as the birthplace of the MBA, Backhill lies deep in the heart of the Galloway hills. This heavily glaciated land of bare granite, lonely lochs, floating bog and tussocky moor was once the most isolated area of S Scotland and home of hardy hill folk who sustained a life based on sheep farming. Swathes of conifer plantations now dominate the landscape and forestry tracks have improved access, but the high ridges to the W and E have retained a sense of remoteness, intrepid walkers drawn in by names which evoke an of mystery and intrigue: Dungeon Hill, Murder Hole, and Rig of the Jarkness. Known as 'Back Buss', Backhill of Bush served as an outlying dwelling for the main farm at Backhill of Garrary. A collection of anecdotes by Dave McFadzean, whose great uncle was one of the last shepherds to live in the cottage, describes a simple, self-sufficient life of long days on the hills, gathering in the flock in all weathers. Visitors were few and the evenings were spent playing the fiddle and knitting. The isolation of the farm, especially in the long, hard winters, finally took its toll and the last occupants packed up in the late 1940s. The building was left as an open shelter and by the early 1950s was an established refuge for visitors as well as for locals fishing in the lochs and *stravaigers* (vagabonds) who roamed the hills. One regular, Kenneth Mcarthur, made a comment in the logbook about maintaining the region's bothies that fired the imagination of Bernard Heath, the founder of what became the Mountain Bothies Association.

The building is a typical *but and ben*, though originally there were also 2 rooms in the attic. A storm porch leads into a small lobby with communal areas leading off to L and R. The LHR has a small Dowling stove, a collection of tables and chairs, and a large platform at the back that can comfortably sleep 6. The RHR also has a stove, and a built-in bench extending along 2 walls. For a while the place lost its lustre, but recent maintenance work including replacement windows is making a difference.

The hills surrounding the bothy have a unique character and are well worth cimbing, although if you are heading W you do have to negotiate to blanket bog. Care is also needed crossing the Saugh Burn, and there are many water-filled holes to avoid. But in the summer months, once you are into the uplands of the Silver Flowe Nature Reserve, you will see beautiful wild flowers, rare butterflies and dragonflies. It is rough but rewarding walking from here, and, as well as the summits of Craignaw and Dungeon Hill, the great attraction is the Devil's Bowling Green (NX 456 386), a spooky collection of rocks and boulders deposited on a flat table of granite by the retreating glaciers at the end the last Ice Age. There are also several aircraft crash sites across the moor, which was under the flight path of many missions and training sorties from Prestwick up to and during World War II. The family living at Backhill were called upon 6 times in as many years to help locate wreckage and carry out survivors. More recently, a memorial cairn has been built close to the crash site of an American F111 near the summit of Craignaw. The Rhinns of Kells ridge is also close to the bothy and can be accessed via the old pony track that crosses the saddle between Millfire and Corserine, following the catchment of the Downies Burn.

Cautionary Note: When the MBA first took on the maintenance of Backhill, it was relatively remote and access was difficult. In the 1970s, after a forestry track was built running straight past the bothy, it became far too easy to drive a vehicle there. Sadly, the shelter gained a reputation for heavy drinking and associated vandalism, which made the place

unpleasant and unwelcoming for others. The MBA worked closely with the Forestry Commission and the police in an attempt to solve these problems but reluctantly relinquished responsibility for the building's upkeep in 2010. The Forestry Commission, however, is determined to maintain Backhill and spent a significant sum on a new roof and patching up the bothy's exterior and interior. The situation is now in flux, yet many local people are very protective of the place and the outlook seems positive. Go with an open mind and, hopefully, you will be pleasantly surprised.

ROUTE 1

The walk in to the bothy is very straightforward, hiking along forest access tracks all the way from the road end at Craigencallie. Heading N and then E, the track contours round the hillside. Turn R here to join the route of the Southern Upland Way (SUW) for a few hundred yards, down to a bridge over the Black Water of Dee. At the T junction, bear L, away from the SUW, and push on through the plantations, turning L again past McWhanns Stone and out towards the Silver Flowe river. The view opens out once you are close to the bothy, which is a welcome sight after a long trek.

DISTANCE 4½ miles

TIME 1½ to 2 hours

TERRAIN Forestry access road all the way

PARKING Road end just beyond Craigencallie Outdoor Centre (NX 503 780)

FUEL SUPPLY Some fallen timber in surrounding plantations.

KEY ATTRACTIONS The Silver Flowe W of the bothy is a National Nature Reserve and home to a number of rare species. Splendid ridge-walking along the Rhinns of Kells and Craignaw, which receive few visitors.

PUBLIC TRANSPORT None.

SPECIAL NOTES Open throughout the year. If the forest gate is open at Craigencallie, it is possible to drive all the way to the bothy, although this has led to problems and is discouraged by the Forestry Commission. Follows part of the National Cycle Route 7 from Loch Trool to Gatehouse of Fleet, and easy to mountain bike the rest of the way to the bothy.

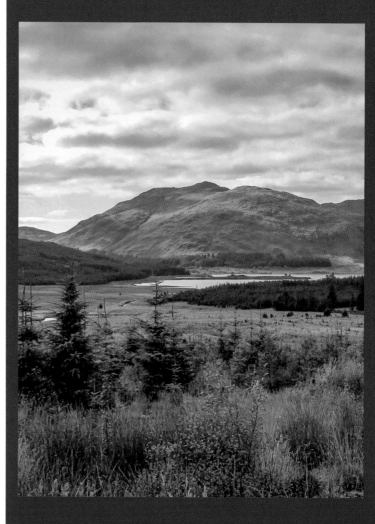

FUEL SUPPLY Fallen wood in the surrounding plantations.

KEY ATTRACTIONS Great walking country with 2 other long-distance paths running close by – the Romans and Reivers Route, and the Annandale Way. Moffat is a lively Borders town with a museum, theatre and art galleries. It has a distinctive wide thoroughfare where sheep and cattle were once herded, as well as many independent local shops and good pubs.

PUBLIC TRANSPORT No direct link. Nearest bus route Stagecoach service X74 Glasgow–Moffat–Dumfries, stops at Beattock.

SPECIAL NOTES Open throughout the year. No vehicles beyond public road end at Cloffin Cottage (NT 046 066). Please ask at the cottage before parking.

BRATTLEBURN

Superior and easily accessible on the Southern Upland Way (1984)

SIZE Medium; sleeping platform for 2, plus attic space
LOCATION LAT/LONG 55.3464, -3.5537, NT 016 069, 275m, LR Map 78

Discreetly located in the Greskine Forest, Brattleburn offers a warm welcome to weary travellers on the Southern Upland Way (SUW), as well as a perfect spot for a weekend getaway. Historically, the upper Annandale Valley, was strategically important, controlling access N, and S to the English border. The route of a Roman road can be traced right through the region and you will see the outlines of forts, castles and tower houses dotted through the glen. A *bailey* and *motte* lies close to Holmshaw on the walk in, and there is a fort on top of Beattock Hill. Homesteads local to the bothy date back to the time of the Border *reivers* (raiders), who held sway in the region from the late 13th century until the Scottish union with England in 1603.

The bothy is an old shepherd's cottage and there is an authentic feel to the interior, which has many homely touches. There are 2 bright, whitewashed downstairs rooms, and a large open sleeping space in the attic, accessed by a wooden ladder. The LHR, the main communal area, has a stove, comfortable chairs, tables, and a narrow sleeping platform in a recess. The sparser RHR, where the fireplace has been bricked up, provides useful overflow space.

ROUTE 1

From Cloffin Cottage (NT 046 066), head up the track along the burn, turning R at a junction, past a quarry and onto Mosshope. The stream has to be forded twice before you cross over the SUW (NT 019 072), and the bothy comes into view soon after. Easy to mountain bike.

> **DISTANCE** 2 miles
> **TIME** 45 minutes maximum
> **TERRAIN** Easy. Track, path for last 500 yds. 2 fording points
> **PARKING** Middlegill (NT 046 066)

ROUTE 2

From the car park, take the signposted SUW through the forest plantation, passing close to Holmshaw Farm. Leaving the trees to cross Garpol Water by a footbridge you return to the forest,

passing the crossroads down to Rivox. After a steep walk up Craig Hill you descend into the glen, then just before the SUW crosses the Cloffin Burn, turn L along a small clearly defined path. There is even a sign to the bothy.

> **DISTANCE** 4 miles
> **TIME** 1½ to 2 hours
> **TERRAIN** Easy. SUW until last 500 yds
> **PARKING** Easter Earshaig (NT 050 024)

ROUTE 3

Park under the dam, take the SUW signposted path above the dam and climb up Sweetshaw Brae. Swing S over Hods Hill and Beld Knowe, following the Greskine Forest boundary fence. Continue down through a boggy gap in the trees, following a gas pipeline, before turning R at a crossroads just before Cloffin Burn. The bothy is signposted to the L.

> **DISTANCE** 4½ miles
> **TIME** 2 to 2½ hours
> **TERRAIN** Easy. SUW until last 500 yds
> **PARKING** Daer Reservoir (NS 972 096)

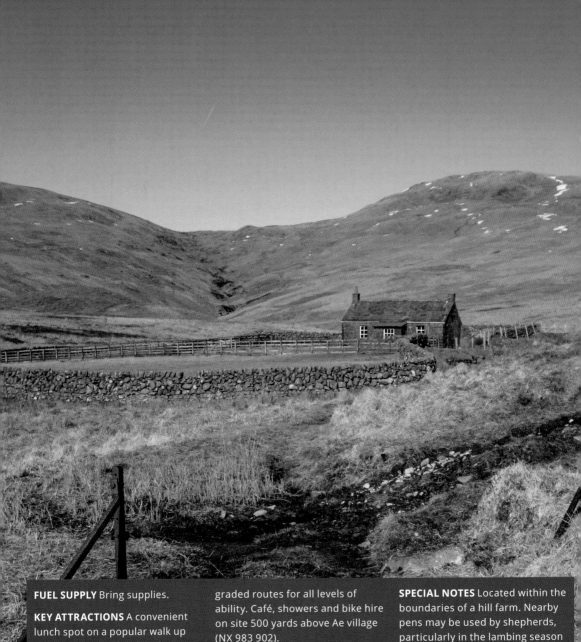

FUEL SUPPLY Bring supplies.

KEY ATTRACTIONS A convenient lunch spot on a popular walk up the fine Donald of Queensberry (697m), the highest point in the area. The Forest of Ae is one of the hubs for the 7Stanes mountain biking network, a nationally renowned facility providing graded routes for all levels of ability. Café, showers and bike hire on site 500 yards above Ae village (NX 983 902).

PUBLIC TRANSPORT No direct link. Nearest bus route Stagecoach service X74 from Moffat to Dumfries, stops at Beattock.

SPECIAL NOTES Located within the boundaries of a hill farm. Nearby pens may be used by shepherds, particularly in the lambing season from April to mid-May. Keep dogs under close control at all times. Easy to mountain bike.

BURLEYWHAG

Snug bothy on a working hill farm (1979)

SIZE Small; 2 rooms, 1 with a platform sleeping 2
LOCATION LAT/LONG 55.2842, -3.6216, NS 971 001, 360m, LR Map 78

Overlooked by a round of gently sculptured hills in a rather neglected corner of Dumfriesshire, E of the sprawling expanse of conifers that make up the Forest of Ae, Burleywhag is a working bothy maintained by the sheep farm at Mitchellslacks, part of the Duke of Buccleuch's huge Queensbury Estate. A network of sheep pens extend to both the front and back of the building, enclosed by a low stone boundary wall, and livestock roam freely in the surrounding sheep walk. Locations in the open hills around the farm were used in the 1978 film adaptation of John Buchan's classic novel *The Thirty Nine Steps*, and it is easy to imagine the stiff-upper-lipped hero, Richard Hannay (played by Robert Powell) on the run, tramping across the moors and spying the cottage as a place where he can escape from his relentless pursuers. Although the Southern Upland Way (SUW) is just 2 miles away, Burleywhag receives far fewer visitors than its neighbour, Brattleburn

(p239). However, the bothy still has a reputation as a place for weekend revelry, and has held its fair share of New Year celebrations and Burn's Night suppers.

The cottage is a typical *but and ben*, consisting of 2 compact rooms accessed from a small vestibule. The LHR has a small but efficient stove, wood-panelled walls, a table and a couple of benches. Off this is a snug partitioned sleeping area for 2 with a raised floor. The RHR is used by the estate to store farming equipment. The roof was replaced in the spring of 2016 and the interior has been spruced up.

ROUTE 1

Take the winding single-track road from the small Dumfries village of Thornhill to the farm at Mitchellslacks. There is space for a couple of cars close to the farm access road, besides a Scottish Rights of Way signpost to Branrig and Beattock (NX 964 961). Head down from the signpost to a bridge that crosses Capel Water and

follow the track up to Mitchellslacks. Turn L through the farm buildings and then climb steadily up into the glen following a track that runs along the valley side following the course of the Capel Burn. The track turns into a muddy path for the final mile, just after passing 2 farm properties that are in a clear state of disrepair. Very soon, the boundary wall and the bothy come into view.

DISTANCE 2½ miles
TIME 45 minutes to 1 hour
TERRAIN Easy. Track all the way
PARKING Farm layby (NX 964 961) close to Mitchellslacks

CLENNOCH

Small, homely bothy, well cared for by dedicated volunteers (1975)

SIZE Small; single room with sleeping platforms for 6
LOCATION LAT/LONG 55.2756, -4.2005, NS 603 002, 416m, LR Map 77

Tucked away in a hollow behind Cairnsmore of Carsphairn, on the outer reaches of the Glenkens Hills in Dumfrieshire, Clennoch is a real gem. And its charm comes as a pleasant surprise, given the reputation of the neighbouring bothies in the Galloway Forest Park. What sets it apart is the care invested in the building by the 'Friends of Clennoch', who have not only kept the bothy spick and span but turned it into a little haven. Happy times spent here are celebrated in past bothy books, which have been laminated and left for posterity, along with a potted history of the steading. Birdfeeders in the trees close to the bothy attract various native species, there are communal binoculars for spotting local birdlife, plus a handy identification poster. Other personal touches include the planting of daffodil bulbs just beyond the boundary wall, and there is even a push lawn mower. The encroachment of the forestry plantations and the presence of the wind turbines have inevitably lessened its charm, but it is still very much worth a visit.

The bothy was once part of one of the most remote sheep farms in southern Scotland. Dane Love, a member of the first MBA work party, interviewed Thomas Murray, the last tenant at the farm. His first-hand account of the difficulties of sustaining a living here were transcribed and put on a display board in the bothy, along with photocopies of 19th-century census details. In one memorable anecdote about an exceptionally bad winter when the roads were blocked and no provisions could be transported to nearby Carsphairn, Murray describes how the villagers walked up to Clennoch to buy essentials when their food ran out. They knew the farm would be well supplied, since the family never ventured far during the winter months. The farmstead was finally vacated in the 1930s, and the building lay empty for 40 years before it was adopted by the MBA. Over that time, forestry has covered the grazing land and on the adjoining hill, appropriately called Windy Standard, wind turbines have been erected.

The farmstead, originally a typical *but and ben* with an attic, was in a ruinous state by the time the MBA stepped in, and the bothy was rebuilt on just a small section of the original foundations. In its single whitewashed room, accessed through a generous porch, there are bunk-beds stacked along 2 of the walls, a small table and some chairs. At a pinch there is probably space for 6 people though it is rarely full, principally because there is no stove. Although this has probably spared the bothy unwanted attention, the interior gets very cold in the winter months. Typically visitors just go for the day, combining a refreshment stop with a walk over Cairnsmore or Moorbrock Hill.

A short wander up the hillside of Dugland, a few hundred yards N of the bothy, brings you to a small stone (NS 605 005) with a memorial plaque commemorating a World War II plane crash. 'Blue Peter', a spitfire named after a Derby winner, came down in the glen and lay undisturbed for decades before the children's TV programme Blue Peter took an interest in the story. Filmed by the BBC, the local aviation society searched the area and eventually found the wreckage. The inscription on the plaque reads: 'Near this spot on 23rd May 1942 Pilot Officer David Hunter-Blair aged 19, a Scot from Ayrshire, was mortally wounded after parachuting from Spitfire MkV AD540 "Blue Peter". He died that others may live. Lest we forget. 1993.'

ROUTE 1

Approaching from the S, park on the verge by the house at Craigengillan then follow the track that runs alongside the Polifferie Burn. When it swings L into the conifer plantation, continue straight on over an old bridge and along an overgrown path that brings you to Moorbrock Farm. Once through the farm, turn sharp L onto a track that heads steeply uphill before turning 90 degrees L and contouring round Green Hill. At the next junction turn L to follow a recently constructed forestry road that passes by the bothy. The previous rough path for the final ½ mile was not even marked on old versions of the 1:50,000 map.

> **DISTANCE** 4½ miles
>
> **TIME** 2 to 2½ hours
>
> **TERRAIN** Easy. Vehicle track all the way
>
> **PARKING** Roadside verge by Craigengillan (NX 636 948)

ROUTE 2

From the Glen Afton side, the route is more of a hike. Park at the end of the reservoir road and follow the track a short way before taking a waymarked path to the R and heading up to the distinctive rocky outcrop known as Castle William. It is named after the infamous William Wallace who, along with Robert the Bruce, sought refuge in this glen during the first Wars of Scottish Independence in the late 13th and early 14th centuries. Here you join a track that has contoured round the hillside from Craigdarroch Farm (an optional starting point of the route). Turn L onto the track and take the R fork at the next junction, climbing steadily up towards Black Hill, before striking S along an ATV track which runs along a boundary fence up

to Lamb Hill, and on to Wedder Hill, Millaneoch Hill and the wind farm on Windy Standard. On the shoulder of the final hill, pick up a new access road which heads down past a distinctive rock called the Devil's Putting Stone before contouring L round to Hog Hill and down towards the Clennoch Burn. Take the obvious final L turn onto the plantation track and on to the bothy. These new tracks are marked on the 1:25000 map sheet no. 328 Sanquhar and New Cumnock.

> **DISTANCE** 4 miles
>
> **TIME** 2 to 2½ hours
>
> **TERRAIN** Straightforward. Track and ATV tracks up to the wind farm and down to bothy
>
> **PARKING** Just after Afton Filter Station (NS 627 054)

FUEL SUPPLY No stove or fireplace.

KEY ATTRACTIONS Cairnsmore of Carsphairn (797m) is a stand out Borders' Corbett with fine views over to Galloway. Take a leisurely walk round Afton Reservoir taking in the history of the glen, which Robbie Burns immortalised in his poem '*Flow Gently Sweet Afton*'.

PUBLIC TRANSPORT None.

SPECIAL NOTES Open throughout the year. Route 1 easy to mountain bike.

FUEL SUPPLY Plenty of timber in the surrounding wood.

KEY ATTRACTIONS Call into the long-established Tibetan Buddhist monastery of Samye Ling at Eskdalemuir for some tea and contemplation. For the more energetic, the mountain-biking loop, which takes in the bothy, starts and ends at the monastery.

PUBLIC TRANSPORT Scotrail train service from Edinburgh to Carlisle, stops at Lockerbie. Houston Coaches/McCalls Coaches service 124/112 Lockerbie–Eskmuirdale–Langholm stops at Boreland.

3 mile walk from here to the road end at Waterhead.

SPECIAL NOTES Open throughout the year. Please do not drive on forestry tracks unless by prior arrangement.

DRYFEHEAD

Charming old forest cottage tucked away in the Borders (2014)

SIZE Medium; 3 rooms each with a raised platform, sleeping 6
LOCATION LAT/LONG 55.2864, -3.3078, NY 170999, 310m, LR Map 79

Dryfehead lies in a small secluded dell on the western fringes of the Eskmuirdale Forest. Before the conifers brought dramatic change to the landscape, the area was steeped in a culture of sheep farming. Further up the valley Garrowgil and Craigbeck was once the largest in the sheepwalk country, and census records of tenant farmers from Dryfehead go back to the 1600s. When the cottage was first offered for renovation it was in a perilous state, but after more than 2 years of hard labour, the building has been brought back to life.

The bothy sits close to the confluence of two tumbling streams, overshadowed by sycamores, and has the luxury of its own grassy lawn. Inside there are 3 compact rooms, each with fixtures shoehorned into every available space. Pride of place in the LHR is a bespoke stove made out of an old gas cylinder. There are 2 single sleeping platforms, which double up as benches during daylight hours, and a built-in table beneath a window. In the RHR, where the original fireplace is intact, there is a 2-person, L-shaped sleeping platform, plus another under the window, as well as a freestanding bench and a couple of comfy chairs. A partition in the hallway has created space for a single platform bed beneath another window, with a small shelf to store possessions.

ROUTE 1

From the road end at Waterhead Farm, take the track leading off L at the last bend, signposted Dun Moss, and head steadily uphill. Go straight across the first junction and turn L at the second, as the track winds its way down along Dryfe Water to Finniegill Farm. Here the track deteriorates into a boggy path, which continues along the R bank before crossing a ford to the L bank. This can be an obstacle in times of spate. There are a couple more streams to cross before you see the bothy.

DISTANCE 4 miles
TIME 1½ to 2 hours
TERRAIN Straightforward. Forestry track, boggy path. River crossing
PARKING Roadside at Waterhead Farm (NY 188 942)

ROUTE 2

From Over Phawhope Bothy (p255) below the headwater of the Ettrick, take the SUW heading S from the bothy. Walk up through the conifers to Ettrick Head and, once over a stile, where a signpost welcomes you to Dumfries and Galloway, leave the path and head along the boundary fence up and over Loch Fell and down into the Dryfe Water valley. Pick up the forestry track between Cowan Fell and Dun Moss that heads L and continue downstream to the bothy.

DISTANCE 6 miles
TIME 2 to 2½ hours
TERRAIN Straightforward. Follows SUW, faint path and track to bothy
PARKING As for Over Phawhope Bothy (p255) (NT190093)

FUEL SUPPLY No stove or fireplace.

KEY ATTRACTIONS There is a sprinkling of Donalds and Corbetts to climb in the area, including White Coomb (821m), Molls Cleuch Dod (785m) and Cape Law (722m). Keen cyclists might like to try the testing route from Tweedsmuir to St. Mary's Loch, up a 15 degree slope. The Tibbie Shiels Inn, a popular weekend destination by the loch, is a good place for refreshment.

PUBLIC TRANSPORT No direct link. Nearest bus route: Stagecoach service 101/102 from Edinburgh to Moffat, stops at Tweedsmuir.

SPECIAL NOTES Open throughout the year. Located on a sheep farm and the adjacent pens may be used by shepherds, particularly in the lambing season from mid-April to end of May. Dogs must be kept under strict control at all times. Bothy is owned by the Borders Forest Trust who are responsible for various native tree planting initiatives in the region, including on the Talla and Gamehope Estate. Easy to mountain bike.

⏶ GAMESHOPE

Simple bothy in quiet glen (2005)

SIZE Small; platform beds sleeping 8
LOCATION LAT/LONG 55.4529, -3.3707, NT135 185, 419m, LR Map 79

Gameshope Bothy is located in a lonely, secluded glen that on the surface appears to be a timeless Borders backwater, but in the late 1700s this was one of a number of places associated with the field-preaching of the outlawed Presbyterian minister, Reverend Alexander Peden. A leading light in the Covenanter movement, Peden campaigned against the religious reforms imposed in Scotland by Charles II. Numerous stones in the region are called Peden's Pulpits, but the precise location of a nearby 'pulpit' has never been firmly established. Another preacher, Donald Cargill, was also connected to the valley and Donald's Cleuch, a hill close by, is said have been named after him. Gameshope Glen is also mentioned in James Hogg's writings. In the *The Bridal of Polmood (from Winter Evening Tales)*, the glen is the scene of an ambush. In the Victorian era, stone from the glen was used in the construction of the dams that formed the nearby Talla, Fruid and Megget reservoirs. These supplied Edinburgh's drinking water.

The original cottage, now a ruin next to the bothy, was built by a local stonemason in the last years of the 19th century for a tenant shepherd. The last permanent residents left in 1919. Constructed from the remains of a byre, the bothy is just one large room with a low ceiling. The distinctive cobbled floor, which was laid on the building's foundations, remains intact. Much of the space inside is taken up by 2 long platform bunk-beds, adorned with fading Tibetan prayer flags. These can accommodate up to 8 people lying head to toe. There are 2 sturdy tables, one with a shelf resting on the old ceramic insulators from an electricity pylon. A plaque on the wall commemorates the life of Andrew Jenson, who died on the Cuillin Ridge on Skye in 2002 and whose memorial fund assisted with the renovation. The major drawback of the bothy is the lack of a stove – this was stipulated by the estate as part of its agreement with the MBA. The evenings in this uninsulated stone bothy can get pretty cold so it is best to visit in warm weather or stop off on a day spent walking the hills.

ROUTE 1

Start just beyond the farm at Talla Linnfoots at the end of the reservoir. Follow the track as it climbs steadily into the glen, running close to the course of the Gameshope Burn, which narrows through a small ravine or *linn* before widening out again by the bothy. The easy-paced walk is complicated by the need to ford the stream just across from the bothy, which could be problematic when in spate. There is a depth gauge on the opposite bank so you can judge whether it is safe to cross. As a rough guide, when the level is up it registers as approximately 50cm, or just over a foot on the staff.

DISTANCE 1½ miles
TIME 30 to 45 minutes
TERRAIN Easy. Good track. Ford
PARKING Talla Linnfoots SE of Tweedsmuir (NT 134 202)

FUEL SUPPLY Plenty of wood in the surrounding woodland.

KEY ATTRACTIONS Visit the Telford Cairn built in 2007 to commemorate the 250th anniversary of the great engineer's birth. It overlooks the car park at the start of the walk in.

Stop off at Samye Ling Tibetan Buddhist monastery W of the bothy; the tea room is decorated in traditional Tibetan style.

PUBLIC TRANSPORT Scotrail train service from Edinburgh to Carlisle, stops at Lockerbie. Houston

Coaches/McCalls Coaches service 112/124 Lockerbie–Eskdalemuir–Langholm stops at Bentpath (6 mile walk to the road end).

SPECIAL NOTES Open throughout the year. Easy to mountain bike.

△
GREENSYKES

Out-of-the-way woodland retreat with a simple walk in (2011)

SIZE Medium; 3 rooms, 2 with raised platforms, sleeping 8
LOCATION LAT/LONG 55.2897, -3.0841, NT 312 000, 268m, LR Map 79

Concealed in a small clearing within the extensive Eskmuirdale forest, on the northern side of the picturesque Eskdale Valley, Greensykes is a great place to escape the relentless pace of the modern world for a while, much like its near neighbour the Samye Ling Tibetan monastery located just over the hill. Like so many remote outposts in the Borders, the bothy was originally a shepherd's cottage, and much of its history can be found in the local parish records. From the photocopied selection tucked into the bothy book, the earliest entry dated 1826 records the birth of Michael, son of James Anderson, and the youngest of 7 children. The family lived in the farmstead for more than 70 years, before the Jacksons and then the Pringles took over the shepherding duties, remaining until the 1940s. Jamestown, at the road end, was originally built to accommodate miners who worked periodically at Antimony mine in nearby Glenshanna until 1921-22.

There is also an information board and plaque commemorating the great civil engineer and surveyor Thomas Telford, who was born at Glendinning in 1757.

When the MBA began renovating Greensykes in 2011, it took a great deal of effort to get the cottage into a habitable state, including removing 2 outhouses as well as other add-ons made over the years. When work was complete, one local man visited and remembered living in the cottage with his grandfather until the age of 4. The inside of the bothy is fairly basic and consists of 3 rooms connected by a long corridor. The RHR is the main communal area, a large space that has an unfinished feel with OSB board, some exposed brickwork and a cement floor. However, there is an excellent stove, wide shelving on the back wall for kit storage and cooking, plus a new single-person raised platform along the back wall. The LHR has a more intimate feel, with a working fireplace and raised platforms along 2 recently lined walls sleeping 4. The central room is a dedicated dormitory, with a sleeping platform for 3 people.

ROUTE 1
From the small car park at the end of the single-track road from Westerkirk Mains, follow a well-maintained vehicle track up into the glen. When it splits, take the L fork that follows the W side of the river. After a gentle climb and the negotiation of a number of gates, you reach the edge of the forestry plantation, where there is a final, firmly locked gate. Once over this, the next 200 yd section is partly overgrown but then the track re-emerges at another junction. Take the track on the R, trending initially downhill to a clearing, where the bothy comes partially into view. It lies off the track towards the side of Meggat Water, which at this point is little more than a stream.

DISTANCE 2½ miles
TIME 1 to 1½ hours
TERRAIN Easy. Track all the way
PARKING By the farm at Jamestown (NY 299 969)

FUEL SUPPLY Bring supplies.

KEY ATTRACTIONS Picturesque Durisdeer has a fine parish church, Kirk of the Queensbury Estate, and you can also walk along the Well Path to the Roman Fortlet. Take a tour of Drumlanrig Castle, the spectacular home of the Duke of Buccleuch, the largest private landowner in the UK. Walking routes, an adventure playground and mountain bike trails within the Castle grounds.

PUBLIC TRANSPORT Stagecoach service 100/101 from Edinburgh to Dumfries, stops at Durisdeer.

SPECIAL NOTES Located within the boundary of a hill farm. The nearby pens may be used by shepherds, particularly in the lambing season from April to mid-May. Dogs must be kept under close control at all times. Easy to mountain bike.

KETTLETON BYRE

A cosy billet in the rolling Lowther Hills (1983)

SIZE Small; sleeping platform for 4 people
LOCATION Lat/Long 55.3006, -3.7156, NS 912 020, 356m, LR Map 78

Kettleton Byre is a wee shack squeezed into a steep notch above the sleepy hamlet of Durisdeer. It lies on the W side of the lonely Lowther Hills that overlook Nithsdale and Dumfries, at the watershed of Glenaggart and the Kettleton Burn. The simple, functional-looking building was much improved by a major MBA renovation in 2008, and also benefited from the demolition of an ugly bungalow close by a couple of years later. Originally there was a staircase leading to a loft but this was removed and the attic

blocked off. Renovations also included the addition of a compact inner porch, which considerably reduced the problem of draughts. From here, you enter a small cosy room, slightly cramped by an L-shaped sleeping platform, which can accommodate 4 people at a push. There is an armchair, a table and a couple of chairs, and taking pride of place below the single W-facing window, a sweet little stove which makes the place pretty snug if you are planning an overnight stay. Next door, the small locked storage space is used by the estate. Despite its new home comforts, most people just use the bothy as a convenient lunch spot before heading on to the surrounding hills, including local Donalds Scaw'd Law (663m) and Wedder Law (672m).

ROUTE 1

Parking at Durisdeer, walk back to the cemetery (NS 894 036) and take the track that leads up onto the moor. (Ignore a track that leads off L straight up the slope onto Blackgrain Shoulder, just after you cross the

bridge 500 yards from the road.) Follow the track as it heads into Glenaggart, continuing on across a small ford and up into the tightening slopes of the glen. After another ½ mile the track curves to the S and reaches the watershed. The bothy now comes into view on the R.

> **DISTANCE** 2 miles
> **TIME** 45 minutes to 1 hour
> **TERRAIN** Easy. Track all the way
> **PARKING** Village square, Durisdeer (NS 894 037)

FUEL SUPPLY Fallen timber in plantations; extra supplies easily carried in.

KEY ATTRACTIONS After reading his books, visit the James Hogg memorial in Ettrick churchyard. Stop at the Tushielaw Inn, an old coaching house on the banks of Ettrick Water, for fine food and a fireside drink.

PUBLIC TRANSPORT None. Stagecoach service X74 Glasgow–Moffat–Dumfries. From Moffat walk along the Southern Upland Way (SUW).

SPECIAL NOTES Open throughout the year. Located on a working sheep farm so keep dogs on a lead at all times. No vehicles beyond the end of the tarmac road up Ettrick Valley. Timber felling currently in progress near the bothy: please heed advisory signs. Easy to mountain bike.

OVER PHAWHOPE

MBA-owned bothy, recently lavished with attention (1982)

SIZE Medium; 3 rooms, 2 with raised platforms, sleeping 8
LOCATION LAT/LONG 55.3606, -3.2925, NT 182 082, 395m, LR Map 79

High in the upper reaches of Ettrick Water, at the end of a long winding glen, Over Phawhope is the only bothy actually owned by the MBA. Bequeathed by the late Harry Fairhurst, the organisation has embraced the opportunity to lavish attention on the property. The bothy now has a new roof, the 2 dormitories were upgraded, insulation added to the ceiling, and new pieces of furniture acquired for the living room. It is also hoped to plant native trees in the flats around the perimeter, perhaps compensating for the loss of the huge pine tree which was a defining feature of the bothy, deemed to be damaging the foundations and dispatched into the annals of history. The stump has been carved into a seat. The beautiful valley setting is matched by the fascinating history and connections of the area's past inhabitants. One Ettrick farmer, William Laidlaw, aka Will O'Phaup, was said to converse with the fairies. The Ettrick Valley is also the birthplace of Laidlaw's cousin, the 'Ettrick Shepherd' James Hogg. He was

a remarkable self-educated writer and poet, and a friend of Sir Walter Scott. In addition, *The View from Castle Rock* by Nobel Prize-winning Canadian author Alice Munro features stories about the Laidlaws, her distant relations. Celebrated 20th-century Scottish painter William Johnston also lived for a time at Potburn, the house just down the glen from the bothy.

The bothy has a welcoming, comfortable feel, and retains much of the cottage's original character. From the spacious porch and small hallway, you enter the communal living space on the L, where the ancient cast iron range, fronted by a woodburning stove, has a surround with 2 carved cherubs. The fire surround and woodwork is painted a bright, cheerful red. There is a plush 3-seater sofa and other seats, a table under a S-facing window, and a long breakfast bar. To the back is a newly wood-panelled dormitory with a large sleeping platform for 6 that even has curtains. A small room has been transformed

into a cosy wood-panelled retreat with a sleeping platform for a solo traveller – useful if the main room gets too boisterous. Down from the bothy there is a long outbuilding with a stone floor and platform that is occasionally used as an overflow shelter but is sometimes locked. Hopefully, the accessibility of the bothy by car will not lead to any abuses.

ROUTE 1
The bothy is a natural stopover on the SUW, but the simplest approach starts at the road end from Ettrick. With the bothy in view, walk down the forestry track that runs below the house at Potburn, past a small quarry and onto the bothy. The track has been significantly widened to allow access to the conifer plantations around the head of the valley, which are in the process of being felled.

DISTANCE 1 mile
TIME 30 minutes
TERRAIN Easy. Forest access road
PARKING End of track (NT190093)

FUEL SUPPLY Some dead timber; supplies easily carried in.

KEY ATTRACTIONS An excellent base to traverse the rugged summits of the Awful Hand; climb Corbetts Merrick (843m), and Shalloch on Minnoch (775m); a trip to the Donalds of Kirriereoch Hill (786m) and Tarfessock (697m) is also worthwhile. A shorter walk up the Donald Mullwharchar (692m) and on to lonely Loch Enoch is less taxing but equally rewarding. Excellent coffee shop in picturesque Straiton.

PUBLIC TRANSPORT No direct link. Scotrail train service from Glasgow Central to Stranraer, stops at Ayr and Maybole. SPT (Strathclyde Partnership for Transport) service 361 Dunure–Ayr–Maybole–Straiton.

SPECIAL NOTES Open throughout the year. Easy to mountain bike.

TUNSKEEN

The first MBA project (1965)

SIZE Small; single room with raised platforms, sleeping 6
LOCATION LAT/LONG 55.1841, -4.4758, NX 425 906, 324m, LR Map 77

Out in the northern periphery of the Galloway forestry, where the plantations end and the wild ice-scoured granite begins, lies a tough old shepherd's croft which has distinction of being the inspiration of the future MBA. In the summer of 1965, a number of hill-walkers and cyclists resurrected the crumbling building, which had lain empty since the 1930s. After a famous meeting of like-minded individuals in nearby Dalmellington Village Hall, the MBA was born. In its halcyon days in the 1960s, the bothy still had its original wood panelling, a number of comfortable chairs, and often a supply of food. Those days are long gone, and today the bothies of Dumfries and Galloway are at risk of being closed down because of vandalism and errant behaviour. Tunskeen remains open, though it is best to be a little wary if you are planning an overnight visit.

The shelter is a single functional room with a low ceiling, a concrete floor and a new stove. A double bunk-bed sleeping platform takes up one wall, and there is another single-berth platform – together comfortably sleeping 6 people. The bothy is a bit rough and ready, and you may find rubbish left behind by thoughtless visitors. You will also notice that a strand of wire has been fixed along all the obviously burnable bits of the building, to stop them being chopped up and fed to the fire. Fortunately, a destructive attitude is the exception rather than the rule, and Tunskeen is still a popular destination. It also receives many lunchtime visitors out for a day's walking.

ROUTE 1

From Ballochbeatties (S of Straiton and by Loch Bradan) follow the forest drive for a mile or so before parking at a junction (NX 428 944), where there is a sign to the bothy, or at an official parking bay 500 yds further on by Loch Riecawr (NX 434 941). From the junction, pass through the forestry gate and follow the track S, to Loch Slochy and the shieling at Slaethornrig. Before the loch, a small path heads into the woods to a large rocking stone, deposited at the end of the last Ice Age. It no longer rocks but is a bizarre sight and worth a detour. The location is marked on the 1:50,000 OS map (NX 422 928). Just beyond Slaethornrig where the track forks, bear R and continue S parallel to the forestry boundary fence until the bothy comes into view.

DISTANCE 4 miles
TIME 1½ to 2 hours
TERRAIN Easy. Track all the way
PARKING Loch Riecawr (NX 434 941)

WHITE LAGGAN

Popular Galloway bothy on the Southern Upland Way (1973)

SIZE Medium; 2 rooms both with raised platforms sleeping 6
LOCATION LAT/LONG 55.0679, -4.4034, NX 466 775, 264m, LR Map 77

Instantly recognisable by the large Saltire (Scottish flag) painted on its north gable end, White Laggan bothy stands proudly on the S flank of the mysterious and neglected Galloway hills, a granite land scraped clean in unsentimental fashion by successions of ice sheets. The bothy was home to a tenant shepherd in the early 19th century, and later served as the workplace and sleeping quarters of staff catering for shooting and fishing parties organised by the Kirroughtree Estate. Guests stayed in a pre-fabricated lodge built in front of the cottage, though this was eventually removed and the present building adapted to accommodate both guests and servants. The rebuild of the tumbledown byre was the fourth and – at that time – the most ambitious MBA project, and it took 20 work parties over 2 years to get White Laggan into a habitable state. In those days before the MBA organised helicopter uplifts, most of the materials were carried in on foot, initially from Craigencallie, before the Forestry Commission pushed the track through to Glen Trool. The opening ceremony was conducted by Sir Robert Grieve, a University of Glasgow professor and former chairman of the Highlands and Islands Development Board. He remarked that, as a youth, he had visited every bothy within a half-crown bus ride of Glasgow, sleeping in barns, behind dykes and under hedges when no other accommodation was available. He judged that White Laggan merited a 5-star rating. Reading working party reports in old MBA newsletters, the rebuild of White Laggan stands out for its clear illustration of the commitment, team spirit and camaraderie that was fostered within the organisation.

Once through the bothy's bright-red front door, there are 3 rooms accessed in sequence. The first room is a sleeping area with platform beds along 2 walls and a small table tucked into the remaining space. A second door leads into the main communal area, again with 2 platform beds, and also a small Dowling stove set within a large fireplace. Inglenooks on either side of the hearth provide additional seating. A small conservatory-like structure extending out from the E wall is used as a kitchen, and a long work surface sits below a big window that frames the lovely view across the glen. Large windows in the other two rooms also help to brighten the bothy; and the place is generally well cared for. Just across from the main entrance there is a corrugated-iron shed, used as a wood store.

Within the Borders region, White Laggan is one of the best-known bothies, and can get quite busy. However, there is enough space to squeeze in several bodies, and the stove provides a welcome focal point. The monotony of the endless conifer plantations does feel oppressive at times, but the area still retains a wilderness feel, especially when you head into the rugged surrounds of Loch Enoch. The bothy is a natural stopping-off point on the Southern Upland Way (SUW), and there is a small area of flat ground outside if you choose to camp.

The bothy is located 500 yds above a wide, unmetalled forestry access route that runs through the S section of the Galloway Forest Park from Loch Trool to Craigencallie House, close to small, picturesque Loch Dee. This route is not only part of the SUW but also an off-road section of the Sustrans National Cycle Network Route 7, and is extremely well signposted. The walk in from Glen Trool is a little more scenic but takes longer and involves a steady amount of climbing. Loch Trool is a popular local beauty spot, and the initial section of track passes through a lovely ribbon of birch and oak woodland along the banks of Glenhead Burn.

ROUTE 1

From a layby just beyond the Outdoor Centre at Craigencallie, head N and then W, contouring round the hillside before reaching a junction, where a track leads down to a bridge over the River Dee (and on to Backhill of Bush Bothy p235). Ignore this and go straight on through the forestry, passing close to Loch Dee. The bothy soon comes into view on the L, 500 yds up a boggy path.

> **DISTANCE** 3 miles
>
> **TIME** 1 to 1½ hours
>
> **TERRAIN** Easy. Forestry access road, then path for last 500 yds
>
> **PARKING** Craigencallie Outdoor Centre (NX 503 780)

ROUTE 2

Start from the Bruce's Stone car park at the E end of Loch Trool, where the road ends. The stone commemorates Robert the Bruce's victory at the Steps of Trool in 1307, the initial skirmish of the War of Independence. From here, follow the track as it rounds the head of Loch Trool to Glenhead Farm, where the route of the SUW crosses the track and heads up the N side of the glen. This is an alternative route to the bothy but a little longer and more undulating. Ignoring this alternative, descend to a bridge crossing Glenhead Burn before climbing up to the narrow upper reaches of the valley. Ignore 2 tracks entering from the R and persevere. Soon, the SUW joins the track, which levels off, and Loch Dee comes into view. Just before the loch you pass a smooth stone with runes carved into it. This is the Glentrool Stane, which marks the cycle route that is part of the 7stane network of bike tracks located across the Borders. Soon after, the track turns to the S and the bothy comes into view on the R, 500 yds up a boggy path.

> **DISTANCE** 4 miles
>
> **TIME** 1½ to 2 hours
>
> **TERRAIN** Easy. Forestry access road, then path for last 500 yds
>
> **PARKING** Loch Trool (NX416 803)

FUEL SUPPLY Some wood in plantation; best to bring supplies.

KEY ATTRACTIONS The Donalds, Millfore (657m) and Curleywee (674m), plus Lamachan Hill (717m) and Larg Hill, (676m) lie to the S while Merrick (843m), Craignaw (645m) and Dungeon Hill (620m) are to the N. Take the opportunity to stargaze in Britain's first designated Dark Sky Park. Galloway Forest Park Visitors' Centre, just beyond Glentrool Village, has a café and interpretation boards.

PUBLIC TRANSPORT Scotrail train service from Glasgow Central to Stranraer, stops at Barrhill. Local bus service 359 run by Kings of Kircowan, Newton Stewart to Girvan, stops at Barrhill and Glentrool Village.

SPECIAL NOTES Open throughout the year.

Through an initiative by the Forestry Commission, Galloway Forest Park was designated as the UK's first Dark Sky Park. Scotland has some of the darkest skies in Europe and so few people live within the 75,000 hectares managed by the estate that on inky-black, cloud-free nights, this really is a brilliant place to enjoy the stars.

FUEL SUPPLY Fallen timber in the surrounding plantation.

KEY ATTRACTIONS Visit the nearby old railway village of Riccarton Junction which evokes the bygone era of steam.

PUBLIC TRANSPORT Telford's Coaches Ltd service 128 runs from Hawick to Newcastleton stopping at Whitrope Tunnel.

SPECIAL NOTES Open throughout the year. Easy to mountain bike.

WILL'S BOTHY, LEYBURNSFOOT

Bothy near a deserted railway village (1994)

SIZE Large; although no sleeping platforms
LOCATION LAT/LONG 55.2712, -2.7313, 250m, LR Map 79/80, NY 536 978

Once thought of as one of the best bothies in S Scotland, Leysburnfoot – renamed Will's Bothy in 1994 – has been subject to ongoing abuse and at the time of writing is at risk of closure. Set in woodland just down from the old Borders railway line from Edinburgh to Carlisle, the bothy lies close to Riccarton Junction. Here, there was once a thriving community with over a hundred residents, a school, grocery store and police station. The bothy was restored and renamed by the friends of Will Ramsbotham, an athlete and mountaineer who died in a climbing accident in 1993. There are 2 large rooms, one with the original range, a number of comfortable sofas, shelving and a large dining table. There is a plumbed toilet in a separate room at the E gable end, and an open wood-sawing area at the W gable end.

In 2004 a group of enthusiasts attempted a major restoration of the station at Riccarton Junction and used the bothy as a base. With its location now more widely known, difficulties arose and by 2009 the MBA decided to hand over control to the Friends of Will's Bothy, but they, too, were unable to continue maintenance. Continuing reports of errant behaviour and rubbish mean the bothy's fate is now in the hands of the Forestry Commission. Although a pleasant backwater, you should be cautious about staying over.

ROUTE 1

Park just N of the Heritage Centre at Whitrope Tunnel (on the B6399 from Hawick). It is also is possible to drive ½ mile along the track to the locked gate. From here follow the old railway track over an embankment and through a cutting until you see a gate on the L. Go through and down towards the bank of the Leys Burn. After 200 yds you see the bothy through the trees.

DISTANCE 2 miles
TIME 45 minutes to 1 hour
TERRAIN Easy. Old railway line, path
PARKING Heritage Centre at Signalbox Cottage (NT 526 003)

The current status of 3 other former MBA properties is also worth clarifying:

BURNS
LAT/LONG 55.3467, -2.5548,
NT 649 060, LR Map 79,80

This bothy in Wauchope Forest plantation has become increasingly dilapidated since the MBA relinquished responsibility for its upkeep in the last decade. A sign indicates it is now closed.

MINCH MOOR
LAT/LONG 55.5919, -3.0221,
NT 356 336, LR Map 73

Minch Moor log cabin on the Southern Upland Way was demolished in 2015 because serious rot was discovered, making the building unsafe.

SHIEL OF CASTLEMADDY
LAT/LONG 55.1834, -4.2957,
NX 539 901, LR Map 77

This old shepherd's cottage had been maintained by the MBA since 1974. It was demolished in 2011 after persistent abuse. A sad loss.

ISLANDS

FUEL SUPPLY Peat supplies until end of September.

KEY ATTRACTIONS The traverse of Beinn Bhreac, Sgorr nam Faoileann (429m) and Glas Beinn (472m) makes a fine day out or tour the world-renowned Islay whisky distilleries.

PUBLIC TRANSPORT Citylink bus from Glasgow to Kennacraig twice a day timed to meet the Calmac Ferry from Kennacraig to Port Askaig/Port Ellen. Islay Coaches service 450/451 Port Ellon–Bowmore–Port Askaig (except Sundays).

SPECIAL NOTES Open all year round. Stalking season runs from 20 September to 20 October. Contact Dunlossit Estate (01496 840 232) if planning a visit. Water supply: nearest stream is 300 yards S along the shore. Small bothy: be prepared to camp.

AN CLADACH, ISLAY

A shoreline haven by the Sound of Islay (1999)

SIZE Very small; single room with 2 bunk-beds, sleeping 4
LOCATION LAT/LONG 55.7855, -6.0853, NR 439 623, 2m, LR Map 60, Explorer 353

An Cladach is one of the sweetest bothies you could ever wish to visit. Perched almost within touching distance of the shore S of Rubh' a' Chladiach, 'the Point of the Stony Beach', on the east coast of Islay, it offers splendid views of Jura and the Kintyre peninsula. According to local folklore, the last inhabitant of the bothy was Baldy Cladach, who ran an illicit still and was eventually transported to Canada in the 1850s. The croft remained derelict until it was rebuilt by the MBA with the support of the Dunlossit Estate in 1999, which was made possible by a bequest from the Chadwick family, in memory of their son Mike who died in a climbing accident in Glencoe in 1998. A new building was fashioned using one of the original gable ends and a chimney was added to the back wall. Inside, there are 2 sturdy bunk beds, a work surface, shelving (with a small library), seating and a fireplace. The cosy shelter also boasts kitchenware, board games, a fishing rod, even a pair of binoculars. The leeward coast of Islay is surprisingly untouched, and you may see otters on the beach. Oystercatchers, terns and gulls patrol the shore, while golden eagles and buzzards soar in the remote glens. The ferry passes twice a day and the lights of habitation across the sound mediate any feeling of complete remoteness. Any visit here always seems too short.

ROUTE 1

From the small layby you can either plough through the heather and peat bogs into Glen Logan, or head down to the smallholding at Storakaig and pick up a faint ATV track, which winds along the fringes of the open bog. Aim for the ruin at Goirtean an Uruisge by Coire Sgiathach (NR 419 624) where the ATV track is more obvious down to the coast. Aim to reach the outflow of the Lùb Gleann Logain (NR 436 629) to avoid cliffs, then continue along the rocky shore. Some scrambling is required at high tide or in stormy weather. Once round Rubh' á Chladaich the bothy soon comes into view.

DISTANCE 2½ miles
TIME 1½ to 2 hours
TERRAIN Challenging. Open moor and faint trails to coast. Shore-side path difficult at high tide
PARKING Layby at the turn to Storakaig (NR 401 625)

ROUTE 2

From Lossit Farm take the track that winds down to the shore at Tràigh Bhàn, then head S along the coast following a faint path to the burn, Abhainn Gleann Logain. This may be impassable at Lùb Gleann Logain when in spate, so you may have to make your way back upstream and find somewhere to cross safely. Once over, pick your way along the rocky shore as described in Route 1.

DISTANCE 3½ miles
TIME 2 to 2½ hours
TERRAIN Straightforward. Track and faint shore-side path. River crossing. Final section difficult at high tide
PARKING Lossit Farm (NR 413 655)

FUEL SUPPLY Bring your own supplies.

KEY ATTRACTIONS The Old Man of Hoy, a 137m sea-stack seen from the ferry from Scrabster, but much more impressive close up, is a must. Cra'as (Crow's) Nest Museum and the Dwarfie Stane, a Neolithic tomb, are also worth visiting. Beneth'ill café, just before the pier, is very good.

PUBLIC TRANSPORT Scotrail Highland line from Inverness to Thurso. Bus from Thurso to Scrabster, then 2 miles to Northern Line ferry to Stromness. Passenger ferry from Stromness to Moaness Pier on Hoy leaves every morning, returning in the evening. On Hoy, minibus to Rackwick Bay Hostel co-ordinates with the ferry. Vehicle ferry from Houton to Lyness.

SPECIAL NOTES Open all year. Bothy provided by the Hoy Community Trust with honesty box for donations. Boil water from tap or stream. Rackwick Outdoor Hostel (April to September) has 2 rooms with bunk-beds plus washing and drying facilities. Simple cycle along the road from Moaness to Rackwick.

BURNMOUTH COTTAGE, HOY

Stunning beachside bothy you won't want to leave

SIZE Medium; 2 rooms, one with raised stone platform sleeping 6
LOCATION LAT/LONG 58.8685, -3.3808, ND 205 987, 5m, LR Map 7

Orkney starts seducing you as soon as you step onto the pier at Stromness, but its soulful serenade begins in earnest once you land on Hoy. On this island of towering sandstone cliffs, rolling peaty moorland, and one showstopper of a bay, Burnmouth Bothy is the icing on the cake – a fairytale stone cottage with a heather-thatched roof right above the shore. Outside, a drystone wall encloses the front lawn, creating a campsite for up to a dozen tents.

The Orkney archipelago was settled by the Vikings in the 13th century, and elements of their language and culture remain. Hoy, for example, is 'high' in Old Norse, and Rackwick, means 'rock bay'. The fertile pastureland supported a scattered crofting way of life, as preserved in the remarkable Cra'as Nest Museum. The main attraction is the Old Man, an impressive red sandstone sea-stack teetering on a black basalt base, first climbed by Chris Bonington in 1966. The bothy sees a steady stream of

climbers, psyching themselves for the ascent, returning in quiet ecstasy and reliving their exploits.

The bothy consists of an elongated communal room, with a separate store, toilet and plumbed-in sink at the N gable end. There are raised stone sleeping platforms running the length of both walls, which double up as seating, a stove at one end and a large dining table and twin benches at the other. A couple of comfortable armchairs are set in front of the hearth, and the W-facing windows bring light into what would otherwise be quite a gloomy interior. Clothing lines adorned with paper lanterns add a cheery touch, but with exposed stone walls and a concrete floor, it can be chilly at night if the stove is not lit.

ROUTE 1

From the car park at Rackwick, the bothy is already in view. A track on the L leads off to the cottage, becoming a grassy path for the final stretch.

DISTANCE 500 yards
TIME 10 minutes
TERRAIN Easy. Path across field
PARKING Rackwick (ND 202 993)

ROUTE 2

From the pier, head up the B9047 through the houses. As the road turns 90 degrees L towards Lyness, continue straight on to the next sharp bend 500 yds later, where you pick up a signposted path to Rackwick Bay. Contour round and down into Rackwick, where the path rejoins the single-track road from Moaness. Ignore the turning to Rackwick Hostel and make your way down to the end of the road, with the bothy in view, then continue as for Route 1.

DISTANCE 4 miles
TIME 1½ to 2 Hours
TERRAIN Straightforward. Metalled road, track and signposted path
PARKING Moaness pier (HY 245 039)

FUEL SUPPLY Peat cutting just above the bothy.

KEY ATTRACTIONS Discover secret caves and raised beaches along the coast. Wonderful wild swimming in waterfall plunge pool on burn above plantation. Jura whisky distillery offers tours.

PUBLIC TRANSPORT Citylink bus service 926 from Glasgow to Lochgilphead and Kennacraig connects with Calmac Ferry from Kennacraig to Port Askaig on Islay. Regular service on to Feolin Ferry. Garelochhead Coaches (01436 810200) run bus services Monday to Friday from Feolin Ferry to Craighouse, Lagg and Inverlussa. Alternatively, Jura passenger ferry from Tayvallich to Craighouse runs from Easter to September.

Advance booking only (07768 450000). West Coast Motors service 426 from Lochgilphead to Tayvalluch.

SPECIAL NOTES Open throughout the year. Deer stalking between July and February. Call Ruantallain Estate (01496 820287). Campsite outside Craighouse Hotel.

CRUIB LODGE, JURA

One of the finest and most unforgettable bothy experiences (2012)

SIZE Medium; 2 rooms with sleeping platforms for 5 people
LOCATION LAT/LONG 55.9770, -5.9015, NR 566 829, 2m, LR Map 61, Explorer 355

Sitting above the tideline in one of Loch Tarbert's numerous hidden coves, Cruib Lodge is a very welcome outpost on this particularly wild and rugged stretch of coast. The bothy was a well-established open shelter sorely in need of an upgrade when the MBA took it on in 2012. The original lodge was a summer house set a few hundred metres N of the bothy. This was a timber folly on stilts shipped over from America which attracted Victorian tourists, who arrived by steam yacht from the Clyde.

The bothy served as accommodation for the estate's stalker and pony man, the stables, as well as a larder where deer carcasses and game birds were hung. The middle room was the living quarters, with the stables to the E and the meat store to the W. The central room remains the bothy's communal space. It has a well-drawing hearth, long library shelf and even an oil painting above the mantelpiece. In the far corner is a generous single-person sleeping platform. The light and airy W wing has a fireplace and a sleeping platform for 4 running the length of 2 walls. The stables are locked and used by the estate for storage.

ROUTE 1

From the layby, follow a track with a line of white-painted stones down to the mudflats at the head of the loch. At low tide it is possible to walk straight across to the far shore. The alternative is to cross the Abhainn Ghlean Aoistail (NR 598 842) via stepping stones, close to a weir marked on the 1:25,000 OS map, and round the head of the loch. From here, walk to the end of the woodland fence, and climb steeply to the top of the slope. One recommended route is to head WNW across the undulations to the N end of Loch na Pearaich, 'Parrot Loch', and make your way down to Sàilean nam Màireach cove, and from there continue round the coast. Alternatively head more directly W, staying on high ground, especially in wet weather when you are well advised to tackle the numerous water crossings as far upstream as possible.

Set your route to aim for the patch of deciduous woodland planted above the bothy, which is visible from the top of the first line of hills. Once across the Abhainn a' Ghlean Duirch either head down to the salt marsh at Learadail and pick up a faint track round the shoreline, or strike uphill to an ATV track that leads down to the trees. The bothy is hidden between the water and a low grass cliff and does not come into view until the very last moment.

DISTANCE 4 miles

TIME 2 to 3 hours

TERRAIN Very tough. Marked path to head of Loch Tarbert, then no recognised route across to the bothy. Follows intermittent deer and ATV tracks. River crossings. Difficult navigation

PARKING Layby just beyond Tarbert on A846 (NR 605 828)

FUEL SUPPLY Bring supplies.

KEY ATTRACTIONS The Rùm Cuillin ridge walk takes in Ainshval (781m) Trollabhal (702m) and Askival (812m) – 2 Corbetts and a Graham. Kinloch Castle offers tours.

PUBLIC TRANSPORT Scotrail West Highland Line from Glasgow Queen St. to Mallaig. Citylink Coach service 915/916 Glasgow–Fort William; daily bus from Fort William to Mallaig (Shiel Buses 01397 700 700). Train and bus co-ordinate with Calmac Ferry to Eigg, Muck, Canna and Rùm. Fiendishly complicated timetable. 5 sailings to Rùm a week in summer.

SPECIAL NOTE Open all year. Stalking activities are displayed in Kinloch, or contact the Reserve (01687 462026). Avoid the potentially dangerous fissure 100m from the bothy, closer to the coast.

DIBIDIL, RÙM

Amazing location between mountains and sea (1970)

SIZE Medium; 2 rooms, both with sleeping platforms
LOCATION LAT/LONG 56.9522, -6.2891, NM 393 927, 29m, LR Map 39

Rounding the steep S slope of Beinn nan Stac, where the path is alarmingly close to the cliff edge, a fabulous view opens up of the craggy volcanic caps of Ainshval, and Trollabhal, with the Rùm Cuillin beyond, where Dibidil bothy is a tiny speck in the shadow of the peaks, looking out across the sound to Eigg and Muck. Its setting is breathtaking, an irresistible combination of mountains and sea. Dibidil derives from the Norse for 'deep valley', and the cottage was built in 1848 to house a shepherd and his family when sheep were introduced after the Clearances, and most of the population were forced to emigrate to Nova Scotia. Originally the dwelling had 3 rooms, with a cellar, ash pit and a privy at the back. It was occupied for just 40 years before the island was turned into a sporting estate. Subsequently Rùm became the private retreat of the Bullough Family, who built Kinloch Castle in 1902.

The building was rescued from ruin by the MBA in 1968 and the renovation was challenging: many of the materials were brought in by boat in difficult weather conditions. Irvine Butterfield, author of the classic Munro reference book *The High Mountains* was part of the working party and wrote an account of the rebuild in *Dibidil, A Hebridean Adventure*. There is a memorial to Butterfield just above the new pier at Kinloch, and all profits from the book go to the MBA. A second renovation took place in 2005, when the interior was spruced up and the roof replaced. The layout is a typical *but and ben*, with 2 cosy, low-ceilinged rooms R and L. The RHR has a large fireplace, wood-panelled walls and a 2-person sleeping platform tucked into an alcove. The LHR has a multi-fuel stove and alpine-style bunks along the wall sleeping 4. Each room is self-contained so the bothy can accommodate 2 independent groups. It is a natural base for a traverse of the Rùm Cuillin, or wander along the wild stretch of coast to Loch Papadil and beyond.

ROUTE 1

From the new pier, head up the track past the first houses in Kinloch, then after 500 yds take the obvious path L, signposted to Dibidil. Walk up the steep slope before contouring above the Sound of Rùm, fording several streams en route and skirting round Beinn nan Stac. The initial section is well maintained but then deteriorates into a boggy morass. As you descend, the final obstacle is the Dibidil River just before the bothy, which can be a serious challenge after heavy rain.

DISTANCE 5 miles

TIME 3 to 4 hours

TERRAIN Straightforward/ Challenging. Established path, boggy in places. Serious river crossings if in spate

START New pier Kinloch (NM 411 992)

FUEL SUPPLY Bring your own supplies - wood only, no coal.

KEY ATTRACTIONS Stac Dhòmhnaill Chaim, a fortified promontory 500 yds S of the bothy, was built in the 17th century by local hero and clan chief, Donald Cam Macaulay. Visit Tràigh Uig, a fantastic crescent-shaped bay 5 miles N, and make time to stop off at the Callanish / Calanais Stones, a Neolithic stone circle, located just off the A858.

PUBLIC TRANSPORT Calmac ferry from Ullapool to Stornoway. Western Isles bus W4 daily from Stornoway to Mangurstadh.

SPECIAL NOTES Open all year. If you want to stay overnight, please contact the Norgroves in advance to book via the Linda Norgrove Foundation website: www.lindanorgrovefoundation.org, the bothy is free but donations to the Norgrove Foundation are appreciated.

EAGLE'S NEST, LEWIS

An exhilarating and extraordinary cliff-edge retreat

SIZE Very small; single room with small sleeping platform for 2
LOCATION LAT/LONG 58.1755, -7.1027, NB 001 317, 40m, LR Map 13

Picking your way down through the shattered pink Lewisian gneiss to the tiny beehive bothy at Mangurstadh, you feel like you have reached the edge of the world. Teetering on the cliff edge, waves crashing over the skerries and zawns below, the vast wild Atlantic stretched out before you, it is a most breathtaking spot. On a clear day you can see St. Kilda and the Flannan Isles, while in the evening the blink of the lighthouse on Eilean Molach is a comforting friend. The bothy was designed and built by John and Lorna Norgrove more than 30 years ago and at first its construction aroused little interest, but then people began to visit and admire it. More recently, the bothy became a poignant memorial to the Norgroves' daughter Linda, an aid worker in Afghanistan who died in 2010 in an attempted rescue by US forces following her kidnap. The Linda Norgrove Foundation, a trust that funds education, health and childcare for women and children affected by the war in Afghanistan, continues her excellent work.

The bothy is a simple structure of wood and stone with two small windows facing W out to sea and 2 skylights in the roof. From a tiny entrance, you step down into a cosy but fairly cramped space with a raised platform to the L that can sleep 2, a separate bench, and a wee fireplace and grate. The stone roof is supported by a central wooden stake, with a wigwam of beams radiating from it.

ROUTE 1

Park in a layby just beyond No.3 Mangurstadh, John and Lorna's home. Visitors can use a toilet in a turreted outbuilding near their house – it is polite to ask them first. Make your way across the open fields along the fence line to a pedestrian gate. Here, a wooden arrow points directly to the bothy. Carefully skirt round the steep edge until you see a stretch of shattered rock. The stone bothy is on a small ledge below, beautifully camouflaged and a little difficult to pick out.

DISTANCE ½ mile
TIME 15 to 30 minutes
TERRAIN Easy. Faint path across fields. Keep away from cliff edge
PARKING layby at Mangurstadh (NB 007 317)

FUEL SUPPLY Storm beach 1 mile W. Best to bring supplies.

KEY ATTRACTIONS Barnhill, where George Orwell wrote 1984 is further up the coast. The infamous Corryvreckan whirlpool lies between Jura and Scarba.

PUBLIC TRANSPORT Citylink bus service 926 from Glasgow to Lochgilphead and Kennacraig connects with the Calmac Ferry from Kennacraig to Port Askaig on Islay. Regular ferry here across to Feolin Ferry. Jura bus service Monday to Friday from Feolin Ferry to Craighouse, Lagg and Inverlussa (Garelochhead Coaches 01436 810200). Alternatively, Jura passenger ferry from Tayvallich to Craighouse from Easter to September (advance booking only 07768 450000). West Coast Motors service 426 from Lochgilphead to Tayvallich.

SPECIAL NOTES Not officially available during stag stalking August to mid October but in practice it is left unlocked. Contact Ardlussa Estate (01496 820 323).

GLENGARRISDALE, JURA

Isolated crofter's cottage in beautiful wild bay (1972)

SIZE Medium; 2 rooms both with raised platforms, sleeping 4
LOCATION LAT/LONG 56.1069, -5.7902, NR 644 968, 7m, LR Map 61, Explorer 355

Sheltered in the secluded bay from which it takes its name, Glengarrisdale lies on the far NW coast of Jura, a magnetic location with views out to Mull, Scarba and the Garvellachs. With its distinctive red roof and whitewashed walls, the bothy is a cheering sight after the challenging walk in. Although now a very remote outpost, this valley once supported a large community and was the site of An Aros, stronghold of the Macleans, a clan loyal to Bonnie Prince Charlie and the Stuarts. Maclean's Skull, possibly a relic of a battle between the Macleans and the Campbells, once lay in a cave here but was spirited away in 1976.

The old crofter's cottage is a typical *but and ben*, its 2 main downstairs rooms separated by a small tool store. Upstairs there is an attic with velux windows. At present it remains open but may be blocked off owing to fire-safety concerns. Both ground floor rooms are quite basic with small NE-facing portholes that let in little light. Each has a rudimentary sleeping platform, a single in the RHR and a double in the LHR. The LHR has a small Dowling stove and the RHR an excellent little hearth that makes it very snug in the evenings. Spend a little time here and you may see otters and seals, as well as the friendly local deer and wild goats attracted by the salty kelp. There are also nesting sea eagles up the coast towards Corryvreckan.

ROUTE 1

From the parking bay in a small disused quarry, follow the private road and at the end of the tarmac take the track signposted to Barnhill, Kinuachdrachd and Corryvreckan. After about a mile take the prominent ATV track which heads up onto the moor, at the point where a chain bars the way for unauthorised vehicles. Follow this track over boggy ground up onto the hillside, crossing a couple of streams, and then take a less distinctive path L round a craggy knoll that skirts above the N side of Loch a' Gheòidh and drops down to the N tip of Loch Doir na h-Achlaise. Contour round the flank of Clachaig Mheadhoin, and Garrisdale Bay comes into view. Before reaching the safety of the floodplain, you have to negotiate a passage down through a low escarpment. There is a well-used path but it is difficult to spot, especially in the summer when the bracken is high, or after dark. If in doubt it is best to head SW, down to the foot of the cliff, and follow the Glengarrisdale River, although the going is very boggy. Once onto the flat expanse of former cultivated fields, with the bothy in view, make for the gap in the drystone wall by the water. Walk down to 2 trees that mark a set of stepping stones across the channel.

DISTANCE 4 miles

TIME 2 to 3 hours

TERRAIN Challenging. Follows ATV track, faint trails and open ground. River crossings

PARKING Road end, 4 miles N of Ardlussa House (NR 670 930)

GUIRDIL, RÙM

Shoreside croft with stunning views to Canna and Skye (1982)

SIZE Medium; 2 rooms plus 4-person sleeping platform in the roof
LOCATION LAT/LONG 57.0254, -6.4183, NG 319 014, 21m, LR Map 39

Watching the sun setting behind Canna from the shingle beach below the bothy at Guirdil is a life-affirming experience. It also brings back happy memories for the many people whose first experience of bothying was here, as part of an organised field trip or wildlife tour. Tucked into a tight crescent bay on the W coast of Rùm, in the shadow of the conical peak of Bloodstone Hill, Guirdil takes its name from the bay's tumbling burn: in Norse, *Giùadal* means 'deep chasm'. The ruined houses nearby are all that remains of a small crofting community, but people were living on Rùm considerably earlier. A Mesolithic (Middle Stone Age) site that was uncovered near Kinloch is thought to be one of the earliest discovered so far in Scotland, dating back over 7500 years. People said to be largely nomadic visited the bay for the rare bloodstone, a type of green chalcedony, which they mined from the rock, the tiny red flecks of iron giving the stone and nearby hill their

names. This valuable commodity was carved into tools as a replacement for flint, which is rare in the Hebrides. Bloodstone was also fashioned into jewellery and ornaments: artefacts originating from Rùm have been found across the W coast from Torridon to Ardnamurchan as well as locally in the Small Isles.

The bothy itself is a former shepherd's cottage, built in 1848 like its more southerly neighbour Dibidil (p275), after the forced exodus of the entire population of crofters to Nova Scotia and the Americas from 1826. A passage in *The Limping Pilgrim* (1883) by poet Edwin Waugh, who visited Guirdil, desribes the plight of the tenant shepherd's wife and the harshness and isolation of life. The rebuilding of the ruined cottage remains one of the MBA's most cherished projects. It not only commemorates the work of Tom and Mary Brown, both founding members of the organisation, but also serves as a memorial to Peter Davis, who fell to his death on Askival in 1996.

Unlike Dibidil, the interior of Guirdil has been left as an open shell divided by a single wooden partition, while the roof space has a neatly designed sleeping platform for 4, accessed by a ladder. The RH section is the communal space, the main focus a large well-drawing hearth with an impressive stone mantlepiece and a fine set of antlers above. A worktop runs the length of the partition and there is another shelf on the back wall. There is a low table, chairs and a couple of benches, and often an accumulation of fish boxes and floats from the storm beach, where you can sometimes pick up driftwood. The LH section is sparser and the fireplace has been blocked up, but the wooden floor is a better choice for sleeping on if upstairs is occupied. There is also plenty of flat ground to camp on closer to the beach. Wander along the coast in either direction to discover a wealth of impressive geological features, from tunnels and caves to natural rock arches, and enjoy the beautiful view from the slopes of Bloodstone Hill.

ROUTE 1

From the new pier, walk through the village, past Kinloch Castle and turn L at the junction just before the bridge over the Kinloch River that heads to the community centre and shop. Follow this track as it gently winds its way up through the trees out into the upper reaches of Kinloch Glen, and the interior of the island. Take the R fork at the junction (NG 371 001), walk down over a bridge and then take the L fork just before the woodland plantation, following the pony path over a low bealach and into Glen Shellesder. Once in the valley there are many streams to cross, which could present difficulties, but the main obstacle is the ford at the mouth of the Glen Shellesder Burn. Once you have waded through the channel, it is a gentle walk along the coastal path, with one final fording point before the bay where the bothy comes into view.

DISTANCE 6 miles

TIME 2½ to 3 hours

TERRAIN Straightforward/ Challenging. Track and clearly defined path all the way. River crossings

START from new pier at Kinloch (NM 411 992)

ROUTE 2

A much more strenuous alternative is to take the L fork at the junction (NG 371 001) in Kinloch Glen (see Route 1). You then pass a quarry and follow the track as it loops round to Malcolm's Bridge. Do not cross the bridge, instead take the faint path along the W bank of the Abhainn Monadh Mhiltich and contour up and round to the Bealach a' Bhràigh Bhig and down into Glen Guirdil. Skirting the scree below Orval, the path then curves round to Bloodstone Hill. The extra effort expended on this route is rewarded by spectacular views over to Skye and Canna, but you will need to pick your way carefully down the final slope to the bothy and the Guirdil River can be difficult to cross when in spate.

DISTANCE 7 miles

TIME 3 to 4 hours

TERRAIN Challenging. As for Route 1 then track and faint path over the Bealach a' Bhràigh Bhig (360m) and Bloodstone Hill (388m). River crossings

START from new pier at Kinloch (NM 411 992)

FUEL SUPPLY Some driftwood. Best to bring supplies.

KEY ATTRACTIONS A National Nature Reserve and an outstanding location for observing wildlife including golden and white-tailed sea eagles as well as dolphins, porpoises, and the world's largest colony of shearwaters. Tours are offered by the Community Ranger Service.

PUBLIC TRANSPORT Scotrail West Highland Line from Glasgow Queen St. to Mallaig. Citylink coach service 915/916 Glasgow–Fort William. Daily bus from Fort William to Mallaig (Shiel Buses 01397 700 700). Train and bus co-ordinate with Small Isles Calmac Ferry to Eigg, Muck, Canna and Rùm. Fiendishly complicated timetable; 5 sailings to Rùm per week in the summer months.

SPECIAL NOTES Open all year. During the stalking season, daily activities are displayed on map boards in Kinloch or contact Reserve Office (01687 462026).

FUEL SUPPLY No fireplace.

KEY ATTRACTIONS Walk straight out of the door to climb S ridge of Blàbheinn (928m) or along the coast to Loch Coruisk via the infamous The Bad Step. From Elgol, take boat trip to Loch Coruisk. On the route of the Skye Trail. The Blue Shed in Torrin, has excellent cakes.

PUBLIC TRANSPORT Scotrail service from Inverness to Kyle of Lochalsh. Citylink coach service 915/916 Glasgow–Fort William–Uig stops at Broadford. Stagecoach service 55 Kyle–Broadford–Elgol, stops on request.

SPECIAL NOTES Open all year. Please respect the privacy of the lodge and old bothy. Strictly no fishing in nearby lochs and rivers. Crossing the Abhainn Camas Fhionnairigh by the old bothy is difficult at high tide or when the river is in spate.

NEW CAMASUNARY, SKYE

Modern bunkhouse with an amazing view (2016)

SIZE Medium; 2 rooms, dormitory with bunk-bed platform for 16
LOCATION LAT/LONG 57.1902, -6.1115, NG 517 184, 5m, LR Map 32, Explorer map 411

If you were to pick just one spot in the Highlands to be the showcase for Scotland's natural beauty, you might well choose Camasunary, 'the Bay of the White Shieling'. Lying on the NW curve of the Strathaird peninsula, it is overlooked by the sentinels of Blàbheinn and Sgùrr na Stri and the views of Skye's jagged peaks on both approaches to the bothy are exhilarating. There has been an open bothy here since the late 1970s, but in May 2016 owner Alan Johnson reclaimed it as a private dwelling. He did, however, provide funds for a replacement – the first new build undertaken by the MBA and carried out enthusiastically by 59 Commando Squadron Royal Engineers as a community training exercise.

The new bothy consists of 2 rooms: a kitchen/dining area with an amazing view of islands and peaks and, leading off it, a dormitory. Inside, an alpine-style bunk-bed that can sleep up to 16 runs the length of the back wall. The building has been well insulated but there is no fireplace or stove, a stipulation by the owner following several instances of people breaking into the farm house looking for fuel. The whitewashed walls have no homely touches and, all in all, this is a functional building which does not encourage a lengthy stay. The project was dedicated to the memory of Neil Mackenzie, who died in a climbing accident on Joffre Peak, British Columbia in 2015.

ROUTE 1

Take the track signposted to Camasunary and Sligachan that rises up the glen to the bealach of Am Màm. There are a couple of stream crossings but they are normally fordable without difficulty. As you round the shoulder of the hill, the view opens up dramatically. Descend steeply taking a sharp L down to the flats, where a path leads towards Sligachan. Leave the track before the bridge over the Abhainn nan Leac, and head over to the bothy. Possible to mountain bike but steep sections to negotiate.

DISTANCE 3 miles
TIME 1 to 1½ hours
TERRAIN Easy. Track. Ascent to 180m
PARKING Car park Kilmarie (NG 545 172)

ROUTE 2

From the car park, head back up the steep section of the B808, then turn L along a lane. Leaving the last houses behind, proceed onto the open moor. The path contours along some vertigo-inducing cliffs below the crags of Càrn Mòr before descending into Glen Scaladal. Ford the burn, an obvious obstacle in times of spate, then climb up the lower slope of Beinn Leacach and contour round the edge of the cliffs. Traverse a final obstacle of rocks and reach the safety of the bay and the bothy door.

DISTANCE 5 miles
TIME 2 to 2½ hours
TERRAIN Straightforward. Skye Trail all the way. Close to cliff edge. River crossings
PARKING Car park Elgol (NG 488 299)

FUEL SUPLY Bring supplies.

KEY ATTRACTIONS Clan Macleod territory and you can visit their ancestral home, Dunvegan Castle. The flat-topped hills, Healabhal Mhòr and Healabhal Bheagh, are known as Macleod's Tables, and Macleod's Maidens are impressive sea-stacks at Idrigill Point. The lighthouse at Neist Point is worth visiting and the Talisker whisky distillery at Carbost is a good wet-weather option.

PUBLIC TRANSPORT Citylink coach service 915/916 Glasgow–Fort William–Skye stops at Portree. Stagecoach service 56 Portree–Dunvegan–Glendale.

SPECIAL NOTES Open all year. Bothy occasionally used by shepherds to whom priority should be given. Please keep dogs under control, close all gates, and respect all notices. For enquiries contact Glendale Estate (01470 511340).

OLLISDAL, SKYE

Old Viking long house on spectacular stretch of coast (1985)

SIZE Small; single room
LOCATION LAT/LONG 57.3596, -6.6361, NG 213 394, 89m, LR Map 23, Explorer 407

At the S end of the Duirinish Peninsula, the small Viking long house at Ollisdal looks out towards the Uists and Benbecular in the Western Isles. On this spectacular stretch of coast, one of Skye's hidden treasures, is a wealth of sea-stacks, caves, and arches. The traverse from Ramasaig to Orbost ranks as one of the most dramatic cliff-top walks in Britain, but remarkably few venture along it. Ollisdal combines the name of a Viking notable with *dal*, meaning 'dale' or 'valley'. The area has lush grazing and was once home to a number of crofting communities. Evidence of settlement is scattered here and all along the coast. Today, the peninsula is owned by the Glendale Estate and its sale in 1908 was Scotland's first community land buy-out. About half the 18,000 acreage still supports crofts and common grazing.

The bothy is a simple affair comprising 2 rooms. A workroom with a dirt floor leads into a snug wood-panelled communal room, dominated by a large fireplace. Ollisdal makes an excellent base for an exploration of the cliffs. Among the highlights is the impressive waterfall and arch in Lorgasdal Bay. The path N to Orbost from Macleod's Maidens passes by the fenced-off Rebel's Wood, planted in memory of The Clash's lead singer, Joe Strummer.

ROUTE 1

Follow the track down to Loch Bharcasaig. By the edge of the woodland, 200 yds before the farm, take the R-hand path, signposted Macleod's Tables, which zigzags up the hill. Climb steeply and then keep to the forestry plantation boundary fence before ascending to the Bealach Bharcasaig. Here the path dissolves into the bog. Make your way past the Ollisdal Lochs and then pick up a faint trail through the bluffs of Coire Mòr and down to the bothy.

DISTANCE 5 miles
TIME 2½ to 3½ hours
TERRAIN Challenging. Paths, faint trails, boggy in places
PARKING Road end Orbost (NG 257 432)

ROUTE 2

Take the track onto the moor that descends to the ruined village of Lorgill. A footbridge has been washed away, so you have to ford the Lorgill River. If in spate, cross downstream towards the beach. From here, follow the faint path up to the cliff top of Biod Boidheach. After a short distance a deep gorge necessitates a detour inland NE for about ½ mile before you head back towards the sea. Continue along the cliff top to Glen Dibidal, then steeply downhill to the Geodha Mòr. Ford the Dibidal River, which may be difficult when in spate. Climb back up to the cliff top before reaching a level section where the bothy comes into view.

DISTANCE 6 miles
TIME 3 to 4 hours
TERRAIN Challenging. Paths, faint trails, boggy in places. River crossings
PARKING Road end Ramasaig (NG 164 443)

FUEL SUPPLY Driftwood in An Sàilean bay.

KEY ATTRACTIONS Excellent wildlife (red deer, wild goats, otters and seals) and geology.

PUBLIC TRANSPORT Citylink coach service 926 from Glasgow to Lochgilphead and Kennacraig then Calmac Ferry from Kennacraig to Port Askaig on Islay. Regular ferry from Port Askaig across to Feolin Ferry. Jura bus service Monday to Friday from Feolin Ferry to Craighouse, Lagg and Inverlussa (Garelochhead Coaches 01436 810200). Jura passenger ferry from Tayvallich to Craighouse runs from Easter to September (advance booking only, 07768 450000). West Coast Motors service 426 from Lochgilphead to Tayvallich.

SPECIAL NOTES Open throughout the year. Contact Ruantallain Estate (01496 820287) if planning a visit during deer stalking between July and February. Water can be fetched from a freshwater lochan 50 yds S of the bothy.

RUANTALLAIN, JURA

Bothy frozen in time in a magical coastal location

SIZE Small; single room with 3 iron bedsteads
LOCATION LAT/LONG 55.9773, -6.0014, NR 505 832, 10m, LR Map 61, Explorer 355

There is something about arriving at Ruantallain that never leaves you. With all the tenacity it takes to reach this wild stretch of pristine coastline, you are rewarded by a vista of mountains and sea that is simply magical. The view S is framed by Loch Tarbert and the Paps of Jura, and from the headland at Rubha an t-Sàilean there is a rare glimpse of Colonsay. In the far distance is the coastline of Islay, where the beam from the Rhuvaal lighthouse is a nightly reminder that civilisation is not so far away. Along with the ubiquitous red deer, wild goats, otters and seals are regular visitors, while cormorants and shags often lurk on the rocks and skerries. It is also a geomorphologist's paradise, dotted with textbook examples of raised beaches and wave-cut platforms.

This remote outpost was an important meeting point for travellers sailing to and from Colonsay and Oronsay, and there was an inn on the site of the bothy. Now only a single cottage remains, one of only 4 buildings along the entire 50 miles of Jura's W seaboard. One end of the building is kept locked by the estate for use during the deer-stalking season, the other is left open to all comers. This old-school refuge feels a little eerie, like entering a time-capsule. Much remains from bygone days including some antique plates, and an oval mirror. The small room is lit by just one tiny S-facing window and the dark, smoke-stained wood-panelling adds to the gloom. A picture of a former laird, partly hidden by a collection of antlers, hangs above the fireplace, and a table, chairs, and 3 ancient iron bed frames have been shoehorned into the space. But once a driftwood fire is crackling in the hearth and your candles are lit, any lingering unease is forgotten. If you prefer to camp, a drystone wall in front of the bothy encloses a level grassy area.

ROUTE 1

The journey to Ruantallain is taxing. Allow plenty of time as it is easy to miss the path in places, and if you do so, the ground is pretty unforgiving.

From Cruib Lodge (p273), head for the outflow of the Garbh Uisge, adjacent to Eilean Aird at NR 557 824, which is the widest and shallowest point. Continue on a vague ATV track up through the undulating moor away from the coast which skirts to the S of 3 small lochans and eventually on to Gleann Righ Mòr and the beach. Cross the track that heads up from the beach (to the boathouse on Loch Righ Beag) and continue along the cliffs to Ruba an t-Sàilean. As you approach the point, the track becomes more obvious, although it is still easy to get disorientated, as the bothy is hidden below a low bluff. It comes into view only at the very last moment.

DISTANCE 7 miles
TIME 3 to 4 hours
TERRAIN Very tough. Marked path to head of Loch Tarbert only, then intermittent deer and ATV tracks. River crossings. Difficult navigation
PARKING Layby just beyond Tarbert (NR 605 828)

FUEL SUPPLY Occasional driftwood. Bring your own supplies.

KEY ATTRACTIONS Amazing views from Raasay's distinctive table-top summit Dùn Caan (444m). Warm hospitality in Raasay House, with good restaurant, café and bar.

PUBLIC TRANSPORT Scotrail service from Inverness to Kyle of Lochalsh. Citylink coach service 915/916 Glasgow–Fort William–Uig stops at Sconser. Calmac Ferry from Sconser on Skye to Inverarish on Raasay runs daily. No bus service on Raasay.

SPECIAL NOTES Open all year. For enquiries contact Raasay Estate (01478 612516). Community shop in Inverarish.

TAIGH THORMOID DHUIBH, RAASAY

Enchanting with end-of-the-world feel (1995)

SIZE Medium; open-plan room with raised platform, sleeping 6
LOCATION LAT/LONG 57.4985, -5.9883, NG 611 524, 15m, LR Map 24, Explorer 409

Taigh Thormoid Dhuibh, 'Black Norman's House', is one of those out-of-the-way places you can't quite believe exists. Located on the N tip of Raasay, the beautiful, understated island between Skye and the Applecross peninsula, the bothy was an old homestead in a crofting community that endured well into the 20th century. The evidence of ruined houses and sheilings is clearly visible as you walk through An Caol towards the headland. The bothy, a solid stone cottage, has a large, open-plan interior with a fireplace at one end and a long sleeping platform for up to 6 people at the other. It was restored in memory of Graham Lipp, an Outward Bound instructor who died in 1992. There is a table under one of the W-facing windows, a couple of chairs, plus fish boxes and other flotsam and jetsam. A skylight in the boarded ceiling helps to brighten the interior. A stream runs outside the bothy down to Caol Eilean Tigh, but this is not always reliable in dry weather, so it might be useful to fill up water bottles on the way.

The last 2 miles of tarmac before the road ends at Arnish form the famous 'Calum's Road'. Over the decades the local community had campaigned unsuccessfully for a road to be built, and in frustration, assistant keeper of Rona Lighthouse Malcolm MacLeod, Calum to his friends, decided to do it himself. From 1965 to 1974, with the help of some initial blasting work by the Department of Agriculture, he constructed the road – complete with passing places and culverts – by hand, using little more than a pick, shovel and wheelbarrow. The road was finally adopted by the local council, and Calum was awarded the MBE. Calum's achievements are related, along with the wider history of the island, in Roger Hutchinson's book *Calum's Road*.

ROUTE 1

From the road end at Arnish, take the signposted track to Torran, where a path leading off to the R is the shorter route to An Caol and the bothy. The detour round the shore to Caol Fladda, on the L-hand path is a delight and well worth the extra half hour. From Caol Fladda the path zigzags back up the slope to join the main path. From here, the trail is faint and a little difficult to follow as it meanders N through the abandoned settlements, but becomes more obvious as you approach the headland. With about ½ a mile to go you pass a ruined croft in reasonable condition and you might well mistake this for the bothy. But press on and the bothy finally comes into view, though only at the last moment. It is tucked away in the fold of a hill and would certainly be difficult to find after dark.

DISTANCE 3 miles
TIME 1½ to 2 hours
TERRAIN Straightforward. Signposted path, turning into faint trail, then more distinct towards the bothy
PARKING Ardnish (NG 594 480)

FUEL SUPPLY No Fireplace.

KEY ATTRACTIONS Whale and dolphin watching from the window. There are binoculars in the bothy. Exhilarating walk round the high cliffs of the Quiraing at the top of the Trotternish Ridge.

PUBLIC TRANSPORT Citylink coach service 915/916 Glasgow–Fort William–Uig. Stagecoach service 57a/57c Uig-Flodigarry-Staffin-Portree, stops on request.

SPECIAL NOTES Open all year. No fresh water within ½ mile of the bothy. Take care on the cliff close to the bothy.

THE LOOKOUT, SKYE

Panoramic views from the northern tip of Skye (2007)

SIZE Small; 2 rooms, including dormitory with bunk-bed sleeping 3
LOCATION LAT/LONG 57.7013, -6.3444, NG 413 763, 82m, LR Map 23

The stunning 180-degree view from the bay window at The Lookout certainly gives the bothy its wow factor. This former coastguard watch station, positioned precariously close to the cliff top above Rubha Hunish, offers a panorama encompassing the entire Western Isles, and on a clear day, the profile of the mainland all the way to Cape Wrath. The bothy is also a fantastic spot for whale and dolphin watching: schools of migrating minkes pass through the Minch in the autumn, and various other sightings are recorded in the log book. The watch room was built in 1928 and the station operated until the 1970s when advances in radio technology superseded the need for a duty officer. The building was then adopted as an open shelter, but a violent storm in January 2005 smashed the W-facing windows, damaging the interior and leaving its long-term future in doubt. The MBA took on the renovation with support from the local community around Kilmaluag, following the design of the original structure as closely as possible. The work was dedicated to the memory of David JJ Brown, an MBA stalwart, and a plaque in the bothy describes him as an 'anti-materialist and wilderness lover'.

From the entrance lobby, there is an open dormitory to the L, a galley kitchen facing you, and to the R, the communal area with the impressive bay window. There is some seating, a coffee table and a small blocked-up fireplace in one corner. An old-style telephone hangs on the wall, along with an information board and a poster identifying different whales, dolphins and porpoises. The only drawback is the ½ mile walk to the nearest stream, which can run dry. The best option is to visit the Trotternish Art Gallery, Solitote (NG 428 742) where the bothy's MO Bill Lawrence and wife Susie will fill water bottles and chat, especially if you purchase one of their beautiful prints. Although The Lookout is very close to civilisation, Rubha Hunish is still a wild and exposed spot. It is well worth heading down the steep descent under the cliffs to walk round the point, but you do need to watch your footing.

ROUTE 1
From the car park, marked by an old red telephone box, take the path signposted to Rubha Hunish, which rises gently up the slope and along a low escarpment. Below is the outline of the abandoned crofting community of Erisco and, further off, the cliff-edge ruins of Duntulm Castle. Once through a kissing gate, where you see the small water-supply stream, head straight up to the cliff edge. Ignore the path that leads down a steep slope in a gap between the crags, and continue along the cliff top. The bothy comes quickly into view and it is only now, when the view opens up dramatically, that you realise the building's original purpose.

DISTANCE 1½ miles
TIME 30 to 40 minutes
TERRAIN Easy, path all the way
PARKING Car park just after Shulista turn-off (NG 422 723)

FUEL SUPPLY Bring supplies.

KEY ATTRACTIONS Climb Beinn Talaidh (761m) and the hills to the S or join a guided visit at Mull Eagle Watch. Stop at the Coffee Pot in Salen or The Mediterranea Restaurant for a drink and local sea food.

PUBLIC TRANSPORT Scotrail train service from Glasgow Queen St. or Citylink coach service 975/976 from Glasgow Buchanan Street to Oban. Calmac ferry from Oban to Craignure. On Mull, West Coast Motors service 95/495 Craignure – Salen–Tobermory. Trains co-ordinate with ferries; cycles are free.

SPECIAL NOTES Open all year. Stag stalking from 15 August to 20 October and hind cull from 21 October to 15 February. Contact Glen Forsa Estate (01680 300674) for hill access. Easy to mountain bike.

TOMSLEIBHE, MULL

A very accessible cottage escape (1980)

SIZE Medium; 3 rooms, 2 with raised platforms, sleeping 10
LOCATION LAT/LONG 56.4664, -5.8689, NM 617 372, 109m, LR Map 49, OS Explorer 375

Beginning the trip up to Tomsleibhe along the fertile, billiard table flat floodplain of Glen Forsa, in the heart of the hills to the east of Mull's distinctive volcanic peak of Ben More, it becomes apparent quite early on that the building spied on the lower slopes of Beinn Talaidh is indeed the bothy. It is a most reassuring sight, knowing that no epic route-finding will be necessary after the long journey out west beyond the mainland. *Tomsleibhe* is Gaelic for 'mountain knoll', a description of the fine hill that overlooks the shelter, also known as Bentalla Cottage. It was once a small farmstead; the ruin of the byre is just up the hill and the remnants of a protective wall and sheep pens are still obvious. The bothy is very well maintained, and although very accessible, does not receive the visitor numbers you might expect. One reason is the walking distance from the headline Munro of Ben More, which takes a day. If the bothy was located in Glen Cannel, on the classic route by Loch Ba and up the peak, the footfall would be much higher.

A classic *but and ben* comprising 3 well-appointed rooms with white-washed walls, the bothy is comfortable and the small front porch provides extra draught protection. The RHR contains the original fireplace, 2 high-sided benches, a table and shelf with some kitchen equipment, and a small library. The LHR has another working hearth, windows front and back, and a sturdy bunk-bed sleeping 8 that runs along the interior wall. There is also a table and a bench, so 2 parties could co-exist quite independently. The middle space is another dormitory, a very cosy affair with a 2-person sleeping platform and a fine view from the window.

ROUTE 1

After turning off the A849 at Pennygown, the parking area is a short way along the lane just before a gate. From here, head along the farm road which runs parallel to a large conifer plantation, past the cottage at Killbeg and out to the open pasture. A herd of highland cattle often graze here, and it is difficult to avoid an encounter, as they are naturally curious. Eventually the track runs close to the River Forsa and passes through some more forestry, crossing a wooden bridge over the Gaodhail River. Carry straight on past a ford to the L leading to some large metal cowsheds and sheep pens, before the path curves round 90 degrees and starts up the slope. Cross a ford with concrete sleepers below the channel, and also some stepping stones if the water level is high, and just beyond this the track forks. A striking memorial with a mangled propeller has been built here, commemorating a Dakota aeroplane that crashed into Beinn Talaidh at the end of the World War II. Take the R fork signposted to the bothy. The track becomes decidedly steeper and rougher over this last stretch and, if you are on a bike, you might have to get off and push.

DISTANCE 4 miles
TIME 1½ to 2 hours
TERRAIN Easy. Track all the way. River crossing
PARKING Pennygown, Glen Forsa road (NM 595 427)

FUEL SUPPLY Some driftwood, best to bring supplies.

KEY ATTRACTIONS Climb Donalds Beinn Mhòr (620m), Beinn Choradail (527m) and Hecla (606m). From Hecla's summit there are spectacular views N over the sunken waterscape of Benbecula.

Marvel at the Stevenson lighthouse S of the cliffs at Creag Dhùghail.

PUBLIC TRANSPORT Calmac ferry from Oban to Lochboisdale. Aitken Island Travel service W17 serves Lochboisdale, Howmore and Benbecula (01878 710333).

SPECIAL NOTES Open all year. During stag stalking check hill access with the South Uist Estate (01878 700301). Gatliffe Trust Hostel at Howmore is a useful base.

UISINIS, SOUTH UIST

Tiny bothy in Western Isles wilderness (1978)

SIZE Very small; single room with bunk-bed sleeping 4
LOCATION LAT/LONG 57.2804, -7.2309, NF 850 333, 24m, LR Map 22, Explorer Map 453

Even by Scottish standards the E coast of the Uists is remote and the bothy above Bàgh Uisinis is in a truly magical location. An expedition to explore this rarely visited area is a real privilege. Sea eagles nest further up the coast, and curious grey seals often bob up in the bay. Uisinis is a traditional stone-built refuge set beneath rugged Hecla, 'the hooded mountain', and Beinn Mhòr. The name derives from the Old Norse but the documented history goes back to the Iron Age, when the sea was the main highway round the Western Isles. Robert Macfarlane explores these 'paths across the sea' in *The Old Ways*. Archaeological digs have recorded the remains of a round or wheelhouse (NF 843 332) under the crags of Moaladh na h-Uamha below Hecla, and a more intact souterrain or earth house at nearby Scalavat (NF 849 340).

Uisinis has two compact rooms, the first used for storage by the MBA. Much of the communal single space is filled by a sturdy double bunk-bed, plus a kitchen area and 2 benches. Over the years, winter storms battered the cottage but a 2012 work party made the building watertight again, and installed a small Dowling stove.

ROUTE 1

There is no easy way to the bothy – the most forgiving route is from Loch Sgioport. Start along a good path round the coast past a number of old sheilings, before it peters out at the old settlement above Caolas Mòr. From here, pick your way across the blanket bog, past the W shore of Loch nam Faoileann and the S side of Loch Bèin, continuing along the line of crags underneath Maol Martaig. Aim for the old sheiling at Rubha Roiseal (NF 858 365). Continue down the coast to the cove of Mol a' Tuath, cross the footbridge below the boatshed, and briefly follow the track that heads NE to the Uisinis Lighthouse. At the sharp turn head out across the open moor again, following a vague ATV trail into Bàgh Uisinis. Traverse the boggy land above the bay, crossing a couple of streams, and reach the bothy.

DISTANCE 6 miles
TIME 3 to 4 hours
TERRAIN Challenging. Path, vague trail and pathless open moorland
PARKING Loch Sgioport, small layby (NF 826 386)

ROUTE 2

Alternatively, head in from Mill Croft, the usual launch point for an ascent of Beinn Mhòr. The track stops after less than a mile, so you must tramp across Glen Dorchaidh and up to the bealach between Hecla and Beinn Choradail, before descending on a faint trail into Glen Uisinis, keeping to the L of Loch Coradail, and the Abhainn Aon-uillt below. There are a number of streams to cross, which could be challenging in times of spate.

DISTANCE 5 miles
TIME 3 to 4 hours
TERRAIN Challenging. Track, pathless open moorland, faint trail
PARKING Roadside off A865, Mill Croft (NF 768 345)

DONALDS, GRAHAMS, CORBETTS AND MUNROS

Although this sounds like the name of a well to do Scotsman it is in fact a system of height classifications of the country's mountain summits. These form lists of objectives that can be ticked off when ascended, and give an incentive to hill walkers to travel round the Highlands and islands rather than climb favourite peaks time and again. The hobbyists are known as 'baggers'. By far the most popular is Munro bagging, and finishers are referred to as compleaters. There is a tradition of celebrating your final Munro with friends and relations. The Scottish Mountaineering Club has produced separate guides for Munros and Corbetts, and recently a new one for Grahams and Donalds. It also holds a record of all Munro compleaters, which currently stands at just above 5500.

Walking out from Gorton Bothy with Beinn an Dothaloth in view, SW Highlands

Munros

Scotland's highest mountains are named after Sir Hugh Munro, who listed peaks that he judged to be over 3000ft (914m) in a book of tables in 1891. His total of 236 separate summits has been superseded thanks to modern survey techniques, and now stands at 282. There is also the concept of a Munro top, which is a peak that is not regarded as a separate mountain, but is within the height range. Tops apply to each of the other categories. It is a little subjective, but has been agreed by all participants. The highest Munro is Ben Nevis, the most southerly Ben Lomond.

Corbetts

These are Scottish mountains over 2500ft (762m) and below 3000 feet (914m) as compiled by John Rooke Corbett in the 1920s. The definition of a Corbett is based on there being at least 500ft (152m) of ascent on all sides. In total there are 221 Corbetts.

Grahams

These are summits between 2000 and 2500ft (609 to 762m) with a drop of at least 500ft (152m) all round. Both Fiona Torbet (née Graham) and Alan Dawson published lists in 1992, the latter in his book *The Relative Hills of Britain*. Torbet and Dawson subsequently met and agreed on a definite list, deciding that the category should be named for Fiona's maiden name: to avoid 'Torbets' being confused with the Corbetts! There are 219 Grahams in all.

Donalds

Finally there are the Donalds which are a collection of hills in the Scottish lowlands over 2000ft (609m) compiled by Percy Donald in 1997. This list was devised to encourage eccentrics to climb peaks of lesser 'status' than the other lists. They are also closer to Glasgow, Edinburgh and the Scottish Central Belt, and thus more accessible to a wider population. Whether a high point is a Donald has been open to debate and follows a complicated formula. A prominence of at least 1000ft (30m) is automatically designated a Donald, but in various cases ones with a relative height of 50ft (15m) have been accepted if they

are of 'sufficient' topographic interest. A number of 140 Donalds has been established for all concerned.

A' Chùil Bothy, a *but* and *ben*

GAELIC GLOSSARY

Many landscape features and places in the book are in Scots Gaelic. Place names and other Scottish words that occur most frequently are listed here.

allt	stream, river
abhainn	river
bàgh	bay
beag	small
bealach	saddle, pass
beinn	mountain
black house	traditional long house with a byre at one end and a thatched roof
broch	prehistoric circular stone tower
buidhe	yellow
burn	stream
but and ben	a dwelling that has two rooms, the but referring to the kitchen and living room, and the ben the bedroom
byre	shed or barn for cattle
camas	channel or bend
coire	hanging valley, corrie
Corbett	mountain with a summit of 2,500–3,000ft (762–914m) named after Scottish mountaineeer John Rooke Corbett
crannag	ancient fortified dwelling constructed in a lake or marsh
creag	crag, rock, cliff
croft	tenanted smallholding
Donald	hill above 2,000ft (610m) listed by Percy Donald
dubh	black
eilean	island
ghillie	male attendant or guide on a hunting or fishing expedition
gleann	glen, valley
Graham	mountain with a summit of 2,000–2,499ft (610–761m)
howff	rough and ready shelter, on the lower end of the bothy scale
laird	owner of an estate
lochan	small lake, tarn
machair	coastal grassy plain
mòr, mhòr	great
meall, mheall	round hill
Munro	mountain over 3,000ft (914m): original list compiled by Sir Hugh Munro in 1891
press	inset cupboard usually shelved, often without a door
ruadh	red
rhubha	point or headland
sgor	rocky peak
sheiling	shepherd's shelter
stane	stone
steading	farmstead
strath	wide valley
stravaig	wander, roam
traigh	beach
uaimh, uamh	cave
uaine	green

Open door policy at Strathchailleach Bothy, Northern Highlands

BIBLIOGRAPHY

Elizabeth Allen. *Burn on the Hill: the Story of the First "Compleat Munroist."* Bidean Books, 1985.

Rab Anderson and Tom Prentice. *The Grahams and The Donalds: Scottish Mountaineering Club Hillwalkers' Guide.* Scottish Mountaineering Club, 2015.

Donald J. Bennet. *The Munros: Scottish Mountaineering Club Hillwalkers' Guide.* Scottish Mountaineering Club, 2006.

Alastair Borthwick. *Always a Little Further.* Diadem Books, 1983.

Dave Brown and Ian Mitchell. *Mountain Days and Bothy Nights.* Luath Press, 2008.

Hamish Brown. *Hamish's Mountain Walk and Climbing The Corbetts.* Baton Wicks Publications, 1996.

Irvine Butterfield. *A Survey of Shelters in Remote Mountain areas of the Scottish Highlands.* Ian Mackenzie, 1979.

Irvine Butterfield. *Dibidil, a Hebridean Adventure.* Irvine Butterfield, 1972.

Irvine Butterfield. *The Call of the Corbetts.* David & Charles, 2007.

Irvine Butterfield. *The High Mountains.* BCA, 1986.

James Carron. *A Ceiling of Stars: The Remarkable Life of a Highland Hermit.* CreateSpace Independent Publishing Platform, 2012.

Mike Cawthorne. *Wilderness Dreams: The Call of Scotland's Last Wild Places.* The In Pinn, 2007.

Daniel Craig. *On the Crofter's Trail.* Birlinn, 2006.

Peter Edwards. *The Hebrides: 50 Walking and Backpacking Routes.* Cicerone Press, 2015.

Peter Edwards. *Walking on Jura, Islay and Colonsay.* Cicerone Press, 2010.

Affleck Gray. *Legends of the Cairngorms.* Mainstream Publishing, 1988.

Iain Harper. *The Cape Wrath Trail.* Cicerone Press, 2013.

Roger Hutchinson. *Calum's Road.* Birlinn, 2008.

G. Scott Johnstone. *The Corbetts and Other Scottish Hills: Scottish Mountaineering Club Hillwalkers' Guide.* Scottish Mountaineering Club, 2002.

Eric Langmuir. *Mountain Craft and Leadership.* Mountain Training Boards of England and Scotland; 4th edition, 2013.

Dave McFadzean. *Tales o'the Back Buss: A Short History of Blackhill of Bush.* GC Books, 2004.

Robert Macfarlane. *The Old Ways: A Journey on Foot.* Penguin, 2013.

Patrick MacGill. *Children of the Dead End.* Birlinn, 2000.

Ian MacKay. *The Last Family at Maol Bhuidhe.*

W.H. Murray. *Undiscovered Scotland: Climbs on Rock, Snow & Ice.* J.M. Dent & Sons, 1951.

Ian Nimmo. Walking With Murder: On the Kidnapped Trail. Birlinn, 2005.

Tom Patey. *One Man's Mountains: Essays and Verses.* Canongate, 1971, 1997.

Paul Gordon Seton. *The Charm of the Hills.* Cassell, 1951.

Nan Shepherd. *The Living Mountain: A Celebration of the Cairngorm Mountains of Scotland.* Canongate, 2011.

Alex Sutherland. *Shenavall – A Brief History.*

Iain R. Thompson. *Isolation Shepherd.* Birlinn, 2007.

David Maclean Urquhart. *Miss MacKenzie couldn't see the wind.* David Maclean Urquhart, 2010.

Adam Watson. *It's a Fine Day for the Hill: Hills, Folk and Wildlife 1935–62.* Paragon Publishing, 2011.

Edwin Waugh. *The Limping Pilgrim.* John Heywood, 1883. On line at www.gerald-massey.org.uk

Ken Wilson and Richard Gilbert. *Classic Walks: Mountain and Moorland Walks in Britain and Ireland.* Diadem Books, 1982.

Ken Wilson and Richard Gilbert. *The Big Walks: Challenging Mountain Walks and Scrambles in the British Isles.* Diadem Books, 1980, 1989.

Ken Wilson and Richard Gilbert. *Wild Walks: Mountain, Moorland and Coastal Walks in Britain and Ireland.* Hodder & Stoughton, 1988.

Ken Wilson, Dave Alcock and John Barry. *Cold Climbs: Great Snow and Ice Climbs of the British Isles,* Diadem Press, 1990.

Luib Chonnal, Central Highlands

The Scottish Bothy Bible
The complete guide to
Scotland's bothies and
how to reach them

www.geoffallan.co.uk

Words
Geoff Allan

Photography
Geoff Allan

Editing
Anna Kruger
Hilary Chung

Proofing
Candida Frith-Macdonald

Design and Layout
Sue Gent
Marcus Freeman
Tania Pascoe

Distributed by
Central Books Ltd
1 Heath Park Industrial Estate,
Freshwater Road, Dagenham
RM8 1RX, United Kingdom
Tel +44 (0)208 525 8800
orders@centralbooks.com

Published by
Wild Things Publishing Ltd.
Freshford, Bath, BA2 7WG,
United Kingdom
www.wildthingspublishing.com
hello@wildthingspublishing.com

PHOTOGRAPHS AND MAPS

All photographs © Geoff Allan. Maps contain data © Ordnance Survey 2016.

AUTHOR ACKNOWLEDGEMENTS

Mister Geoff Associates would like to give a heartfelt thank you to everyone for their help, advice, support and inspiration in bringing this project to fruition:

Mum, Hil, Mia, Trevor, Ruth and Stuart, Adam and Ali, John and Katherine, Jamie and Anna, Phil and Elly, Nick and Suze, Dave R, Ant, Eileen, Frances, Jo, Al Reid, Paul, Chris and Val, Ann Beth and Tom, Kerstin and Mark, Kat and Ruedi, Dave C, Karen Fairhurst, Imelda, Paul T, Dave and Jo, Struan and Karen, Celia and Alberto, Brad and Heidi, Doug, Sarah, Phoebe, Hanna, Isabel, George and Pam, Jacqui, Mark R, Simon K, Martin P and Kate, Paul G, Colin H, Brian and Jane, Alistair B, Laurel, Sarah, Kate S, Stevo and Justine, Pete and Juliette, Ally D and Jess, Simon and Jana, Donald, Davie, Nick G, Tim, Sam, Jim, Tom and Alyson, Jane, Tommy, Catherine, Chris and Ray, James Edwards, Greg Macvean, Dan Bailey, Jake Macmanus, Blair Urquhart, Alec Finlay, Geoff Sample, Bill Anderson, Jennie Renton, Sara Hunt, Dixe Wills, Dave Robertson, and Dave Donaldson. Daniel Start and Tania Pascoe for giving me the opportunity to publish and, most importantly, the MBA and the estates who make available and maintain these wonderful shelters.

I would also like to thank all the staff at the National Library of Scotland, and the Blue Blazer for their smiles and kind words in the last 18 months of hard labour, plus JP Camera's, The Bike Station, and The Bicycle Works for keeping me on the road.

WILD THINGS PUBLISHING